blue tomorrow?

the football, finance and future of Chelsea Football Club

Mark Meehan

First published in 2000

EMPIRE PUBLICATIONS LTD
1 Newton Street, Manchester M1 1HW

Front Cover Photo: © Atlantic Syndication Partners
Gianluca Vialli and Ken Bates celebrate a good end to the 1999/2000 season.
Back Cover: The author with the FA Cup..

ISBN 1-901-746-16X

Typeset by Ashley Shaw and Stuart Fish
and printed in Great Britain
by Redwood Books,
Kennet Way, Trowbridge,
Wiltshire BA14 8RN

I would like to dedicate this book to my late father, William Meehan, who in January 1970 brought home from work the Chelsea programme for the following day's fourth round FA Cup tie with Burnley. As a result I have been a Chelsea supporter ever since – thanks very much Dad.

Contents

About the Author

Mark Meehan was born in London in 1962 and saw his first match at Stamford Bridge in April 1971. No sooner did he start going regularly to Stamford Bridge, when Chelsea's years of success quickly became a distant memory. He has a perverse memory of the gloomy years and looks back nostalgically to the days of the formidable Chelsea defence of Graham Wilkins, David Stride, Micky Nutton and John Sitton.

His most memorable moments as a Chelsea fan include Clive Walker's goal at Burnden Park that kept Chelsea out of the Third Division in 1983, being snogged by Chelsea programme editor Neil Barnett in Stockholm in 1998 when Zola scored the winner and being barred from drinking with Tommy Baldwin (aka The Sponge) for getting the ex-Chelsea star the worse for wear one evening after a drinking session in Chelsea.

He keeps going to Chelsea in the belief that Eddie McCreadie will one day return as manager and believes the greatest player he has ever seen, Pat Nevin, will one day become Chelsea chairman, just as he will one day win the lottery and buy a millennium suite in the West Stand with his windfall . He has had the honour of treading on the hallowed turf of Stamford Bridge himself but his only attempt at goal ended up nearer the top tier of the Shed than the back of the net.

Mark was the editor of the highly-influential *Chelsea Independent* fanzine between 1994 and 1997 and has since written for various publications including *Football Monthly*, *Action Replay*, *FourFourTwo* and the official Chelsea magazine to name a few. He lives in West London with his wife and two young daughters.

Acknowledgements

I would like to thank Ashley Shaw and everyone at Empire Publications and Tom at Solo Synidcations for their help in getting this book finished.

I would also like to thank Graham Bell, John Hollins, Tommy Langley, Pat Nevin, Peter Osgood, Mark Sandom, John Spencer, Garry Stanley and Clive Walker for the assistance they have given me. In addition, I must acknowledge the countless Chelsea websites out there for providing useful information, gossip, statistics, facts and figures that helped me get this book completed. Thanks to you all and let's hope a Blue Tomorrow is getting closer each day.

Mark Meehan
Greenford, Middlesex

October 2000

Introduction

Tuesday 18 April 2000. 10.23pm local time. Chelsea lead Barcelona 4-3 on aggregate in the Nou Camp and are seven minutes away from the semi-final of the Champions League when disaster strikes. Barcelona score a third goal to level the tie 4-4 on aggregate and take the game into extra time. Sadly the Catalans are too strong and, handicapped by the sending off of Celestine Babayaro, the Blues are eventually beaten 5-1 after extra time. If Chelsea had held out for seven more minutes, they would have made the last four of the world's most prestigious club tournament at their first attempt. Yet despite their disappointment, most fans are of the view that while Chelsea may have been only seven minutes from glory, a loss to Barcelona in extra-time is an accurate measure of just how far the club and its supporters have come.

Only seven years before, almost to the day, on Saturday 17 April 1993, Chelsea travelled to Old Trafford to face champions- elect Manchester United. United were about to win the first-ever Premier League title but it would be their first league title since 1967 – a lengthy twenty-six year gap. Chelsea, on the other hand, had only just dispensed with Ian Porterfield and drafted in Chelsea old boy David Webb as manager. By the time they travelled to Old Trafford, Webb had succeeded in his task. Chelsea were firmly rooted in mid-table but the 3,000 travelling supporters made the journey north in expectation rather than hope. Other than a defeat during the John Hollins reign, the Blues had not lost at Old Trafford in the league since 1965. A remarkable record and one that an ex-Blue such as Webb should have known about.

Sadly, Chelsea showed little interest on the day and the fans sitting were forced to watch their side lose 3-0 with the third an embarrassing own goal by Steve Clarke. Team captain Andy Townsend was playing like a man who wanted to leave the club at the end of the season, and of the current players still at Chelsea, while Dennis Wise is the only Chelsea player remaining of the eleven who played that day.

The most embarrassing moment for the travelling Chelsea fans came in the 60th minute when promising youngster Neil Shipperley, in only his second game for the club, was substituted for Steve Livingstone. With United already 3-0 up, Webb pinned his hopes on the only signing he made for the club. Livingstone had been signed by Webb in a swap deal which had seen promising youngster Graham Le Saux go to Blackburn Rovers in the opposite direction. Le Saux went on to England caps, a Premier League title and an eventual transfer back to Chelsea for an expensive £5 million. Livingstone never played for Chelsea again other than two substitute appearances in friendlies against Reading and West Bromwich Albion at the start of the next season.

The 1992/93 season petered out disappointingly as the Blues finished eleventh in the table, their long-suffering fans forced to endure a 21st consecutive season without a trophy. Those same Chelsea fans still believed that things could only get better and that the next season would be their year.

At times Chelsea fans have resembled the Trotter brothers in the BBC's successful long-running comedy *Only Fools and Horses*. The final sentence uttered by most Chelsea fans when the last ball was kicked at the end of every season began with the immortal line 'this time next year we'll be.......' It is perhaps no coincidence that the first series of *Only Fools and Horses* coincided with Chelsea's gloomy years and that when Del Boy and Rodney finally struck it rich, the Blues were celebrating success on the football pitch by winning the FA Cup in 1997.

When I started writing this book at the beginning of last season I optimistically envisaged writing about our first league title for 45 years and intended that it would celebrate the Blues first season in the Champions League. I had planned for the book to be a history of the club culminating with the final chapter being a review of an all-conquering 1999/2000 season. Clearly, events did not quite work out like that and as the season progressed bits were added and bits were taken away. One of the final additions was the title of the book *Blue Tomorrow*.

I was aware of the programme on Channel Chelsea bearing the same name that few people outside South West London had seen and before anyone gets the idea, this was not my reason for the book title. When looking at the chapters in the book, and after some early efforts at encapsulating the Chelsea experience, *Blue Tomorrow* seemed to have a nice ring to it. No sooner had I agreed on the title than Chelsea released their FA Cup final record under the same title!

Nevertheless, *Blue Tomorrow* sums up what Chelsea fans have always yearned for over the years. No matter how bad things have seemed, the fans have remained loyal in the hope of better times around the corner. We have always been optimistic fans, we have always believed that silverware is just around the corner and as each trophy-less year passed by, and a few more fans would reluctantly stop going, the rest of us continued to believe that we would see our *Blue Tomorrow*.

So why are we like this? Why the optimism? Many outside observers would have said that, until the historic 1997 FA Cup final win, the most optimistic supporters in the land still lived in the past rather than the future. We harked back to the days of the 1970s, the days of Osgood, Hudson, Cooke and Harris.

The days when Chelsea ruled the roost and were one of the top sides in the country. On reflection I suppose we did. Most Chelsea fans started going regularly during that era and therefore retained a strong affinity with that side, as it was the only really successful period in the club's history. But the adversity which followed created an optimism that made fans believe our glory days would return.

Even when it all went horribly wrong, and the club severely tested the loyalty of the most ardent fans, the supporters remained loyal. After the success of the seventies the board, looking to build on that success, embarked on an ambitious plan to build the best stadium in the country. The building of the East Stand was proposed as the first stage of full ground redevelopment that would see Chelsea playing in a brand new 60,000 all-seater stadium.

Sadly, the three-day week, rising building costs and regular industrial disputes saw the stand go over budget. Its construction also coincided with a disastrous period on the pitch, as the star team of the early 70s grew old and in some cases angry. So by the time the new stand was opened for the opening of the 1974/75 season, Chairman Brian Mears' words that the new stadium represented 'the beginning of a new era in the history of Chelsea Football Club' seemed to have more than a hollow ring. By the end of the season Chelsea were not only relegated, but over £3m in debt.

Indeed during the mid-70s it took a miracle for the club to survive. The era was characterised by two relegations, the departure of Osgood, Hudson, Webb, Hollins and eventually Dave Sexton and nearly a decade of mediocre football played mainly in the Second Division, with only the 1976/77 Eddie McCreadie promotion-winning side worth remembering.

However, from a fan's viewpoint, it was during these years that Chelsea's away following mushroomed to the extent that we seemed to take more fans away some weeks than we were getting at home. I remember being there in the early 80s when we had 6,000 for a home game with Leyton Orient, when as many fans the week before had travelled up to Hillsborough. These times are not known as the gloomy years for nothing.

In the early seventies, Chelsea had become one of the biggest clubs in the country and even during the gloomy years, most Chelsea fans believed that their side was still one of the big teams, irrespective of whatever predicament the team found itself in at the time. If we were patient, we thought, our time would come. In the meantime, we had to suffer lesser lights like Coventry, Luton, Wimbledon, Ipswich and Southampton winning at Wembley while we put up with embarrassing early-round exits at the hands of Cardiff, Scunthorpe, Scarborough and Reading.

On this evidence, the title *Blue Tomorrow* could not be more apt. One of the early chapters examines the history of Chelsea Football Club. A history that is littered with ifs, buts, maybes and might-have-beens but this has not stopped the supporters of this great club retaining a level of optimism unsurpassed by any other group of supporters in the country. It made no difference how bad things got on or off the field, we all believed that good things were just over the horizon. A change of playing personnel, a change of manager, a change of chairman, a different stadium. We have seen them all and come through the other side – now we are enjoying the most successful time in our history.

Then there have been the moments when Chelsea managed to pluck defeat from the jaws of victory. Chapter Two, *Appetite for Destruction*, is not an appreciation of the only decent album released by Guns N' Roses but something that defines Chelsea over the years. It looks at how the history of the club has been littered with serious disagreements between key personalities at the club just when we appeared on the verge of great things. For instance, there was the Docherty–Venables spat in the sixties. In 1965 Chelsea were closing in on a treble. Having won the League Cup, they were in the semi-final of the FA Cup and top of the league with six games to go. They lost to Liverpool in the FA Cup and fell away in the run-in, allowing Manchester United to snatch the title.

Docherty had a young side at the time, skippered and inspired by Terry Venables and matters came to a head when Chelsea travelled north for their last two league games at Burnley and Blackpool.

Docherty sent home eight players, including Venables, George Graham and future Chelsea manager John Hollins, for breaking a curfew in Blackpool. With reserves brought up from London at the last minute, Chelsea were humiliated 6-2 by Burnley, ending any remaining hopes of the title. Venables and Docherty continued to clash after the Blackpool affair until he was stripped of the captaincy and quickly sold to rivals Tottenham.

If that was not bad enough, there was the Sexton–Osgood–Hudson row in the 70s. Having started the decade winning trophies in successive seasons, the club was thrown into turmoil when the two stars of the side, Peter Osgood and Alan Hudson fell out with manager Dave Sexton. When the board backed the manager there was only going to be one winner and within weeks of being dropped both players were transferred. Throw in the row between Eddie McCreadie and the Chelsea board in 1977 and Ruud Gullit and Ken Bates in 1997 and history does seem to have a habit of repeating itself.

To cap it all, just as I was completing the book, Chelsea sacked the most successful manager in their history. Had the Blues pushed the self-destruct button once again? Or had Bates pulled a masterstroke by appointing the relatively unknown Claudio Ranieri in his place?

Chelsea Football Club have come a long, long way in the past seven years and nobody wants to go back to the half-empty Stamford Bridge and midtable obscurity with which supporters were familiar in the early 90s. Can it really only be seven years ago that things began to change at Chelsea? David Webb was replaced as manager by Glenn Hoddle and what has now become known as the 'Chelsea Revolution' began. Hoddle changed the club inside and out and began a process that his successor Ruud Gullit carried on, culminating in the FA Cup win in 1997. This revolution is covered in Chapter Three. The arrival of Hoddle paved the way for Gullit and led eventually to Gianluca Vialli becoming the most successful manager in the club's history.

Glenn's arrival also saw European football return to Stamford Bridge for the first time since John Hollins put a penalty wide against the part-timers of Atvidaberg 23 years earlier. In Chapter Four I examine the Blues' European record, in particular those heart-breaking last seven minutes in the Nou Camp last April. Chelsea could have been the first club to enter the European Cup and who knows how our history would have panned out had we followed Hibernian into the competition that same year. Hibernian made the semi-finals and a few quid on the way but Chelsea bottled it in 1955 when the FA asked them to withdraw. Manchester United were made of sterner stuff, entered it the following season and have been in it once or twice since, I gather. We had to wait over forty years to get another chance. A tomorrow that took a long time coming.

The last five years have seen Chelsea playing in European competition on a regular basis and with the atmosphere at home games now a shadow of its former self and domestic away match tickets harder to get hold of, Europe is now the place to have the 'craic' away from home and Chelsea fans now travel in greater numbers to places like Mallorca, Seville, Vienna, and Milan than to many Premier League grounds. In recent years Chelsea fans have had the opportunity to visit such cities as Prague, Stockholm, Vienna, Seville, Copenhagen, Barcelona, Rome and Berlin to name but a few. From the four hundred who froze their rocks off in Tromso, to the twenty thousand who went to Stockholm there have been many memorable moments on and off the field.

If you relied on the press for information on Chelsea last season, you would be forgiven for thinking that any memorable moments were few and far between. However although a final finish of fifth may disappoint some, if you look back seven years to that Old Trafford game, significant progress has been made during that time. Chelsea have not finished out of the top five in the last four seasons, and Chapter Six looks back on a varied and successful season at Stamford Bridge.

Among the headline-grabbing accusations aimed at Chelsea last season, the club's so-called foreign policy came in for most stick. In Chapter Five I take a closer look at the youth policy and focus the spotlight on the young players currently at the club in an attempt to explain why so many are optimistic about the most promising set of youngsters since Eddie McCreadie's promotion- winning side of 1977. It only seems like yesterday that the English press were writing positive things about the youth set up at Chelsea after the arrival of Glenn Hoddle as manager and the appointment of Graham Rix as youth team coach. A huge restructuring programme was implemented at youth level. With the same playing set-up throughout the club from first team to youth team, the idea of a completely foreign Chelsea team seemed an anathema.

The final chapter examines Chelsea Village. Set up by Ken Bates in the early nineties, it seems the future of Chelsea seriously depends on its success. Like his predecessor Brian Mears, Bates has always believed that football clubs can no longer survive on income derived solely from the turnstiles on 25-30 days a year. His vision for Chelsea Village was that it would provide the club with vital income streams to support the core business – football. Thus Bates was attempting to insure the club against a return to the gloomy years. So the theory goes, that if Chelsea are ever relegated or attendances drop significantly, the club will be supported by the income generated by the bars, restaurants, car parks, shops, hotels and travel agencies.

However, the most successful part of the business at the moment seems to be the football club, with season tickets at record levels and every home game a sell-out – except UEFA Cup games, it would seem! Clearly, most Chelsea fans go home happy each Saturday if the Blues have got three points or if there is a trophy to cheer at the end of the season. Although they know and love Chelsea Football Club, few supporters are aware of the importance of the Village and how it affects the playing side of things.

At the moment, Chelsea Village have a £75 million bond

that needs repaying in seven years time along with the £6 million odd interest required to finance it each year. For the future of Chelsea to be secure then like it or not Chelsea Village has to be successful. At present Chelsea Village are paying out approximately £16,000 every day in interest payments alone. That is more money than even some Chelsea fans earn in a year. You also have to consider that Ken Bates is not getting any younger and that he might not be around in seven years time when the loan needs to be repaid. By then he would be 75 years of age and even if he is still alive, would he still want to be Chairman at that age? He had previously planned to step aside in 2002 with the intention that the late Matthew Harding would be groomed as his successor. Whether or not he still intends to retire only he knows but whether he stays or retires, one thing is for certain – the loan needs to be repaid and there is still £117 million outstanding including interest payments.

The clock is ticking.

Chelsea: From Genesis to Revolution

Stamford Bridge was opened for the first time in April 1877 as the home of London Athletic Club. The ground had previously been an area for garden allotments and market gardening before two London businessmen, James and William Waddell, acquired it. They paid the princely sum of £2,599 after their previous site, in nearby Lillie Road, proved unsuitable.

In the early days of the London Athletic Club only one stand existed, where the Shed End Stand is today. It seated 1,000 spectators – a dramatic contrast to the new Stamford Bridge that now seats 42,000 paying punters.

The Waddell brothers were not renowned for their business acumen and soon found themselves in dire straits financially, having to flee the country in disgrace. The next owner was the rather curiously-named Mr Stunt, who had a clause inserted into the lease that the London Athletic Club should be leaseholders at Stamford Bridge for at least two years after his death.

This proved relevant when in 1896 local businessman Gus Mears and his brother Joseph had the idea to turn Stamford Bridge into a ground good enough for league football. They had already purchased a large area next door to the Athletic Club so they could realise their vision of developing their own football club in the heart of London. The Mears brothers were keen football fans and regarded Stamford Bridge as a prime location for a stadium that could eventually hold 100,000 spectators, each of whom would be afforded a perfect view of the game.

Having acquired the freehold of Stamford Bridge, the brothers' dream of owning their own football stadium had to be put on hold for a few years as Mr Stunt survived until 1902, so it was not until 1904 that the brothers owned Stamford Bridge outright and the story of football at the Bridge could begin.

An immediate approach was made to neighbours Fulham Football Club to see if they wanted to move their team from Craven Cottage. One director, John Dean, was initially keen but, in a decision that would be repeated 80 or so years later, the Fulham chairman Henry Norris declined the offer. Perhaps the current Fulham chairman, Harrods boss Mohammed Al-Fayed, would be amused to discover that his predecessor was reluctant to pay the modest rent of £1,500 per annum.

With the ambition to stage football at Stamford Bridge becoming a distant reality, Gus Mears was made an offer to sell the site by the Great Western Railway Company, who wished to turn Stamford Bridge into railway sidings and a goods yard. While contemplating that offer, he met with Frederick Parker, a friend and local financier who had been involved with the London Athletic Club since its infancy. Parker shared the Mears' ambition of having a football club on the site and made a last-ditch attempt to persuade his friend not to sell. As luck would have it, Mears' Scotch terrier attacked Parker at the meeting. The sight of Colonel Parker hopping around in pain caused the Mears so much amusement that, turning to Parker, Gus said, 'Get that bite seen to and we will meet here tomorrow morning and get busy.'

They did 'get busy' and within days they had decided that if Fulham wanted to stay at the Cottage they should form their own football club and, after the names London Football Club, Stamford Bridge Football Club and Kensington Football Club were considered and rejected, they eventually settled on Chelsea Football Club.

They commissioned renowned architect Archibald Leitch to design a new stand on the East Side of the ground. Leitch had an impressive CV as a football stadium designer – he helped many of the cathedrals of British football, including Villa Park, Goodison, Ibrox, and Hampden. By early 1905, the East Stand was under construction, and soon after three huge terraces were begun which, on completion, would give the stadium a capacity approaching 70,000.

The first meeting of Chelsea Football Club took place on 14 March 1905. The first item on the agenda was the election of a chairman, and Claude Kirby was appointed to the post. Recruitment of a manager followed swiftly and in April 1905 John Tait Robertson filled the hot seat. 29-year-old Robertson was appointed as player-manager on £4 per week. His reputation in the game had been established as a Scottish international and he had been a member of the Glasgow Rangers side that had won three titles in a row between 1900 and 1902. He had the reputation of being a shrewd judge of talent and, with the newly-formed Chelsea keen to enter the Football League and possible entry only a matter of weeks away, the Scotsman had his work cut out to assemble a squad fit for league football.

Within a week of his appointment Robertson had signed three players from Small Heath (later to become Birmingham City) and within the month, he had assembled a squad of players that included the legendary Sheffield United goalkeeper, Willie 'Fatty' Foulkes. Although Foulkes only played one season for Chelsea, he became a folk hero among the fans. He was already well known in the game partly because he had played in three FA Cup finals before arriving at Stamford Bridge but mainly because he was such a huge man. At well over six feet tall and twenty-five stones, he was an intimidating figure in goal – it was said that any opposing forward bearing down on him could only see half the goal. Meanwhile, Robertson continued to assemble a talented squad in the optimistic belief that Chelsea would be elected to the Football League – but this was by no means a certainty.

On 29 May 1905, at the Annual General Meeting of the Football League, held at the Havistock Hotel in central London, Colonel Parker gave a three-minute presentation in an attempt to persuade League members to allow his club in. Parker was a shrewd operator and took the precaution of bribing the bar staff to ensure that when rounds of scotch were being bought, his glass would only contain ginger ale. After his three-minute speech, the League Committee retired to discuss Chelsea's membership.

If anything swung the vote, it was probably Stamford Bridge, Chelsea's ready-made stadium. The club was elected to the Football League by two votes and Chelsea's first league match was away to Stockport County on 2 September 1905. Chelsea lost 1-0 but the following Saturday, while still on their travels in the north, they won their first game in the Football League, 1-0 at Blackpool. Two days later, the first-ever league game was staged at Stamford Bridge against Hull City and Chelsea ran out emphatic winners, beating the Tigers 5-1. A crowd of just over 6,000 saw goals from David Copeland (two) and Jimmy Windridge (hat-trick). Chelsea wore blue shirts and white shorts, a home strip they would retain for nearly sixty years until Tommy Docherty changed the kit to all-blue in 1964. At the end of their first season Chelsea's playing record read: played 38; won 22; drawn 9; lost 7. They scored 90 goals, conceded 37. In their first season Chelsea had finished a respectable third in the Second Division.

One notable moment in their first season was the day Chelsea played two matches in one day. When Manchester United courted controversy last season because they withdrew from the FA Cup to play in the World Club Championship in Brazil, the debate at the time questioned why United could not field a below-strength side consisting of reserves and juniors in th FA Cup. Indeed, United have Chelsea to thank for them being allowed to withdraw from the competition. In that 1905/06 season Chelsea's league game with Burnley clashed with their FA Cup tie away to Crystal Palace. Nowadays, the league game would probably be rearranged but then the Football League insisted Chelsea field their strongest side in the league and fulfil the fixture. Chelsea, always a club prepared to obey the rules, complied and beat Burnley 1-0 at Stamford Bridge. A scratch side was dispatched to South London the same afternoon and were hammered 7-1 by Crystal Palace, which remains Chelsea's record defeat in the FA Cup. As a result, the Football Association passed a rule that teams must field full-strength sides in future.

In that first season, it would seem that Londoners took to the new team and Chelsea were well supported with an average attendance of 14,368. Their highest gate of the season was against Manchester United (no change there then), when over sixty thousand spectators went through the Stamford Bridge turnstiles with the gates swelled by thousands of 'cockney reds'.

The following season promotion was gained to the First Division, mainly thanks to an impressive home record and the goal scoring exploits of new signing George Hilsdon, who managed 27 goals including five in one game against Glossop.

Sadly, Chelsea's time in the top flight was short-lived and after only three seasons they had their first taste of relegation, a flavour fans would become accustomed to over the years. However, the relegation run-in was not without its share of controversy. In a stronger financial position than many other clubs in the First Division, the Board attempted to make some last-minute purchases to stave off relegation. Five players were bought in a desperate attempt to avoid the drop but Chelsea were still relegated. As a result, the Football League introduced the 16 March transfer deadline rule which prevented any transfers after that date each season. The same rule exists today to prevent a repetition of what Chelsea had tried to do, i.e. buy their way out of trouble.

Chelsea's absence from the top flight was brief and after only two seasons the Blues were promoted behind champions Derby County in 1911/12.

The following season, Chelsea clung to First Division status by their fingertips but after an encouraging eighth place in 1913/14, optimism rose at Stamford Bridge. Since the club's formation, gates had risen steadily each year so that by 1914 Chelsea had an average gate of 36,131, but even in those days Chelsea fans were cherry-picking their games. A crowd of 61,500 saw Chelsea lose to Tottenham, while two days later only 5,000 fans watched their home game against West Bromwich Albion.

In the event, the 1914/15 season should have been curtailed by war although the Football League insisted the season continue to its conclusion, despite most clubs finding it impossible to field the same side regularly. Chelsea's league form suffered significantly as a result but the FA Cup was a different story. Since entering the Football League, Chelsea had performed badly in the cup with only a semi-final defeat by Newcastle in 1911 to show for their efforts. However, in 1914/15 they embarked on the first of the club's many cup runs.

After beating Swindon in a replay, Woolwich Arsenal were beaten 1-0 by a Harold Halse goal and Manchester City and Newcastle were both beaten 1-0 on their own grounds. The semi-final was played at Villa Park where Halse and James Croal, a schoolmaster by profession, scored to take Chelsea through to their first-ever cup final.

Despite the war and manager David Calderhead not knowing who would be available to play on Saturday from one week to the next, Chelsea managed to field a strong side for the final against Sheffield United. Sadly, with few Chelsea fans able to make the journey to the final at Old Trafford a partisan crowd, made up mainly of Blades' fans, saw a below-par Chelsea comfortably beaten 3-0. It would be 55 years before Chelsea finally won the coveted trophy.

On top of losing the FA Cup final, Chelsea's league form meant that they were relegated but following the cancellation of the 1915/16 season, football fans had to make do with friendly games as professionals guested for clubs offering the greatest financial incentives.

As a celebration to mark the end of the war, Chelsea and neighbours Fulham had the honour of playing in the Victory Cup final at Highbury which Chelsea won 3-0. The club's first trophy was soon followed by the good news that following the reformation of the Football League in 1919, the First Division was being expanded to twenty-two clubs and Chelsea would not be relegated.

The twenties saw little success on the field for the Blues, with another relegation in 1923/24 and Chelsea spent the next six years in the Second Division.

In true Chelsea style they only won promotion on the last day of the season when, despite losing to Bury at Gigg Lane, a defeat for rivals Oldham at Barnsley meant Chelsea returned to the top flight. They would stay in the top division for over thirty years until their relegation in the 1961/62 season.

The thirties saw the departure of manager David Calderhead, in May 1933, to be replaced by Leslie Knighton who had previously managed Birmingham City, Huddersfield Town, Manchester City and Arsenal. Sadly Knighton had little success in his time at Chelsea and was replaced at the end of the 1938/39 season by Billy Birrell, who had previously managed neighbours Queens Park Rangers.

Strangely, Knighton's best season had been the previous year when Chelsea topped the league after only twelve matches. Once more, however, Chelsea's inconsistency saw a run of only two wins in twenty games and the Blues eventually finished tenth.

Birrell was unfortunate that no sooner had he taken over the managerial hot seat at the Bridge than war broke out again. Chelsea played only three league games in the 1939/40 season when league football was cancelled. The last match was a 1-0 defeat at Anfield on 2 September. During the war, football continued at Stamford Bridge, although the odd game did take longer than ninety minutes as there was the small matter of air raids. The most important man in the ground in those days was the member of staff who used to sit on the East Stand during each home game. He spent the entire ninety minutes ignoring the football, watching the skies just in case Hitler sent his Luftwaffe to check on the score!

Chelsea managed to play in two wartime cup finals, losing to Charlton in 1944 in the League South Final, and returning the following year to beat Millwall 2-0. Unfortunately, with so many players away both Chelsea sides were made up of guest players from other clubs, but that didn't stop the crowds – 85,000 attended the Charlton game and 90,000 the following year for the Millwall game. No matter what the occasion, Chelsea fans always love turning up for a Wembley final.

In 1946, league football resumed again and over the next few years, despite the goals of England international Tommy Lawton and his successor Roy Bentley, Chelsea could only finish fifteenth, eighteenth and thirteenth in the First Division. Scoring goals was not a problem, with Chelsea averaging 70 a season, but unfortunately problems continued at the back as the defence habitually conceded more! As an example, Chelsea produced some extraordinary scorelines in this era, losing 7-4 to Liverpool, 6-1 at Stoke City and 6-4 at Wolves.

By 1949/50, some consistency began to appear in Chelsea's play and, although they only managed thirteenth in the First Division, they reached the semi-final of the FA Cup where they were beaten by Arsenal after extra time in a replay at White Hart Lane. However, the following season was one of the most memorable in Chelsea's history. With four games remaining, the club were rooted to the foot of the table, six points below Everton (remember there were only two points for a win in those days) and appeared doomed to relegation. To stand any chance of survival they had to win their four remaining games, a seemingly impossible task as they had failed to win in their last fourteen outings. Liverpool were the first opponents and a 1-0 victory was recorded. Four days later, goals from Ken Armstrong and Roy Bentley gave Chelsea a 2-1 win over Wolves. Local rivals Fulham were then beaten at Craven Cottage and with one game remaining Chelsea were joint bottom of the league along with Sheffield Wednesday, two points behind Everton in 20th place.

As luck would have it, Wednesday were at home to Everton on the final day of the season while Chelsea entertained Bolton. The Blues won 4-0 and Wednesday slaughtered Everton 6-0 so Chelsea managed to stay up by the skin of their teeth – or .044 of a goal on goal average.

The pressure had been too much for manager Birrell and he retired, ending a thirteen-year association with the club. It was time for a younger man to take over and the man handed the task of reviving Chelsea's fortunes was ex-Arsenal striker and England international Ted Drake.

Drake had a huge reputation in the game following his exploits for Arsenal and England and took little time in making his mark at Stamford Bridge. In Drake's eyes Chelsea had gathered a reputation for being a soft touch and their nickname 'The Pensioners' had given many a has-been comedian the odd laugh or two in music halls up and down the country.

First to go was the nickname, it being replaced by the more conservative 'The Blues'. Also, with the demise of the 'Pensioner', Drake introduced a new club emblem – a blue lion holding a golden crozier, a badge later to become an important part of the club's identity. Sadly, Ken Bates replaced the badge soon after he took charge, as the club did not own the copyright and it reminded him too much of his predecessors the Mears family.

Ted Drake continued his Stamford Bridge revolution. He berated the home fans for being too sporting. Chelsea's home support had gathered a reputation as one of the most sporting grounds in the country. Drake felt that matters were difficult enough already, with the fans tucked away so far from the pitch and was appalled to find the home fans applauding the opposition whenever they scored against Chelsea. This welcoming West London attitude held no fears for opponents making their annual visit to Stamford Bridge – from now on, Drake insisted the fans get behind his team and make Stamford Bridge a fortress to put fear into opposing teams.

Drake was quick to ask the crowd for patience however. He committed himself to building a team within three years that could challenge for the title and as the club had not won a domestic trophy since its formation at the turn of the century, few fans quarrelled with this line of argument.

In his first few seasons in charge Drake failed to set the First Division alight. His construction of a championship-challenging side was one of evolution rather than revolution. In his first season Chelsea finished 19th, just above the relegation zone and other than a cup run that took them to the fifth round, the only satisfaction most Chelsea fans got during the season was the Blues doing the double over Tottenham. Nearly forty years on and nothing much has changed there then!

But steadily Drake introduced his own style of play, hard-working players replaced old crowd favourites. For some Chelsea fans, Drake went too far and the style of football Chelsea fans had been brought up to expect appeared to be vanishing. The following season, though, things began to go in the manager's favour. And although there was no apparent reason to crack open the champagne after finishing eighth, it actually represented Chelsea's highest league position for nearly fifty years.

The season had seen its share of problems. By November, Chelsea were bottom of the table and Drake had to endure an 8-1 hammering at Molineux at the hands of Billy Wright's mighty Wolves. This remains Chelsea's record defeat and is perhaps the least- remembered statistic from Drake's reign as manager. Sorry Ted.

However, the following season Drake and his players immortalised themselves in Chelsea history. For the only time in Chelsea history they won the First Division title. The year was 1955, Chelsea's Golden Jubilee – 50 years after Colonel Parker had plied the Football League management committee with drink, Chelsea finally won their first trophy and the most important domestic pot of the lot.

The title win was not without its critics. Many home fans, schooled on a different style of Chelsea football, were disappointed with Ted Drake's management. His Chelsea team were a hard-running, hard-working side who never gave up. Their game was built on a solid defence – a trait more in common with Drake's spiritual home in the marble halls of Highbury.

The press did not take too kindly to Chelsea either. By common consensus, Chelsea were not reckoned to be the best football team in the country, despite their title victory. The pundits reckoned that Chelsea had merely been the best of a bad bunch. Their hard-working brand of football won few fans among Fleet Street purists. The title decider, played in front of 51,421 fans against an already relegated Sheffield Wednesday was won in some style 3-0, with two goals from Eric Parsons and a penalty from Peter Sillett. Drake had kept his promise. Chelsea had won the championship by four points from Wolves, Portsmouth and Sunderland who all finished level on points. Within three years Chelsea had not only challenged for the title they had actually won it. After the game Drake came out to greet the fans, walked up to the microphone and told delighted supporters, 'This is the happiest moment of my life. I was asked would we win the cup? I thought we might. I thought we had a chance of winning the championship even better.'

For many clubs winning the title is the catalyst for the club to go on to greater things but the players Drake had assembled at Chelsea had given their all in winning the championship. The following season proved a struggle for Chelsea. The signs were there for all to see from the first match of the season as they lost 2-0 at home to Bolton Wanderers. A fortnight later, visitors Portsmouth won 5-1. At one stage the Blues were bottom of the table and, though they rallied in the second half of the season, they could only finish sixteenth. The only bright spot on a disappointing season came when the Blues won the Charity Shield for the first time, beating Newcastle 3-0 at Stamford Bridge with goals from Bentley, Blunstone and an own goal from Newcastle defender McMichael. Sadly, only 12,000 fans were there to see it – the game was played on a Wednesday afternoon in September unlike the modern-day curtain raiser it has become.

Drake quickly realised that his players had peaked and given their all in that championship-winning season. He soon began to break up the side with John Harris, Bobby Smith and Stan Willemse the first departures.

The next three seasons saw Chelsea finish eleventh, fourteenth and eighteenth as the Drake championship-winning side became a vague memory and Chelsea spent more time in the lower half of the table, fighting relegation rather than challenging for trophies.

The one bright spot during this period was the discovery of a young striker, Jimmy Greaves. Greaves scored on his debut, away at Spurs in August 1957. Over the next four seasons he scored 132 goals in 169 appearances with Wolves, Preston North End and West Bromwich Albion suffering more at his feet than most when he scored five against each of them in single games. With Chelsea struggling during this period, it is fair to say that without Greaves, the Blues would have been relegated.

The 1958/59 season is a prime example. Greaves scored 32 of the Chelsea total of 77 goals while the defence managed to let in 98. No matter how many goals Greaves scored in a game, he could almost guarantee that the defence behind him would let in one more.

The next two years saw much of the same with Greaves almost single-handedly keeping Chelsea in the First Division. In 1959/60 the Blues spent most of the season fighting relegation and were on the end of some severe hammerings. At Stamford Bridge, Manchester United won 6-3, West Ham 4-2 and Sheffield Wednesday 4-0 in the last home game before Christmas. During the final home game of the season, with Chelsea just about assured of safety, came the ultimate humiliation, a 5-1 defeat to Wolves. Away from home, West Ham won again, 4-2 at Upton Park and Everton put another six past Reg Matthews at Goodison.

Finally, Greaves decided he had had enough and announced before the end of the 1960/61 season that he would be leaving the club. The fans did what they could to persuade him to stay, as they remained unsurprisingly pessimistic about their future in his absence. On the final day of a season that had seen Greaves score more goals than anyone in the club's history before or since, Chelsea made him captain. Nottingham Forest were the visitors and in a game that could have mirrored any one of Greaves' Chelsea appearances, a kamikaze home defence gifted Forest three goals. Fortunately for Chelsea, Greaves went one better and scored all four in a memorable 4-3 victory for the Blues. The crowd carried him off the pitch realising his like would probably never be seen again at Stamford Bridge.

'One wonders with desperation what Chelsea would do without him next year,' said a TV commentator as Greaves bade farewell to Stamford Bridge. Sadly, Chelsea were relegated the following season even though Drake was gone by September 1961. But his replacement Tommy Docherty could not reverse the fortunes of an ailing side that quickly.

Docherty had inherited a squad with a number of senior players and a good crop of youngsters just breaking through or on the periphery of the first team. Docherty put his faith in youth. Many had graduated from the youth team and he dispensed with the services of a number of senior players, including some who had played in the 1955 championship-winning side. Reg Matthews was sold to Derby County, Ron Tindall went to West Ham United, Peter Sillett got a free transfer to Guildford and brother John was sent to Coventry for £3,000.

With a side mainly consisting of former youth team players, Docherty got Chelsea promoted at the first attempt. Although he used 24 players over the season, he tried to stick to the same eleven players unless injury or suspension ruled anyone out. Terry Venables and John Mortimore were ever-present and six others played 36 games or more. By the end of the season, Chelsea had finished second with 52 points behind champions Stoke City but it had been a close call. Until Christmas, Chelsea had been in fine form and were six points clear at the top of the table by Boxing Day, having gone on an eleven-match unbeaten run from October.

The winter of 1963 was one of the harshest on record. As a result the Football League as good as shut down for the months of January and February. Chelsea's first game after Boxing Day was on February 9 away to Swansea and they lost 2-0. Five consecutive defeats followed and Chelsea's promotion campaign was in severe jeopardy. A home defeat by eventual champions Stoke City meant Chelsea needed a win at Roker Park against promotion rivals Sunderland.

A goal off Tommy Harmer's backside secured Docherty's men the points. Three nights later 54,558 fans turned up at Stamford Bridge with Chelsea needing to win the last game to guarantee promotion. Opponents Portsmouth were swept away 7-0 by a triumphant Chelsea, with Bobby Tambling scoring four goals and Derek Kevan, Frank Blunstone and Terry Venables one each. However, despite a return to the top flight, Docherty was not content for Chelsea to just make up the numbers, he wanted them to be challenging for the championship each season.

In their first season back, Chelsea won 20 league games, scoring 72 goals in the process and finished fifth in the table, the highest position in the league since they had won the championship. Over the next three seasons, Chelsea finished third, fifth and ninth and appeared in two FA Cup semi-finals and a Fairs Cup semi-final. They won the League Cup against Leicester City in 1965 and reached the 1967 FA Cup final only to be beaten by rivals Tottenham.

When Docherty finally resigned on October 6 1967, he had experimented with many different formulas in an attempt to build a side capable of sustaining a championship challenge. In his final full season in charge he must have thought he had cracked it when Chelsea went through the first ten games of the season unbeaten and sat proudly at the top of the league. Sadly, it did not last and though Docherty went on to manage Aston Villa, Derby County, Manchester United and Queens Park Rangers, that Chelsea side was the closest he ever got to winning the title.

Under Docherty, Chelsea's support gathered momentum and a group of fans began to congregate at the south end of the ground. As soon as you were old enough to go to football on your own with your mates and away from the supervision of your parents, the Shed was where you stood and as near as possible to the middle as possible. If you were lucky, you would get near to the 'Zigger Zagger Man' and hear him counted down from ten before launching into his song, 'Zigger Zagger, Zigger Zagger, Oi Oi Oi.' The 'Zigger Zagger Man' was Micky Greenaway, probably the best-known Chelsea fan of all time.

Greenaway grew up in Billing Street, a few hundred yards from Stamford Bridge. He was fortunate enough to have been a ball boy during Chelsea's Championship winning season in 1955. However, it was his initiative in being the founder of Chelsea's Shed End that formed his reputation at Stamford Bridge. In the mid-sixties the Football League ran a competition in its magazine *Football League Review* to find which club had the loudest fans. It was round about this time that Greenaway organised a group of Chelsea fans to congregate at the Shed End. Greenaway spent many a Friday night composing and gathering songs for the Sheddites to sing the following day. However, *Zigger-Zagger* was the rallying cry Greenaway would burst into to get his troops behind their team. In the same way that *My Way* will always be associated with Frank Sinatra, then *Zigger Zagger* will always remind Blues fans of Micky Greenaway.

The famous roof on the Shed was constructed in the 1930s but not, as you might expect, to keep the thousands of fans dry. It was actually built to provide cover for the bookmakers who usually stood on the back of the terrace on the nights when greyhound racing was held at Stamford Bridge. As any Chelsea regular will tell you, it often rains when night games are on at Stamford Bridge, so I imagine that the evening weather in SW6 in the 1930s was no different than today. The bookmakers were a powerful lobby and managed to persuade the club to put a roof over the terrace. Although the Shed was born, it was Greenaway and his companions who really brought the place to life, creating a raucous atmosphere at every home game with non-stop singing for ninety minutes. The Shed is as much a part of Chelsea history as players like Roy Bentley, Jimmy Greaves, Peter Osgood or Gianluca Vialli. Chelsea fans have a lot to thank Micky Greenaway for and it is my hope that, in the tradition of naming all the bars at Stamford Bridge after famous players, one day there will be one named after Micky Greenaway.

One man whose picture you can find in a few of the bars at Chelsea is Dave Sexton, who succeeded Tommy Docherty in 1967. Sexton was a popular successor to Docherty, having already been coach at the club and although he inherited a good squad of players, success was gradual as in his first three seasons in charge Chelsea finished sixth, fifth and then third in the table in 1969/70.

Although Sexton's side began to bury the old 'inconsistent Chelsea' jibes, it was in the FA Cup that the side really began to shine. Following Docherty's era, in which Chelsea had made a name for themselves as a useful cup side Sexton, in his first two seasons in charge, took Chelsea to the quarter-finals. However, in 1970 they went two stages better and having disposed of Watford 5-1 at White Hart Lane in the semi-final, reached the FA Cup final to play favourites Leeds United.

Having drawn a classic match at Wembley 2-2, with goals from Peter Houseman and a late equaliser from Ian Hutchinson, both sides had to wait a further 18 days for the replay at Old Trafford.

On Wednesday 29 April 1970, American Judge James Boyle's report into the death of Mary Jo Kopechne the previous year declared that Senator Edward Kennedy was probably driving the car before it crashed into a river in Chappaquiddick Island in July. The judge rejected Kennedy's claim he took a wrong turning on the way home from a party and that he had 'probably been driving negligently'. But if Teddy Kennedy had been 'negligent' in Chappaquiddick, the same night the same word could be used to describe Mick Jones' performance for Leeds United at Old Trafford following his rash challenge on Peter Bonetti after thirty-five minutes of the FA Cup final replay.

Jones' challenge left Bonetti temporarily crippled and Leeds took full advantage. Allan Clarke rode three tackles and put Jones through. His shot flew past Bonetti's shoulder into the roof of the net. Shortly after, Ron Harris did what David Webb had failed to do at Wembley. He clobbered Eddie Gray and made him a passenger for the remainder of the game. Then, with the clock ticking towards a Leeds United victory, Charlie Cooke sprinted forward to pick up a Hudson pass and cross for Osgood to head past Harvey to level the scores.

In extra time, the first period was almost complete when a throw was awarded to Chelsea on the left touchline. Ian Hutchinson, who had earned himself a reputation for having the longest throw in the game, picked up the ball and launched it into the Leeds United penalty area. There, waiting at the far post, was David Webb who gatecrashed a pile of Leeds defenders to head the ball into the net to win the game for Chelsea and give the Blues their first-ever FA Cup.

The following season, in the European Cup Winners' Cup final, Chelsea needed a replay once again to win the trophy. Having drawn 1-1 on the Wednesday, Chelsea returned to the Karaisaki stadium two days later and goals from John Dempsey and Peter Osgood were enough to secure a 2-1 victory for Dave Sexton's men.

The good times were rolling at Stamford Bridge and when Chelsea returned to Wembley the following season, as hot favourites to beat Stoke City in the League Cup final, no one could have expected the outcome. After Terry Conroy had given Stoke the lead and Osgood (naturally) had equalised just before half-time, the stage seemed set for a Chelsea victory. It did not happen. With seventeen minutes left, George Eastham, who even then was close to collecting his pension, scored the winning goal for Stoke and the first cracks appeared in the Chelsea armour.

Having finished sixth in 1971 and seventh the following season, Chelsea's league form deteriorated and twelfth place in 1972/73 was the club's lowest position for ten years. The only saving grace from that season were two cup runs that saw Chelsea reach the quarter-finals of the FA Cup and the semi-finals of the League Cup. Unfortunately, Arsenal and Norwich City ended Chelsea's Wembley aspirations for another year and it would be another 22 years before a Chelsea side graced Wembley in a domestic cup final. In that time Luton Town, Oxford United, Wimbledon, Coventry City and Ipswich Town all went to Wembley and won a trophy.

Chelsea's poor league form continued over the next two seasons and Dave Sexton finally resigned in October 1974 after a seven-year stint as Chelsea manager. Ron Suart, Sexton's assistant at the club, was initially given the job as caretaker manager. His caretaker role went on longer than anyone probably intended but Suart could not succeed where Sexton had failed. With three games to go of the 1974/75 season and Chelsea battling desperately against relegation, the board made a further change, appointing Eddie McCreadie as manager.

McCreadie immediately axed his former colleagues Hollins, Houseman and Hinton from the side and not only recalled Ray Wilkins after a four-game absence, but made him captain as well. McCreadie's three games in charge failed to produce a victory and Chelsea were relegated.

Their first season in the Second Division saw Chelsea finish a disappointing eleventh in the table but McCreadie had been ruthless in managing the side. He had given the youngsters their chance, sold Hollins, Houseman, Hinton and Kember and cancelled the contract of John Sissons.

Amid a heightening financial crisis, chairman Brian Mears optimistically hoped that the next season would be successful. The club was in debt and badly needed to gain promotion but even Mears himself had been overwhelmed by the support and generosity the club had received.

'The main thing we have experienced is that when you are in trouble friends rally round. The goodwill being shown towards the club is staggering and moving. No one is knocking us, no one is gloating over our problems. We have had hundreds of letters containing cheques, postal orders and ready cash – the lot. Most heartening of all is the players' attitude. They even waived their expenses when we toured Sweden for eight days. They were entitled to six pounds a day but none of them took a penny.

'With fans and players like that we must have a chance. If

the crowds do start coming back again they may do so from a variety of motives - goodwill, sympathy, love, morbid curiosity even. But it would be wonderfully poetic, don't you think, if we could hold them here with quality football.'

With the club's financial problems mounting, the club took the hard decision to quit its training ground at Mitcham. Chelsea had been there since 1964, but with the club being run on a shoestring the move would help save somewhere between £10,000 and £15,000 a year.

'The upkeep of the training ground cost a great deal of money.' said Mears. 'It will certainly help if we move to a place which has similar facilities but will not be such a drain on our resources.'

Chelsea started promisingly and by the halfway stage their nearest rivals were Wolverhampton Wanderers. Most pundits already had the rest of the division written off as also-rans, with Chelsea providing the only likely adversaries to Wolves' title aspirations. When Wolves came to the Bridge in December it was already being billed as a title decider.

It was the game of the day in the top two divisions as the ITV cameras and Brian Moore joined the 36,137 throng. A notable visitor to the Bridge attracted even more attention – the international peacemaker and American Secretary of State Dr Henry Kissinger. Stamford Bridge had been used to visits from Hollywood superstars in the days of Osgood, Hudson and co and staff had got used to the hullabaloo that surrounded such visits but no one anticipated the attention Kissinger's visit to the Bridge would cause.

An hour before kick-off a cavalcade of limousines arrived at the main gates. The large crowd mingling around the main entrance were amused and curious as to who all the men in dark glasses were. There were so many Secret Service personnel surrounding Kissinger that even Lee Harvey Oswald would have had trouble making an assassination attempt. With their customary dark sunglasses in place, despite it being not only December but one of the coldest days of the year, the whole affair had more in common with the circus coming to town than an international statesman. Every time the crowd shouted 'shoot', Kissinger's bodyguards squirmed uncomfortably.

The Secretary of State certainly picked the right time to visit the Bridge as the two promotion-chasing sides served up one of the games of the season on a pitch that would not have looked out of place in the Arctic Circle.

With the Blues 3-1 down, things looked grim. But nothing could prepare the American for the last ten minutes when first Ian Britton headed home a Wilkins corner and then, with only three minutes remaining, Steve Finnieston was first to react after Wolves keeper Pierce had saved well from Garry Stanley.

The crowd erupted in the East Stand and as everyone rose to acclaim Finnieston's goal, Kissinger's bodyguards panicked for a few seconds while their view of their man was obscured. One or two slipped their hands inside their pocket in the direction of their holsters but they had nothing to fear. The only 'hitman' was Steve Finnieston who, in scoring his 16th of the season, had salvaged his side's unbeaten home record.

Boosted by the Wolves game, Chelsea continued their promotion charge and were not put off by a hypnotist named Romark. Apparently he had put a curse on Crystal Palace the previous season, after which they were knocked out of the FA Cup and failed to gain promotion from the Third Division, having been runaway leaders for most of the season. Perhaps Chelsea had not given Mr Romark free tickets for a home game but he was in an unforgiving mood as he told *Daily Mirror* journalist and long-time Chelsea fan Nigel Clarke. 'It will be doomsville for Chelsea. They will go downhill just like Palace did. I will stake my reputation on it. They will just collapse. Last season 24 out of my 26 match predictions were right. The other two were draws.'

Chelsea's march towards promotion briefly became irrelevant when news filtered through that their former star player and double cup-winner Peter Houseman and his wife Sally had been tragically killed in a car crash. Houseman, his wife and two friends were returning to his home in Witney, Oxford from an

Oxford United Football Club dance when his white Avenger collided with another car on the A40. The death of both parents had orphaned Matthew (seven), Daniel (five), and Nathan (two).

Peter Houseman was born in Battersea in 1946, joining his local team Chelsea as a junior from Spencer Park School in the summer of 1962. Stamford Bridge remained his football home for thirteen years until his transfer in May 1975 to Oxford United.

'Nobby' Houseman played a total of 343 competitive games for Chelsea, scoring 39 goals and making countless others with his immaculate crosses from the left wing. His honours included winner's medals in the 1970 FA Cup final and a year later in the European Cup Winners' Cup final. His funeral was held on Friday 25 March in Sally Houseman's home town of Cirencester, with over thirty former Chelsea teammates attending.

Within days, Houseman's 'football family' rallied round with Chelsea organising a benefit match to raise funds for the children orphaned by the car crash. Manager Eddie McCreadie agreed to play for 'old' Chelsea against his own 'new' Chelsea.

And by the time minds returned to football, the promotion run-in gave Chelsea a few hiccups but McCreadie was determined to see the task through as he told the *Evening Standard* with six games to go.

'I know I am punishing myself with work and worry, but I am prepared to go to the physical and mental limits to make me and Chelsea winners. I am prepared to drag the team into the First Division if necessary. I'm prepared to do that because I have a strong back. I am a fighter and I am not letting go now. Too much is at stake and though I have never been so tired, I'll drag them along until I bloody well drop. I am determined to stick to my decision to resign if we do not secure promotion in two years. That means that if we do not go up this year, I'll have just one season left to prove myself.

'There would be no point in staying if I fail. I will have done everything possible and it would be someone else's turn. I've caressed, cuddled and kissed my team, which is the best squad of young players in the country.'

It seemed the pressure of getting Chelsea back to their rightful place in Division One was beginning to affect everybody at the club including Ray Wilkins.

'I have never felt so nervous,' admitted Wilkins. 'The pressure has finally caught up with me. What is the point in lying about it? It makes me feel sick inside to think about how I will feel if we fail to get promotion. I try, but I cannot seem to get away from the feeling. The only release comes when the referee blows his whistle to start the match. It is the waiting I hate. For months I never thought about it. I wasn't sure what people were talking about. Now I know.'

Chelsea's promotion dreams boiled down to one game – the return match at Molineux against Wolves. If Chelsea won, they won the league but if Wolves won, Chelsea would have to win their last game and rely on other teams losing. A few weeks before this vital match, the misbehaviour of certain elements in Chelsea's support had led to an away match ban for all Chelsea fans. However, with promotion at stake, all the talk among fans was about getting tickets for the Wolves game. Thousands of fans seemed determined to 'beat the ban' and for many it proved easier to get a ticket than they thought possible. All you had to do was stand outside Stamford Bridge and sooner or later, like a no11 bus, someone with tickets would come along. Terrace tickets for Molineux that were normally 80p were changing hands for between £2 and £3 and there was no shortage of takers.

In the week before the game all the talk was about the so-called 'Kamikaze Kids'. An 'elderly and long time Chelsea fan' had written an anonymous letter to the *Daily Mirror* to warn the authorities of a group of Chelsea fans going to Wolves intent on causing trouble. *The Mirror*, like most tabloids of that era, was obsessed by soccer violence and made the item its back page headline and readers, on the morning of 30 April 1977, turned to the sports pages to be greeted by the headline:

'WAR ON SOCCER KAMIKAZE KIDS'

The story continued. 'There is a gang of nine lads who are

the leaders of the Shed boys. They have been discussing tactics in order to cause as much aggravation as possible at the Wolves match. Led by a youth named Emu they are intending to travel to Wolverhampton then mug Wolves fans and grab their scarves to enable them to pass as Wolves supporters.

'They will lash out with various weapons, causing as much damage as possible to the enemy before either being beaten up by Wolves fans or overpowered by the police,

'Emu has started a new cult, named the Kamikaze Kids, which will go into operation for the first time at Wolves.'

Up in Wolverhampton, the police were ready with hundreds of extra officers, dog handlers and mounted officers drafted in from neighbouring forces for the biggest game the local police had handled for many a year.

'We are bringing in extra men to be ready for every eventuality. We know about the tickets getting into Chelsea supporters' hands. But it is those who are left outside who are our main concern,' said a police spokesman at the time.

Even the players jumped on the bandwagon in appealing for calm before the biggest game of the season. Wolves' striker John Richards spoke for all when he said, 'It is a game of football. So let the players decide who takes the championship.'

Tommy Langley has fond memories of this game and although he scored the vital goal it was for other reasons he remembers that match.

'As everybody knows Chelsea supporters were banned at the time and were not supposed to be at Molineux. Apparently they had been a bit boisterous that year and the FA banned them as a result.' Langley has a quick chuckle at the memory and continues, 'however there were at least 5,000 of them at Molineux that day. The funny thing was we had the pre-match meal at West Brom, we watched *Football Focus* in our hotel as you do, travelled on the team bus to the ground and saw all the home fans and nothing looked any different.

'At Molineux in the Old Stand the dressing rooms used to be in the far end and when we came out of the tunnel we heard this huge roar. We all looked ahead, there was nothing. We looked to the left and then when we looked to the right there was this sea of blue and white. Apparently the police had said there were so many Chelsea supporters in Wolverhampton they thought it would be safer to have them all in the ground, rather than roaming the streets. In a strange sort of way, I don't think our spirits were down beforehand as it was a big game but that sight gave us the extra impetus and we all said we were going to win promotion, not for ourselves but for those fans that had beaten the ban. They were not supposed to be there, and might not have got in, yet they had still travelled to Wolves. Unbelievable support!'

When the final whistle went at the end of a 1-1 draw both teams celebrated. Wolves were Champions but importantly for McCreadie, Chelsea were back in the First Division. No one now could deny him his moment of glory – he would finally earn the acclaim he deserved.

Sadly, McCreadie resigned in the summer and youth team coach, Chelsea old boy Ken Shellito was promoted to replace him.

With few funds in his first season, Shellito couldn't strengthen his side and did extremely well to keep the Blues in the top flight. A final position of sixteenth, although not flattering, remained a credit to him. Sadly, the following season a poor start saw Shellito replaced by the eccentric Irishman Danny Blanchflower. Chelsea embarked on the ultimate of losing streaks, losing 27 league games, including four months without a win at home and were relegated. As someone once said, a losing streak is a bit like joining the Moonies – easy to get into but a hell of a lot more difficult to get out of.

Perhaps the only memorable event of that woeful season was the match against Bolton Wanderers on 14 October. Chelsea were bottom of the league after nine games and had lost all four home games when newly-promoted Bolton came to town. By half time, following two goals from Alan Gowling and a penalty by famed Elvis Presley impersonator Frank Worthington, Chelsea were heading for a fifth home defeat of the season.

Then, with fifteen minutes left, Garry Stanley was replaced

by Clive Walker, who had lost his first team place following the early season signing of Duncan McKenzie.

Amazingly, Walker produced a match-winning performance in those last fifteen minutes that Chelsea fans still talk about today. For most it remains one of their top ten Chelsea games of all time.

Having inspired Chelsea to fight back from 3-0 down with goals from Swain, Langley and Walker, most sides would have been satisfied with a draw. But with a minute to go, the crowd were yelling for the ball to go to Walker every time Chelsea had possession. On cue, Walker cut in from the left and went for goal once more, his low grass-cutting cross came in and Sam Allardyce put the ball into his own net. In the space of fifteen minutes, Walker had won Chelsea the game.

As if to add to the previous season's disappointments, Ray Wilkins went to Manchester United in the close season while the opening day of the new season saw Chelsea pitched against pre-season promotion favourites Sunderland. The Blues battled well and at times had the Wearsiders on the rack, which even inspired the Whitewall to sing 'we don't need Wilkins anymore.' Oh didn't we!!

After a 0-0 draw, Chelsea won the next two games away to West Ham and home to Wrexham, before losing to the Geordies at St James' Park. The following Wednesday, the Blues were at home to Plymouth Argyle in the second round, second leg of the League Cup. Although they drew 2-2 in the first leg and a place in the third round seemed assured, fate once again played a cruel hand and not for the first time, Chelsea were bundled out of a cup competition by a lower division side.

So it was the following Saturday, during a home defeat to Birmingham City, that the Chelsea crowd booed the manager and team all the way to the dressing room. The bizarre substitution of Peter Osgood, replaced by Gary Chivers, when the Blues were losing did not endear Blanchflower to the home fans. That proved to be Peter Osgood's last game in a Chelsea shirt. He would not have wished it that way. Osgood later went to Butlin's holiday camps to coach kids – a shocking waste of a unique talent and it would be some years before he would find himself again welcome at Stamford Bridge. Blanchflower resigned the following Monday, saying that he never intended to stay long-term and that a younger man should take over. Danny Blanchflower sadly died in December 1993 after a lengthy illness.

Geoff Hurst took over as caretaker manager and Chelsea proceeded to win the next five games on the spin. The fans wanted Hurst as manager and it appeared that, over the next five-week period, Mears was stalling in the hope that Hurst messed up so he would have a good excuse not to appoint him. Hurst did not and on 27 October 1979 he became the twelfth manager in Chelsea's history.

The Hurst reign started promisingly but, having failed to win promotion in three seasons in charge, he was replaced by likeable Geordie John Neal. John Neal succeeded where Blanchflower and Hurst had failed and got Chelsea back into the First Division in his third year in charge but the season before promotion had not been short of traumas for the Chelsea boss. When the club lost at Turf Moor with four games to go, Chelsea fell into one of the relegation spots and were in grave danger of relegation to the Third Division.

Two seasons earlier Chelsea had been up to Bolton early in the season and had rejoiced in a 3-2 victory and the debut appearance of Jimmy Clare. Who was Jimmy Clare? The only Chelsea player who will best be remembered, not for his football prowess, but the fact he was best man at Nigel Spackman's wedding. Back to the football, nothing less than a victory would suffice now. Chelsea were fighting to keep their Second Division future alive.

Chelsea had to win. A draw would not be enough. The first half was played in torrential rain and appeared to offer no salvation. Half time was spent with the human calculators working out the implications of only getting a point. Even if Chelsea won their final game they could still go down. Chelsea relegated to the Third Division – who would have thought it ten years earlier? No, Chelsea must win, nothing else would be sufficient.

The second half proved as uninspiring as the first. Colin Lee got through with only Jim McDonagh to beat. With all the Chelsea fans thinking, 'he must score…', Lee and goalkeeper McDonagh collided and the cries for 'penalty ref... surely', fell on deaf ears. However, with the away fans resigned to going home with just a point, instead came a moment in Chelsea history that the thousands present will always remember. It was the moment Chelsea saved their necks from the relegation guillotine.

From twenty-five yards out Clive Walker hit an unstoppable shot into the roof of the net over Bolton goalkeeper Jim McDonagh. Half the ground went mental and for the remaining ten minutes or so the noise was deafening. The final whistle went and the Chelsea players came over in the pouring rain and threw their shirts into the crowd. With half the Chelsea end seemingly glued to their radios the results came in thick and fast. Burnley had drawn at home and were as good as down, Charlton had only been able to draw at Barnsley but with a home game with Bolton the following week and both teams below Chelsea, it worked out that the Blues were as good as safe. For the fans present it felt like Chelsea had won the league – I often wonder how that would feel. The following Saturday Chelsea slugged out a boring 0-0 draw with Middlesbrough to ensure their safety.

It was clear that things had to change. During the pre-season there were a number of new faces at the club but very few of them were household names. With prodigal sons John Hollins and Alan Hudson returning, a link with the great teams of the past was retained but it was the other signings who would create some history of their own.

In came goalkeeper Eddie Niedzwicki from Wrexham. Defender Joe McLaughlin arrived from Morton in Scotland, Nigel Spackman came in from Bournemouth and a young lad called Kerry Dixon was signed from Reading. Sneaking in behind them was a shy nineteen-year-old from Clyde in Scotland. His name: Patrick Kevin Francis Nevin.

The first chance any fans had to see any of the new signings in the flesh was pre-season. For years, Chelsea had spent pre-season training running up and down the sand dunes at Aberystwyth and many Blues travelled down to Newport to see the new-look Chelsea in action against a team soon to lose their league status. Sadly, not all the new signings were on show. Kerry Dixon, Nigel Spackman and Eddie Niedzwicki were all missing and for a while it looked just like the tired old format the fans had been used to during the previous season. Where was the promised brave new era?

John Hollins and Alan Hudson were playing, so many nostalgia buffs hung on their every move but Hudson looked overweight and it was no surprise that he was replaced by Nevin in the second half.

Nevin looked a weedy little fart, the type Rotherham centre halves use as a football in mid-November. He looked like one of the school lads who'd get his head regularly shoved down the toilet on a Monday morning, but for forty-five minutes, Nevin was spellbinding. Although he didn't resemble a modern-day footballer, here was someone who could not only cross a ball but could beat defenders with ease. Having been fed on a football diet of Driver and Rhoades-Brown for the past two seasons, Chelsea fans soon lost their anorexic feelings and regained their appetite for some serious wing play. Nevin had cost just £95,000 at the end of the previous season from Clyde. He was 19 and had played only 39 games for Clyde scoring five goals. He looked a bargain.

Anyone who ever saw Nevin play would probably say their favourite Pat Nevin game was at home to Newcastle in 1983. As Nevin himself once said, 'If we score a goal early, I'm going to take the piss for the rest of the game.' Well he did that and the lasting memory for all Chelsea fans was of the wee man's solo run from one end of the pitch to the other where he seemed to beat half the Newcastle team before slipping up at the last minute. If he had scored after that amazing run, I think I would have happily died there and then.

Sadly the game was not filmed or videoed so modern-day fans have not been able to witness one of the greatest pieces of skill ever seen at Stamford Bridge. Osgood did something similar years ago against Southampton when he finished the move off with a goal but very rarely since Nevin's day has any Chelsea fan been fortunate enough to see a professional footballer produce a moment of skill akin to those few seconds of brilliance. Gullit and Zola are probably two of the best-ever players to wear a Chelsea shirt and neither ever produced a run of such brilliance that could compare with Wee Pat.

Nevin, alongside striking partners Kerry Dixon and David Speedie, were part of the John Neal side that won Chelsea promotion in 1984 and between them they scored 55 goals that season. 1984/85 saw Chelsea establish themselves back in the top flight and a League Cup run to the semi-finals saw them fail at the final hurdle, losing to Sunderland 5-2 over two legs. Former striker Clive Walker was cast as the villain when he scored against his old club, but a good season almost ended with qualification for Europe before a bizarre last home game of the season against Norwich saw Chelsea's European dreams literally washed out.

Norwich were fighting for First Division survival. They were four places off the bottom and six points ahead of Coventry City who had three games remaining. On the night, the heavens opened and it pissed down all afternoon, leaving the pitch flooded by 7.30, as Noah, his Ark and all the animals were assembling in the vicinity for an early evening sailing.

In any other circumstance this match would have been called off but referee Leslie Burden surprisingly deemed the pitch playable – for water polo perhaps – the game went ahead and Chelsea lost 2-1. To this day, many Chelsea fans still believe that the club were victims of a conspiracy to rival the shooting of JFK and that the game should never have been played. But it was played and when Norwich grabbed their winning goal just before full time, Chelsea's European hopes bit the dust while Norwich believed they had ensured their First Division status for a further season. Sadly they were relegated on goal difference and the events at the Heysel stadium a few days later made Chelsea's disappointment irrelevant anyway.

Sadly, John Neal's ill-health had got too much for him by now and popular coach John Hollins succeeded him for the start of the 1985/86 season. Hollins' first term had some highlights as the goals of David Speedie (17) and Kerry Dixon (19) ensured Chelsea a season towards the top of the table, finishing sixth once more. The two major turning points that season concerned injuries to crucial players. The injury to Kerry Dixon in a fourth round FA Cup tie at home to Liverpool put him out of the side for two games but the effects on Dixon's game lasted a great deal longer. His two goals in a memorable win at Old Trafford in April were the only ones he scored between January and the end of the season.

More crucial was the loss of Eddie Niedzwicki with a knee injury following a quarter-final Milk Cup replay defeat at home to nearby rivals Queens Park Rangers.

The knee injury would dog Niedzwicki for the next two seasons. Despite bravely making two comebacks, he had to admit defeat in May 1988 and retire from the game. Niedzwicki was never properly replaced despite the best efforts of Tony Godden, Perry Digweed and Roger (Freddie) Flinstone and there are many who believe that Chelsea would never have been relegated the following season had Niedzwicki been between the sticks.

Hollins' first year became a distant memory as problems in the dressing room spread onto the pitch and the last two years of his reign had few memorable moments. The age-old Chelsea tradition of being knocked out of cup competitions by unlikely opposition continued with Cardiff City and Reading putting Hollins' side out of the League Cup in successive seasons. The press hovered around Chelsea like vultures and with unrest in the dressing room, the back pages of the tabloids had a field day. *The Sun* probably stooped lower than any when they asked Chelsea fans to ring in if they wanted Hollins sacked!

The writing was on the wall for Hollins when Ken Bates brought in his old friend Bobby Campbell as first team coach to replace Ernie Whalley against Hollins' wishes. The two worked together initially but their partnership proved brief.

The damage was done in two successive away games. Leading 3-1 at Coventry, Chelsea somehow managed to let Cyrille Regis and co back in the game to draw 3-3. The Chelsea fans who travelled to Highfield Road optimistic, that Chelsea would win their first away game in six months, returned bitterly disappointed. The following week, when they read Hollins' programme notes, their disappointment turned to anger.

After a woeful second half performance had seen Chelsea throw away their lead, the players were congratulated by Hollins rather than criticised.

'At Coventry last Saturday, the players showed what they were made of with a good fighting performance. Every player deserves congratulation and after the press we endured all week it can't have been easy for them. They showed plenty of character, the sort of grit that will help Chelsea turn the corner.'

Perhaps Hollins was operating some kind of reverse psychology with his players but two weeks later the Coventry draw paled into insignificance when Chelsea travelled to fellow strugglers Oxford. At half time Chelsea were celebrating a 3-0 lead, but again Chelsea threw it away and drew 4-4.

Three days later, on Tuesday 22 March 1988, the club issued a press release that confirmed the departure of one of Chelsea's favourite sons.

'After an amicable discussion Chelsea and John Hollins agreed it would be in both parties' best interests if they end their association. Accordingly Mr Hollins has left the club, and an appropriate payment will be made to him which recognises his past services for which he is sincerely thanked.'

When Hollins left, Chelsea were sixteenth in the table, three places above the relegation zone with six games remaining. Despite his best efforts, Bobby Campbell could not save them and the Blues only managed to win one of their remaining games – relegation confirmed by a play-off final defeat by Middlesbrough at the Bridge. Crowd trouble after the game led to the Stamford Bridge terraces being closed for the first six home games of the following season. It was a sad end to a disappointing season.

Like Docherty many years before, Campbell got Chelsea back into the First Division at the first attempt. After a slow start they won the title by 17 points, amassing 99 points and scoring 96 goals in the process. A plus had been the return to form of Kerry Dixon, who finished the season with 28 goals in all competitions. He was ably assisted by John Hollins' signing Gordon Durie (17 goals) and Kevin Wilson (15). More surprisingly, joint second-highest goalscorer with Durie was new team captain Graham Roberts who hit an amazing 11 from the penalty spot.

In the first season back, Campbell struck gold as Dutchman Ken Monkou and Norwegian Erland Johnsen developed the perfect centre half partnership. This solidity at the back and 21 goals from Kerry Dixon saw Chelsea finish in a respectable fifth place. Another trip to Wembley in the ridiculously named Zenith Data Systems Cup (aka the Full Members Cup) saw Chelsea beat Middlesbrough 1-0 with a Tony Dorigo goal in front of a staggering 76,369 fans. Chelsea were so starved of success by this time that they sold 40,000 tickets – and didn't we all celebrate like mad at the end of the game!

The following season saw the first team squad strengthened by the record signings of Andy Townsend (£1.2 million) and Dennis Wise (£1.6 million) and having finished fifth the year before, fans were optimistic for the year ahead. Two wins in the first ten games saw Chelsea start badly. Despite a five-match winning run in December that included a memorable 6-4 away win at Derby County, things did not improve and the Blues spent most of the season in the lower half of the table.

Although a decent run to the semi-finals of the Rumbelows Cup temporarily distracted most fans, the majority were glad when the season was over. The final away game at Villa Park was designated as a beach party and the travelling army arrived with beach balls, Hawaiian shirts and ludicrous shorts.

What had not helped Chelsea were the cliques developing in the dressing room. The Scottish players, Clarke, Durie and McAllister were in one group; the intellectuals, Monkou, Johnsen and Le Saux were in another and then there was the other group which included Dennis Wise, Kerry Dixon and Andy Townsend. As a result, Campbell was 'promoted' to the board at the end of the season and Ian Porterfield became Chelsea's 16th manager.

One of the worst things Campbell did while manager was claiming that he was proud to have received £925,000 for Pat Nevin. Most Chelsea fans were upset that Nevin had left the club in the same way that they would be today if they sold Gianfranco Zola. Campbell seemed more interested in the money he had got for the player than the fact that the club's best player since the 1970s and one of Chelsea's best of all time, had left the club. Then he unfairly ensured that the blame for Nevin's departure was placed at the door of John Hollins. Of all the decisions Ken Bates has made about his club managers, pushing Campbell upstairs was probably one of the best of them. I would leave the last word on Campbell with current captain Dennis Wise. 'Bobby Campbell was the manager who signed me but I can't honestly say I got on well with him. I didn't really like him and I certainly did not like the way he treated certain players.'

The Porterfield reign at Stamford Bridge did not start well either when, on a pre-season tour to Ireland, Eddie Newton and Damien Matthew were passengers in a car accident that saw a young girl tragically killed. However, Porterfield's first months in the job held a few surprises, in particular the signing of Vinnie Jones who shocked many by winning over Chelsea fans with his solid performances. The arrival of Jones in turn inspired his former teammate Dennis Wise and the double act combined at Anfield to give Chelsea their first win there since the Titanic went down! Chelsea finished the season in fourteenth place, three places lower than in Campbell's last season.

Porterfield had claimed that it would take him three years to build a side that could challenge regularly for honours but the bitter cup defeat at Sunderland not only saw the end of Chelsea's season but a huge fall out between the manager and some of his players. As a result, Porterfield sold Kevin Wilson, Clive Allen and promising youngster Jason Cundy, to Tottenham of all teams, on transfer deadline day.

The next game at Maine Road saw unhappy Chelsea fans protesting about the departure of Cundy. Credit has to be given to Eddie Niedzwicki who came over to the fans and did his best to reassure them that, contrary to what they believed, the manager knew what he was doing, promising 'we're really going to go for it next season, wait and see'.

But by midway through Porterfield's second season there seemed to be little improvement in the league despite the arrival of club record signing Robert Fleck for over £2 million. As hard as Fleck tried, the goals couldn't come and he ended up with the embarrassing record of having scored more league goals against Chelsea than he did for them. Porterfield also added the experienced Mal Donaghy and Mick Harford to the squad and signed John Spencer, whose only claim to fame had been that he was one of the first Catholics to play for Glasgow Rangers.

For some perverse reason, Porterfield rarely played Spencer, but when he did play him, the young Scot reminded many of a young David Speedie. He played like his life depended on it and once again brought back some pride to the Chelsea shirt. To his credit, Porterfield gave young players like Frank Sinclair, Eddie Newton, Graham Stuart and David Lee a run in the side but the biggest mistake he made was selling Chelsea idol Kerry Dixon and replacing him with Tony Cascarino. Dixon had only been nine goals away from equalling Bobby Tambling's club record 202 goals but he was sold in the summer of 1992 to Chelsea-on-sea (aka Southampton), ending the last link with the John Neal era.

Another run in the Rumbelows Cup took Chelsea to a quarter-final with Crystal Palace and once more Chelsea fans were dreaming of Wembley. A torrential downpour on the night flooded Selhurst Park but referee Gerald Ashby inexplicably allowed the game to proceed. Palace adapted to the conditions better and won 3-1. Within a month, Porterfield became only the second manager sacked by Ken Bates.

With thirteen games left, the last thing Ken Bates could afford was for Chelsea to be relegated while he was trying to bring his Chelsea Village dream to reality. He turned to another Chelsea old boy David Webb and gave him a three-month contract with the specific task of keeping Chelsea in the Premier League.

Chelsea won five, drew four and lost four games under Webb's reign. While it was not championship form, had Chelsea reproduced that kind of form over the course of a full season they would have finished sixth in the table rather than eleventh.

Disappointed at not being given the job full time, Webb spent most of the last league game of the season at Bramall Lane in the bar with executive supporters, drowning his sorrows.

Meanwhile, out on the pitch, Chelsea managed to score two late goals to put some gloss on a poor 4-2 defeat to Sheffield United. Following on from the successful beach party the year before, 7,000 fans had travelled north in fancy dress to watch that last day and on the way back to London the majority thought things had to get better than this. As it transpired, Ken Bates thought along similar lines – within weeks the Chelsea Revolution was born.

Appetite for Destruction

As any long-standing Chelsea fan will tell you, the history of their beloved club is littered with ifs, buts, maybes and what-might-have-beens. Every time Chelsea seem to be on the verge of making their mark on English football (or in some cases actually appear capable of winning a trophy) something always goes wrong.

If it isn't the players falling out with the manager, then the manager falls out with the board or the chairman. In other cases players have found imaginative ways of losing to sides they could have beaten in their sleep and shattered our dreams once more.

Looking at the moments when Chelsea pushed the self-destruct button, certain incidents in the club's history are so serious that they set the club back years. Indeed, so severe are they that they should serve as a warning that no matter how good it seems to be supporting your team, there is no telling quite what lies around the next corner.

So let's start our trawl through Chelsea's suicidal years with the first incident of note, which occurred during the somewhat turbulent reign of Tommy Docherty. Following

Chelsea's relegation in 1962, Docherty carried out something of a revolution at Stamford Bridge and they bounced back to the First Division at the first attempt. For the next ten years, and up until the recent departure of Gianluca Vialli, this was probably the best time to be a Chelsea supporter. In the same way that the arrival of Glenn Hoddle began an era that has since seen Chelsea under Vialli win five trophies, Docherty began an era that Dave Sexton then took on to greater things in the early seventies.

Although it was a good time to be a Chelsea supporter, Docherty's four-year reign only produced one trophy, the 1965 League Cup. However, long before Manchester United's manic night in Barcelona in 1999 saw them win the treble, Docherty and Chelsea could have become the first side in this country to win the domestic treble. By mid-March they were going well on all fronts: they led the league, were leading in the first leg of the League Cup final and due to play Liverpool in the semi-final of the FA Cup at Villa Park

However, Chelsea's season swiftly unravelled following Liverpool's victory in the FA Cup semi-final. Chelsea fans no doubt reassured themselves that they would still win the Championship. With ten games to go, Chelsea were top, but following a poor run-in that saw them win only one of their last six games, the Blues finished an deflating third in the table.

Clearly, things were not right on the pitch, but matters were just as grave off it and everything came to a head in Blackpool, just before the season ended. Chelsea had lost to Liverpool at Anfield on the Saturday, a defeat that had as good as killed off any dwindling hopes of winning the title, so the team travelled over to Blackpool for their last two games of the season. They played Burnley on Saturday 24 April 1965 and 48 hours later, were due to visit Blackpool.

Although the title was as good as gone, Chelsea still had a slim chance if rivals slipped up and lost their last two games. In supporters' minds at least there remained the remotest possibility that they could win it.

Docherty had, weeks earlier, promised his players a night out on the town as a reward for the season's efforts. However, after the poor performance against Liverpool, he changed his mind and insisted the whole squad went with him to the cinema instead and were in bed for an eleven o'clock curfew. After his protégés had nipped off to bed, declining the opportunity of a nightcap, Docherty settled down for a drink with trainer Harry Medhurst. He had just opened a bottle of champagne when the night porter, George Honeyman, came over to tell him that his players had gone out again. 'No you must be mistaken,' said Docherty. 'It will be that rugby lot who have gone out, all my players have gone to bed.' The night porter was adamant that the footballers from London had broken fire regulations, opened the fire door and quickly nipped out before they thought anyone had seen them.

Docherty waited in the bar until 3am and had nodded off to sleep once or twice when the porter tapped on his shoulder to tell him 'they're back!' Having had four hours to think about what action he would take, Docherty was in no mood to take prisoners. One by one he went to each room to find all the miscreants asleep in their beds but when he pulled back the bedclothes he found eight culprits fully dressed, including his captain Terry Venables.

Without delay, he sent home George Graham, Terry Venables, Eddie McCreadie, Joe Fascione, Marvin Hinton, Bert Murray, Barry Bridges and John Hollins.

One of the miscreants, John Hollins, was in his first full season at the club having come up through the ranks. Hollins revealed his own views on the Blackpool affair some years later.

'The press made out that we had all gone out drinking. It was never a booze-up. We had, up until a couple of weeks earlier, been going for the treble and we would have been the first side to achieve it but things had gone wrong towards the end of the season. We were in Blackpool for the week so we decided to go out and talk about the season, discuss what had gone wrong before we broke up and went our separate ways for the summer. Many of that group went into management and two of us ended up as manager of Chelsea so we were hardly irresponsible. Yes, we were wrong and we broke the curfew set by the Doc but I think the reports in the press at the time were wildly inaccurate.'

Incredibly four of the 'irresponsible' players went into football management and Venables went onto manage England. Perhaps 'El Tel' remembered his Blackpool run-in with Docherty when, a week before Euro 96, England players flying back from Hong Kong were accused of vandalising a plane following reports that some of them had been seen drinking heavily in the now notorious Jump Club. As the press cried for certain players to be thrown out of the squad, Venables resisted all media pressure and succeeded in creating harmony within the squad in the process.

In contrast, Docherty's punishment was instant. He handed the eight culprits train tickets back to London and told them to be on the first train the very next morning. Although the punishment seemed harsh – with Chelsea still in with an outside chance of the title if both their rivals lost, it seemed insane. Docherty was a strict disciplinarian and felt he had to make a stand. The players were dispatched to London with their tails between their legs and reinforcements sent for to strengthen a now depleted Chelsea side.

The eight miscreants were busy on the train back to Euston when the news broke in London that they had been sent home. Every Fleet Street sports editor sent a reporter to meet the players coming off the train. The 'Chelsea Eight' had a statement prepared, which they read out on arrival at Euston station. 'We are shocked by the punishment, which we believe is out of all proportion. It has not been in our nature to misbehave, and anyone who has seen us play should know that we are dedicated to fitness and to the game. We are too professional to do anything that would ruin our reputations.'

If the eight players had not upset Docherty enough already, it was fortunate that he wasn't around to see the London evening papers as the 'Eight' announced that they would be returning north to cheer on their teammates for their penultimate game of the season. In the event, they watched Burnley storm into a 4-1 half time lead at Turf Moor before eventually running out 6-2 winners – it was Chelsea's heaviest defeat of the season.

After the match an angry Docherty agreed to meet the eight players and two hours later, elected spokesman Eddie McCreadie read a prepared statement to the press stating that the matter was now closed, that the players had accepted their punishment and in return for their contrition, they would be reinstated for the final match of the season at Bloomfield Road, Blackpool. It need not have mattered. Against a mid-table team Chelsea lost 3-2 and a season that had promised so much had ended in farce.

The Chelsea side of 1965 was far better than the side that had won the league ten years earlier, but after Blackpool, things were never the same again. During the next two seasons Chelsea succeeded in reaching two more semi-finals and an FA Cup final but the seeds of Docherty's demise and the break-up of his 'Diamonds' were sown the moment he handed his players their train tickets back to London.

For his part, Docherty had promised to forgive and forget in a statement after the incident. But while he may have looked satisfied with the outcome on the surface, over a period of time he sold many of the 'Blackpool Eight'. George Graham went to Arsenal in September 1966 in an exchange deal that brought Tommy Baldwin to Chelsea. Bert Murray went to Birmingham City in August 1966 following Barry Bridges, who was sold to them in May. But first out of the door was the man who Docherty perceived as the ringleader, Terry Venables. Docherty let the Blackpool incident stew for twelve months but too many run-ins with his captain on the training ground eventually saw Venables stripped of the captaincy and put on the transfer list. Within a week of Charlie Cooke's arrival in April 1966, Venables was sold to Tottenham for £80,000.

Within a couple of years Docherty himself was out on his ear. Having lost disappointingly to Tottenham in the 1967 FA

Cup final, Docherty took his players to the Caribbean for an end of season tour. In a friendly game against a Caribbean Select XI Docherty made the mistake of telling the referee to 'fuck off' and was promptly reported to the Football Association and received a 28-day ban.

Unfortunately, Docherty's closest friend and ally, chairman Joe Mears, had died in the summer of 1966 and his successor, Charles Pratt, fell out with Docherty. The Scotsman was sacked within weeks.

The departure of Docherty initially appeared to have an adverse effect on his players as the first match after he left saw Chelsea lose 7-0 at Leeds United. The danger signs were there for all to see. With Chelsea looking more like relegation candidates than Championship challengers, Docherty's replacement, the mild-mannered Dave Sexton, slowly began to turn things round. Chelsea finished sixth in Sexton's first season in charge which was a dramatic transformation from the more likely relegation battle they appeared to face following Docherty's departure. They also managed to reach the FA Cup quarter-finals but were knocked out by Chelsea old boy Barry Bridges and Birmingham City. They qualified for Europe at the end of the following season and in 1969/70 Sexton brought glory to Stamford Bridge when Chelsea won the FA Cup for the first time beating Leeds in the replay at Old Trafford 2-1.

When Sexton followed up with a Cup Winners' Cup triumph over Real Madrid the following year, it appeared the Blues could do no wrong. But once again, with the world at Chelsea's feet, it all began to disintegrate – this time in an even more explosive manner than the Docherty era.

Sexton had always got on well with his players but gradually his relationship with Chelsea's star player Peter Osgood began to disintegrate. The first cracks appeared on the way back from Sofia in 1970/71 after the second round of the Cup Winners' Cup. Chelsea had become the first team to beat the Bulgarians on their own patch but on the flight home Dave Sexton was far from ecstatic. Osgood had picked up a booking for kicking the

Sofia keeper and though Dave Webb had also incurred the wrath of the referee, Sexton blamed Osgood. By the time the Chelsea squad arrived back in London, Osgood had had enough and he offered Sexton 'out' for the matter to be settled under Queensbury rules behind the old East Stand.

The matter was defused and no punches were thrown but Osgood and Sexton appeared to be an accident waiting to happen. There were one or two minor disagreements between player and manager during the remainder of that season but nothing could have prepared supporters for what happened at the start of the 1971/72 season.

Double-winners Arsenal had beaten Cup Winners' Cup holders Chelsea 3-0 at Highbury on the opening day of the season in a well below-par Chelsea performance. Four days later, Manchester United arrived in London and in front of 54,763 Chelsea fans, they took the points in a 3-2 victory. Although Osgood scored, Sexton blamed him for the defeat and accused him of 'not trying'. The following day Sexton sensationally placed Osgood on the transfer list. Not surprisingly, the tabloids had a field day and for several days the term 'crisis at Chelsea' made back page headlines. The asking price for Osgood was a then record-breaking quarter of a million pounds.

The reaction from the fans was instant. Petitions were signed, collected and delivered to club chairman Brian Mears. Some fans protested outside the ground, some even slept outside overnight. A famous actress at the time, Judy Geeson, who lived next door to the Bridge, even managed to grab a few back page headlines herself when she came out with hot coffee to help keep the fans warm.

Eventually peace and harmony was restored with Sexton taking Osgood off the transfer list but you have to question his motivation in putting him on it in the first place. Was it a threat? Or was it an attempt to bring Osgood into line?

Bizarrely, throughout his time on the transfer list, Osgood was not dropped at any time and still finished the season as top scorer with 23 goals. So while Sexton may have used the transfer list as a mechanism to bring his star player down to earth it failed to diminish his performance.

Although all appeared to be peaceful, the relationship between player and manager was now held together by the slenderest of threads and things would only remain on an even keel provided the team kept performing. Finally the cracks re-appeared in the last week of February and the first week of March 1972 and things were never the same again. Indeed Chelsea's eventual relegation in 1974/75 could probably be traced back to that week.

Having disposed of Blackpool and Bolton in the earlier rounds of the FA Cup, Chelsea were drawn away to Orient at Brisbane Road in the fifth round. With Chelsea due at Wembley the following week in the League Cup final, the Blues were chasing a cup double. The FA Cup game seemed to be the easier of the two and the Blues were expected to beat the O's easily. The game was going according to plan as Webb and Osgood put Chelsea into a two-goal lead. To most the game seemed won. Then somehow Chelsea managed to push the self-destruct button and throw the game away. Although Orient midfielder Phil Hoadley pulled one back with a twenty-five yarder that gave Peter Bonetti no chance, at half time most Chelsea fans remained confident that the Blues were on course for an easy win.

However, the second half turned into the stuff of nightmares for the travelling Chelsea faithful. Indeed I'm sure that cold, wet February day must come back to haunt some of them from time to time. Soon after the restart, a tame ball into the Chelsea area saw a misunderstanding between David Webb and Peter Bonetti allow Micky Bullock to nip between them to score the equaliser. The rest of the second half was all Chelsea as the Blues tried to restore order but with five minutes remaining Barry Fairbrother had his fifteen minutes of fame when he took advantage of more hesitation in the Chelsea defence to score what proved to be the winning goal.

The following week at Wembley, Chelsea were shocked again, 2-1 by Stoke City, who won their first-ever trophy. The rest of the season petered out with Chelsea finishing in seventh place, their lowest league position since Sexton took over.

Despite this disappointment, Sexton survived the summer. The following season began well with a 4-0 win over Leeds on the opening day, but a run of one win in thirteen matches between October and January saw Chelsea finish a disappointing 12th in Division One – their lowest position in the table since Docherty had brought Chelsea back up to the First Division ten years earlier.

The 1973/74 season represented Chelsea's shortest season since 1961/62 in that they only played 45 competitive games, but for many it felt like the longest season ever, especially as once again, events within the club pushed the club to the verge of destruction.

After Docherty's turbulent reign, Sexton had been brought in partly because of his potential as a manager and partly because he was regarded as steady hand. That he had managed to not only keep Chelsea on an even keel but bring them two trophies spoke volumes for his management skills. But certain events during the 1973/74 season would cause such irreparable damage that Chelsea took years to recover from them.

Matters came to a head during the Boxing Day game against West Ham. At half time Chelsea were two-nil up thanks to goals from Ian Britton and Alan Hudson and with West Ham bottom of the table, the 26,982 crowd looked forward to more goals in the second half. But in eleven crazy minutes they conceded three goals to a very poor Hammers team. First to score was Frank Lampard, whose goals for West Ham were as regular as Halley's Comet and just after that came the turning point in the whole game. John Hollins crossed for Osgood, who turned and fired his shot against the underside of the crossbar, the ball rebounded back into play, West Ham went up the other end and Bobby Gould equalised.

The two goals knocked the Christmas stuffing out of Chelsea and when Clyde Best scored two further goals soon after, Chelsea had crashed to their most unlikely defeat of the season.

After the game, their third defeat in a row, Dave Sexton called Osgood into his office and with the striker anticipating the worst he was stunned when Sexton asked him if he would like to skipper the side.

'Would you like to be captain?' recalled Osgood. 'And I told him that Ron Harris was the captain but Dave told me he wanted me to be captain.' Osgood promised Sexton that he would think about it but with Liverpool visiting the Bridge only three days later, Chelsea at least had an immediate opportunity to make amends for the West Ham fiasco.

Unfortunately, a John Toshack header confirmed their fourth loss on the trot and with games coming thick and fast, Chelsea were due at Sheffield United on New Year's Day. Sexton once again summoned Osgood to his office but instead of offering him the captaincy, he told the star striker that he had been dropped along with Peter Bonetti, Alan Hudson and Tommy Baldwin for a game that Chelsea could not afford to lose. Surprisingly the Blues triumphed 2-1 and Sexton's gamble looked like it had paid off. But if Sexton thought he had turned the corner, his troubles were, in fact, only just beginning.

Perhaps he felt vindicated by the victory or believed that no player was bigger than the club. He might also have thought Chelsea could thrive without star players such as Peter Osgood in the long term. Whatever, he was soon to discover the full extent of the problem just a few days after the Sheffield victory. Osgood and Hudson were training with the reserves when he sent coach Dario Gradi over to fetch them back to train with the first team. He was stunned when they refused. Sexton went over to the pair and a heated argument ensued which culminated with Sexton telling them to 'fuck off', continuing 'if you want to leave the club you can!'

Up until now, most of the disagreements Sexton had were with Osgood but now he found that the striker had an ally in his friend and teammate Hudson. 'We both got into an argument with him and he told us to leave the club,' recalls Hudson. 'He accused us of being drinkers and troublemakers.'

The club responded by suspending both players for a week and placing them on the transfer list, a move which, not surprisingly, made back-page headlines. This was hardly the ideal preparation with a third round FA Cup tie against QPR just forty-eight hours away.

Their early days on the list saw Osgood and Hudson linked with Manchester United, Arsenal and Tottenham but soon after the rumours began to dissolve and the only club who made Chelsea a serious offer for Osgood was Derby County. Osgood was given permission to speak to them but he turned Derby down. On the same day Hudson was first out of the door with a move to lowly Stoke City.

Over the coming months Chelsea's season continued to deteriorate and on March 2, having lost 3-0 to West Ham United at Upton Park, they found themselves one place above the relegation zone. The soap opera took a further twist on the Monday evening when the *London Evening News* announced that Dave Sexton had sensationally resigned as Chelsea manager. Sexton had left Stamford Bridge after the weekly board meeting and bid farewell to his players and backroom staff. Had player power won and would Osgood now be staying?

The soap opera continued the next day when Sexton announced that he was staying following a late-night phonecall with club chairman Brian Mears. Where did this leave Peter Osgood? He had not played in the first team since Christmas and three months later, with Dave Sexton's position at the club apparently assured, he was left with the problem of whether to stay or go. In the event his fate was swiftly sealed. On transfer deadline day Southampton offered Chelsea £275,000 for Osgood and he signed the same day.

Osgood and Hudson were not the only players who fell out with Sexton. At one stage or another, Eddie McCreadie, Marvin Hinton, Ian Hutchinson and Tommy Baldwin had all fallen out with the manager. That is not uncommon at a football club. Managers and players fall out all the time but usually everything is kept behind closed doors and not served up for public consumption. The row between Osgood, Hudson and Sexton was carried out in full view of the media and the majority of Chelsea fans were desperate for both players to stay.

Within months, after receiving the dreaded vote of confidence from the board, Dave Sexton himself left Chelsea and at the end of the 1974/75 season the club were relegated to Division Two. Relegation could not have come at a worse time as mounting costs off the pitch, due to the construction of the new East Stand, had seen Chelsea's debts rise substantially. The East Stand had been constructed with the intention of a successful Chelsea challenging for trophies and playing in Europe every season and filling it every week. The average league attendance in the relegation season had been 27,396 but in the Second Division this plummeted to 18,956, a loss of nearly 9,000 fans every home game.

The construction of the East Stand in 1974/75 was meant to be in chairman Brian Mears' words 'the beginning of a new era in the history of Chelsea Football Club'. Instead, Chelsea were relegated and with over £3 million in debts two years later, Chelsea were in serious financial trouble.

The purchase of the freehold of Stamford Bridge from the JT Mears Trustees had not been scheduled until May 1974. However, with Chelsea apparently riding the crest of a wave both on and off the pitch, the board gave the go-ahead to purchase the freehold for £475,000 and to begin the redevelopment of Stamford Bridge. But the construction of the East Stand hit more trouble as a result of the deepening recession of the mid-seventies, the onset of the three-day week and soaring inflation which led to the stand being over budget and past its deadline. By June 1976, before a ball had been kicked in anger, the club's creditors granted a one-year moratorium and with debts now standing at £3.4 million, manager Eddie McCreadie had only option, he had to get Chelsea back in the First Division.

Another season in the Second Division would probably have put the club out of business. With the tabloid newspapers not failing to write an article about Chelsea without mentioning that the club were '£3 million in debt', it was only going to be a matter of time before some predatory clubs started poring over the array of young talent that McCreadie had in his first team. McCreadie had to get Chelsea back in the First Division and fast. It was a tall order but with the manager unable to purchase players, he made a virtue out of necessity and built his side around youngsters, led by captain Ray Wilkins.

He and his captain won admiration from chairman Brain Mears. 'Whatever our troubles the manager will always be allowed to manage at Chelsea and Butch Wilkins – what maturity and what a sense of responsibility he has shown. But then they all have done that. They have exceeded anything I expected of them. Eddie has always said he would create a great side here within two years. Nobody wants to believe that more than me. But we still cannot afford to have great expectations, not until after our financial position has been reviewed next June anyway.'

A tremendous season saw McCreadie's young side play excellent attacking football and on the penultimate Saturday of the season, Chelsea went to Molineux to play fellow promotion contenders Wolves, needing a point for promotion. A goal from Tommy 'Leather Lungs' Langley ensured Chelsea of the point needed to regain their rightful place in Division One.

After the match, in the pandemonium outside the Chelsea dressing room, McCreadie praised his promotion stars and laid down a warning to the big guns in the top flight that Chelsea were back and would not content themselves with consolidation.

'My magnificent boys will enhance football in this country,' he said, 'Once we have consolidated ourselves, I think in the season after we will terrorise the First Division. I have not always enjoyed being manager but I must admit it brought me a great deal of happiness today.'

Mears held up his champagne glass in the crowded Molineux tunnel and had no doubt as to whom he wished to toast. 'It has been a tightrope without a net. But I never doubted we would get to the other side. I can't believe that any manager in history has been under the sort of pressure that Eddie has experienced.

Those who started this season had to finish it... no matter how bad things got. There simply wasn't a penny available to buy players. Now we can go to our creditors in July and say we have done everything they wanted us to do and more.'

Despite the joy of that moment, few could have foreseen what would happen in the weeks ahead. Within weeks, Mears and McCreadie had fallen over the club's refusal to give the Scot a contract. All season McCreadie had worked day-to-day without a contract and when he succeeded he was disappointed with the club's answer. At the time it was suggested that the real reason for McCreadie's departure was the club's refusal to give him a company car. Whatever, the Scot resigned and walked out on Chelsea, never to return.

Years later, McCreadie broke his silence to *Guardian* journalist and regular matchday programme contributor Rick Glanville. 'It wasn't the money, it wasn't a car, it was the contract. It maybe sounds silly to people. It hurt me really bad. I'd been there for 16 years, I loved my club and still do, and going through in the two years what I went through, knowing what I had to do for my club.... When we finally took them up against Wolves, I thought, thank God! I've got the club back! And then I walked into a situation where the directors of the club are telling me they can't give me a contract.'

So would things have turned out differently had Eddie McCreadie stayed? Tommy Langley for one certainly thinks so.

'I don't know and will never know but Eddie was so special and it was a shame things broke up like they did because, having won promotion we were on a high, we had played together for years and we were looking forward to playing in the First Division. If Eddie had been there then yes, maybe we would have stayed in the top flight longer than we did. Ken Shellito came in and he was okay for me, as I had known him from my days in the youth team. He did a good job but he was a different character to Eddie.

'For player management skills there was no one better than Eddie McCreadie. I had a lot of time for Eddie. It was a shame his relationship with the club ended the way it did. He would come up to you before a game, give you a hug and say, "You are the best centre forward in Europe" – it transpired he told us all the same thing. It is the same old story. If someone tells you that you are the best forward in Europe for long enough it gives you tremendous self-belief. Especially if you are young player, you are so responsive to any kind of encouragement. When Eddie did that you thought, this guy believes in me!'

One of Tommy Langley's teammates, Clive Walker, only made a couple of appearances under McCreadie but he was left with a lasting impression of the man. Walker only has good things to say about Eddie Mac.

'During the period he was in charge we won promotion from the Second Division and the club was on such a high and everybody expected great things in the First Division. Although I did not play in the first team much for Eddie, other than that sub appearance at Oldham, I played with him in the reserves and he had that 'thing' about him that made you want to pull on a Chelsea shirt. You'd put that shirt on whatever you were paid for Eddie. I have heard people say about players playing with pride but Eddie was the only manager at Chelsea that made you feel proud to pull on that Chelsea shirt. I don't know what he had but it was something special.'

In the run-in to promotion, Garry Stanley had actually been dropped by McCreadie but despite that he has fond memories of Eddie Mac. 'Tremendous fellow. He built you up before a game and made you feel important. He would say things like, "I would not want to play against you today, you're on fire" and things like that. He stood for no nonsense though. We all looked up to him. Winning promotion was a big thing for the club but Eddie going was a shame. It would have been nice if Eddie had had one season back in the First Division.'

Ray Wilkins was another of the Chelsea youngsters who could not believe that Chelsea had let their manager go and despite a delegation of players led by Peter Bonetti going to see Brian Mears, McCreadie did not return.

'At the time I could not believe that the club would not give him what he wanted,' says Wilkins. 'He had done a wonderful job and had the utmost respect of all the players and it appeared to us as young men as just a very sad situation. I have spoken to Eddie a few times since then and he has never mentioned it. Not even when he was leaving did he say anything, which I thought highly of him for because it is easy to start having a pop at your employers in that situation.'

Following the departure of Eddie McCreadie, a period of instability quickly followed. McCreadie's replacement, Ken Shellito, lasted just over a season in the hot seat. He was sacked in December 1978 with Chelsea languishing at the bottom of the First Division. While Chelsea were searching for a new manager, Frank Upton was put in temporary charge and told all the players that in future they had to call him 'Boss'. In an attempt to exercise his authority over the senior players, he turned to Peter Osgood and said, 'and that includes you Ossie.' 'Okay, Frank,' replied Ossie.

The next day Peter Osgood was driving into training when he heard on the car radio that Danny Blanchflower was going to be the new manager. He drove into the training ground and the first person he saw was Frank Upton. Osgood walked up to the one-day caretaker manager and said, 'morning Boss,' to which Upton replied, without a hint of irony, 'It's okay Ossie, you can call me Frank!'

If things had gone wrong under Shellito, Chelsea became a disaster area under Blanchflower, with Chelsea on the receiving end of some terrible defeats. A 7-2 loss at Middlesbrough in his opening game was followed by a 5-1 thrashing at Ipswich soon after. A 6-0 annihilation by Nottingham Forest was followed by a 5-2 defeat at Highbury. The game against Arsenal relegated Chelsea to Division Two with five games remaining in the season. Blanchflower lasted only five games into the new season and was replaced by the man he had brought in as coach, England's 1966 hat-trick hero Geoff Hurst.

Hurst's only experience of football management had been a two-year spell in charge of Telford United in the Southern League. Despite this inexperience he started well, however, taking Chelsea from near the bottom of the division to promotion candidates. However, a failure to beat Swansea on the penultimate day of the season cost Chelsea dear and they missed out on promotion when Sunderland beat FA Cup winners West Ham to grab the last spot.

Despite this disappointment, Hurst still had the nucleus of a squad to challenge for promotion the next season. After the traumas of the previous two seasons they should have formed a basis on which to build and ensure promotion back to the top flight.

Unfortunately, Chelsea pushed the self-destruct button once again, this time on a pre-season tour of Scotland. Chelsea had arranged three friendlies in five days and Hurst and assistant Bobby Gould had taken the whole first team squad up there to prepare for what they hoped would be a successful season. But before a ball had been kicked, a dispute between the players and Hurst and Gould almost saw a change in management before the season had begun.

Tommy Langley was at the centre of the dispute, a dispute that led to the end of his Chelsea playing career. Nearly twenty years on, Langley looks back on the chain of events that saw another breakdown between the playing staff and management.

'We had gone up to Scotland to prepare for the new season and our first game was against Hearts. We arrived up in Edinburgh the day before the game and that night we went out for a walk around the town. We popped into this bar and a few of the lads ordered pints, some had orange juice and some ordered coffee when suddenly Geoff and Bobby walked in. We had not even had the chance to have a drink and we were all immediately fined two weeks' wages. Actually, we got in such a row with them that they initially resigned and did not turn up for the game the next day and Norman Medhurst took charge of the team. We won 1-0 and they reappeared the day after but the damage was done.'

A week before the start of the season, the row between Hurst, Gould and the players had simmered on long enough for Tommy Langley. He kicked his last ball for the club in a Friday night friendly at Carrow Road against Norwich City and just as the first team were about to fly to Greece for their last two pre-season friendlies, Langley signed for Queens Park Rangers. The Chelsea propaganda machine ensured that Langley was rather unfairly painted as the villain for daring to want to leave the club. However, the departure of a player who had supported the club as a boy and whose family had been season ticket holders for years did not go unnoticed by his former teammates.

The management and playing staff were by now an accident waiting to happen. The side started badly with no wins in the first seven games and a humiliating second round exit against Cardiff City. However, an eleven-match unbeaten run between September and early November saw Chelsea climb the table, but at the beginning of December the good run came to an end and things started to go wrong. Hurst dropped five players – Ian Britton, Gary Chivers, club captain Micky Droy, Peter Rhoades-Brown and Clive Walker – from the team for the visit to Luton Town on Boxing Day. Not surprisingly, Chelsea lost 2-0 and within a couple of days had recalled all of them to the side but too late, the damage was done. Clive Walker was the first to admit that things began to go wrong after that. 'We had a good run up until Christmas, but we had had a few run-ins with Geoff and Bobby and things were getting tense between them and the players. After we had drawn 0-0 at home to Swansea, Geoff and Bobby told us we were rubbish, which did not go down well I can tell you. The following game they dropped five of us from the team but we lost and we were soon back in the side. By then the damage had been done, the players were thinking "sod you" and with a bad feeling in the dressing room, it was always going to be difficult to turn things around after that. We were top of the league at one stage but won only three more games and Geoff and Bobby got the push at the end of the season.'

Those three games were the only times in the last twenty-two league games that Chelsea scored and the side slipped from top of the table to finish twelfth. The run-in was a desperate time to be a Chelsea supporter. In the last nine games Chelsea failed to score a single goal. Before the last match of the season, Hurst was sacked but he had the nerve to sue Chelsea for unfair dismissal. He later settled for what was described as 'substantial compensation'. The fans had had enough though and a last-day home defeat by Notts County saw a pitch invasion from unhappy fans calling for the head of Chelsea chairman Brian Mears. Many had not forgiven Mears for letting McCreadie go in the first place and the terraces rang out to the cry of 'bring back, bring back, bring back our Eddie to us, to us!'

Within weeks, Mears had resigned his chairmanship and Viscount Chelsea succeeded him. His first appointment was former Middlesbrough manager John Neal, Chelsea's sixth manager in seven years. The damage done to the club would reverberate around Stamford Bridge for three more seasons before the Blues once again won promotion back into the First Division.

It was during these 'gloomy years' that the loyalty of the fans was severely tested. If the 1980/81 season had been a disappointment with Chelsea finishing in twelfth place, the 1981/82 season was little better. Although things were bad on the pitch, off it these were probably some of the best times in terms of Chelsea's support, especially away from home. The support given to the club during these lean seasons was second to none. If Manchester United or Arsenal had endured the kind of performances Chelsea fans had to put up with, then their support would have evaporated.

I know, I went to most games during that turbulent time and the support of some Chelsea fans exceeded even my wildest expectations. They went to every single game Chelsea played, be it a friendly, a testimonial or pre-season tour. Some of the more dedicated ones even travelled up to Sunderland in 1980 to cheer for West Ham in a vital promotion decider. The support was fanatical. More encouraging was the fact that the supporters were acknowledged by the club, players and even the official programme. It was at this time that players started coming over at the end of each game to thank the travelling 'Blue Army' for its support. It was always the whole team and no matter what pokey bit of terrace the home club had allocated the away fans, the Chelsea players would walk right over and acknowledge that support irrespective of the result. It is good to see that tradition continued today but those Chelsea players who cannot be bothered to do it or give a half-arsed wave from the halfway line would do well to learn from their predecessors of twenty years ago.

There was also a regular fan page that Chelsea fans wrote in to and it was rarely censored. It was a proper supporters page, unlike the fans' page in the current Chelsea programme (sorry, *Official Matchday Magazine*) today which appears to be written by members of the programme team or their friends and family. When 200 or so Chelsea fans travelled to Sweden before the start of the 1981/82 campaign, after Chelsea had really hit rock bottom the previous season, the programme even printed some of the photos taken of the fans, acknowledging them and thanking them for their support.

Nor should it be forgotten by modern-day Chelsea fans that the anthem *One Man Went to Mow* was born on that Sweden trip. As the story goes, Micky Greenaway bought an old Wally Whyton tape on holiday and played it at every game. The travelling Chelsea fans were soon joining in the songs and that song in particular struck a chord – we carried on singing through to the following season. Nearly twenty years later, Chelsea fans still sing it and on a good day at the Bridge you can get the whole ground singing it simultaneously.

The club also used to list, at the end of the season, those fans who had travelled regularly on the club train to away games by way of thanking them for their support. The team may not have been doing anything on the pitch but at least the fans felt part of Chelsea and you felt guilty if you actually missed a game, as you were seen to be letting the club down.

With uncertainty hanging over the club, even after a certain white-bearded dairy farmer from Beaconsfield bought the club for £1 in 1982, Chelsea could have gone out of business at any time. Yet every week there were thousands of Blues fans travelling to places like Rotherham, Grimsby, Oldham and Shrewsbury. Despite Chelsea's poor league position during those seasons, it was no coincidence that most clubs Chelsea visited recorded their highest gates of the season, with the terraces swelled by thousands of Blues giving their support to the club when they needed it most. It's relatively easy to support Chelsea now. We have some of the best players in the world in our side, we play fantastic football in an ever-improving stadium but the true test of your support is when your side is 6-0 down away from home at Rotherham and John Bumstead has just missed a penalty. What would some of our present day fans have done then? Would they have left at half time or would they still be there like the thousands at Millmoor singing *One Man Went to Mow* and sitting down on the cold Yorkshire terraces on 'ten', or taunting the home fans by singing louder than them when their team was winning 6-0.

Any Chelsea fan reading this who was there then should pat themselves on the back. Your support kept the club going when they could easily have gone out of business. Any fan that was not there then but knows someone who was, be thankful to them as without their support, who knows where Chelsea would be today... Ken Bates has to take credit for saving the club in 1982 but without the support of the fans in those days, who knows, he may not have had a club to save.

The 'gloomy years' officially came to an end in 1984 when John Neal rewarded Ken Bates' loyalty by getting Chelsea promotion back to the First Division. 'Chelsea are back' was heard as Neal's team established themselves in the top flight by finishing sixth in their first season back.

Sadly, the health of the manager was beginning to suffer. Having had open-heart surgery after promotion from the Second Division, the chain-smoking manager's health was deteriorating fast. In the close season, John Neal joined the board and John Hollins took over as manager.

At the time he was a very popular appointment. Hollins had made 591 appearances for the club and only Ron Harris and Peter Bonetti had made more appearances for the club. His return to Chelsea as player-coach at the start of the 1983/84 season coincided with the club's promotion and a lot of credit was given to Hollins for Chelsea's continued progress in the first season back in Division One. In his first full season in charge, Hollins maintained the status quo and Chelsea once again finished sixth in the table, beating Manchester City 5-4 at Wembley in the final of the first-ever Full Members' Cup competition.

Everything at Chelsea Football Club was looking healthy and optimism was high for the start of the 1986/87 season. The nucleus of the John Neal side was still there but Hollins had recruited some of his own players. He'd signed Jerry Murphy on a free transfer in August 1985, Gordon Durie in April 1986 for £381,000 and Roy Wegerle from Tampa Bay in June 1986. Old boy Steve Wicks returned in July and Steve Clarke in January 1987. The signings were meant to strengthen a Chelsea squad that in 1986 had been title contenders at one stage before two crushing London derby defeats at Easter by West Ham (4-0) and QPR (6-0) had killed off that dream.

However, once more trouble in the dressing room caused problems for Hollins. At times Hollins must have thought he should have a revolving door installed in his office, as an apparently never-ending procession of unhappy players came in and demanded a transfer. If it wasn't David Speedie, it was Kerry Dixon, if not Kerry Dixon then Nigel Spackman and so on and so forth. At one stage open warfare broke out at Stamford Bridge after ten players had put in transfer requests. PFA chief Gordon Taylor was called in to act as peacemaker between players and management but any 'ceasefire' did not last long.

For example, the Kerry Dixon saga dragged on for over a season and despite his popularity with supporters, Dixon himself must have been surprised when he was jeered at Vicarage Road by the travelling support. Arsenal had initially offered £600,000 for Dixon, which they kept raising over the course of the season until their offer finally broke the £1 million barrier. Confusion reigned at Stamford Bridge. Arsenal's version of events is that they had met Chelsea's asking price of £1 million but when

Bates confronted John Hollins as to who had sanctioned the asking price, Hollins denied that he wanted cash and indicated he was only interested in a player exchange deal.

The two seasons that spanned the Dixon transfer clearly had an adverse effect on the Chelsea striker. In the 1985/86 season he scored 19 goals but the following year he only hit the net eleven times. In the relegation season he had managed eight goals by October but only a further five in the remaining seven months of the season.

Off the pitch, the media were having a field day with stories coming out of Stamford Bridge about unsettled players and ex-players leaping to give their fivepence worth. Former captain Micky Droy risked the wrath of Bates by telling the *News of the World* that his former side were a 'sick joke.' Not surprisingly, a week later Bates hit back accusing Droy of disloyalty to his former club. Midfielder John Bumstead was also stung by Bates' comments, when he felt aggrieved at ending up out of pocket after his testimonial against Real Sociedad had attracted only 3,500 spectators.

With the players queuing up to talk to the press and morale low in the dressing room, Bates was in his element in his programme notes.

'I think it is very sad that players find it necessary to make excuses to the public. Everyone has a bad patch from time to time. Instead of blaming others, that is the time to roll up the sleeves, grit the teeth, and try even harder for the team, the supporters, their careers and their self-respect.'

Conscious of the fact that most of Chelsea's dirty linen was not just being washed in public but being hung out to dry there as well, Bates quite rightly reminded the players of the need to keep their mouth shut.

'Recriminations are for the dressing room – and that's where they should stay.'

Despite the rows between Hollins and his players, Bates defended his manager. He regularly complimented Hollins in the press and in his programme column. The greatest compliment

Bates could pay his manager was that in his own words, 'John Hollins is a good manager and works very hard for his players and the good players appreciate this and give their best in return.' However, the 1987/88 season saw Chelsea change managers once more and relegation to the Second Division swiftly followed.

The season had started well enough when, after nine games, Chelsea were second in the table. Hollins had been quick to get rid of some of the players he had fallen out with. Spackman had gone to Liverpool and Speedie had been sold in the summer to Coventry but the discontent among the players was still evident, with most of their venom directed towards first team coach Ernie Whalley.

This had not gone unnoticed by Bates and when he discussed playing matters with John Hollins and Ernie Whalley, he quite rightly expressed his concerns. The coach effectively signed his own P45 at the end of November when he arrogantly told Bates that 'if you are not satisfied by Christmas, you can sack either or both of us.' Bates uncharacteristically bit his lip and bided his time, no doubt hoping that the team's performance would pick up with perhaps an FA Cup run in the New Year to look forward to.

In the FA Cup fourth round, Chelsea travelled to Old Trafford to play Manchester United and took 10,000 fans with them, one of their largest travelling supports in years. Amazingly, Hollins left Hazard and Nevin on the bench, the two players most likely to create a match-winning opportunity for Chelsea. With Chelsea 2-0 down to an ordinary Man United side, Hollins sent both players on late in the game but it was too little, too late and the Chelsea fans were furious, letting their feelings about Hollins known in no uncertain terms.

Having lost to Manchester United in the FA Cup, Bates sought a meeting with John Hollins the following Monday and once again expressed his dissatisfaction with the way things were working out. The following week, Chelsea lost at Nottingham Forest and following another defeat to Manchester United on 13 February, Bates finally intervened.

Once again, he asked Hollins to review his playing and coaching policy and once again Hollins refused. Having not won a league game since October, Bates called an immediate Board Meeting and Ernie Whalley got the red card. Bates' choice of replacement was former Fulham manager and close friend Bobby Campbell. In his book on the 1983/84 season, *My Year*, the chairman said he would never employ him, as he was a friend.

In the first home game following Campbell's arrival, Bates used his infamous programme column to justify the chain of events that had taken place in and around his manager.

'John Hollins' contract gives him full control over coaching, appointment of staff, training and team selection. This is the first time that I have interfered in two years nine months. Anybody who says otherwise is a liar!'

On arriving at Chelsea, Campbell had said that he was there to help John Hollins sort the players out and to try and encourage some team spirit into a demoralised side.

'There is a spirit here but when you go 14 or 15 matches without a win players lose a bit of faith in themselves. You have to pick them up and dust them down and send them out there again. If you have had experience with top quality players then you can help these boys because you have been through the mill before and can pass on your experience.'

But Campbell's plans never came to fruition. After the inevitable departure of Hollins, Chelsea had six games left, four of them at home, in which to beat the drop. Sadly, a Mike Hazard goal in a 1-0 victory over Derby was the only win Chelsea managed and they were thrown into the drama of the play-offs.

Having beaten Blackburn in the semi-finals, it looked as if Campbell could pull Chelsea out of the mire but a below par performance at Ayresome Park saw Chelsea 2-0 down to Middlesbrough after the first leg. Despite an early second-leg goal from Gordon Durie and 40,550 fans cheering them on, Chelsea could not find the elusive goal and were relegated once again.

The heady days of the John Neal promotion team of 1983/84, when the club looked ready to take on the best in the First

Division, had evaporated in the space of four seasons. When Chelsea were relegated in 1974/75 and 1978/79, hard though it was to take for Chelsea fans, if truth be told they had deserved to go down. Many Chelsea supporters were not surprised by the pain of relegation, as they had spent most of those seasons half expecting it. During 1978/79 in particular they were in the relegation zone nearly all season.

However, relegation in 1987/88 season was probably harder to take because it was difficult to explain. After nine games Chelsea had been in second place and all the talk was of a possible championship challenge. It was hard to accept that a season that had started so promisingly had ended so disappointingly. It seemed once more that Chelsea once again had been the masters of their own misfortune.

Scapegoats were quickly searched for... was it Ernie Whalley's fault? Was it down to the players? After all, as Bates had said at the time of all the infighting, 'if those players who are moaning really want to go then they can bugger off to other clubs, then perhaps they will appreciate how well-off they are at Chelsea. The players who have been bellyaching have enjoyed unbroken success for three years. Suddenly they start to lose so they didn't get their win bonuses – so they were unhappy. What do they want, more wages?'

Had Bates stayed loyal to Hollins for too long? When Hollins left, Bates' parting words about him were tinged with regret. 'I still think that one day John Hollins will become a great manager. I have regrets and feel sad about what has happened.'

Clearly Hollins was the fall-guy in all of this and took the brunt of the supporters' criticism, and the media criticism too, but for someone who had been a Chelsea legend it was a sad end to his time at Stamford Bridge. Perhaps John Hollins, who is still one the nicest people I have ever met in football, was too nice for his own good and some of the Chelsea players took advantage of him.

The one certain thing was, having had to endure the 'gloomy years' of the early eighties and the enforced five-year absence from the First Division, few fans relished a return journey to Second Division obscurity.

Although Campbell succeeded in getting Chelsea back up from the Second Division at the first attempt, he only stayed at the club for three years as manager. Things started promisingly at first with promotion in his first year and a fifth place in the top division in his second season but a year later, in true Chelsea style, just when you thought things were turning the corner a woeful end of season run saw the old inconsistency return.

It could have been so much different when on a cold January night in 1991, Chelsea travelled to White Hart Lane to play Tottenham Hotspur in a Rumbelows Cup quarter-final replay. The Blues turned in probably their best performance under Campbell's reign. They took Terry Venables' Tottenham side apart, winning 3-0 with goals from Andy Townsend, Kerry Dixon and Dennis Wise.

The 3,000 fans who were at White Hart Lane were magnificent and with Second Division Sheffield Wednesday waiting for them in the semi-final, many believed that Chelsea would reach Wembley for the first time since losing to Stoke City in 1972.

The first leg on February 24 was due to take place at Stamford Bridge at the ridiculous hour of high noon, 12 o'clock. 'Do not forsake me oh my darling'. The most important match Chelsea had played in years and the police had deemed it sensible to kick off when most of the crowd were still suffering from their previous night's hangovers. The atmosphere in the ground was non-existent. Wednesday had lost 4-0 the previous week in the FA Cup to Cambridge United and so should have been there for the taking in front of 34,000 Chelsea fans. This was a semi-final after all; two steps from Wembley, but by the end of the game Chelsea had blown it again. They lost 2-0 and Wembley seemed a million miles away.

Although disheartened, the mood of the Chelsea support was ridiculously optimistic. Most believed we could still salvage the tie and get to Wembley. After all, the Blues had won 3-0 away from home at Tottenham in the previous round and Sheffield

Wednesday were nowhere near as good as Spurs. The fans who travelled to Hillsborough were convinced they still had ninety minutes to save Chelsea's season and get to Wembley.

The support at Hillsborough for the semi-final second leg was incredible. What other club would bring 5,000 to a game most of the country had already believed was all over bar the shouting? However, although the supporters were magnificent, the players were crap. If they had been bad at Stamford Bridge on the Sunday, they saved their worst performance of the season for probably their most important game of the season.

At half time, Chelsea were 2-0 down, 4-0 on aggregate and out of the cup. Many of the 5,000 Chelsea fans packed up and headed for home but many, myself included, stayed behind and kept cheering until the final whistle. Why did we subject ourselves to this humiliation? Our team was being stuffed out of the cup, not for the first time, by a lower league side and the travelling Blues were bravely taking it on the chin. Why? Because deep down, the Chelsea psychology was at work.

The fans at Hillsborough remembered Chelsea scoring four goals in one half against Sheffield Wednesday in the same competition a few years previously and felt that maybe, just maybe, lightning might strike twice. Back then, Chelsea fans were believers in the impossible dream, we were the Lazarus of the Football League, we all believed we could do it; if we did not believe, why had we travelled to Sheffield in the first place?

Sadly, it was not to be. Despite a scrambled Graham Stuart goal giving everyone a ray of hope, Sheffield got one more before the end. Chelsea had once again managed to fall at the penultimate hurdle. The victorious home fans invaded the pitch and the disconsolate Blues invaded the nearest pubs. Wednesday would go on to Wembley to win the Rumbelows Cup while Chelsea contented themselves with mid-table mediocrity.

A run of one win in twelve games saw Campbell's side slip further down the table and although Chelsea won two and drew one of their final four games, sandwiched in between was a humiliating 7-0 defeat by Nottingham Forest. That was the final nail in Campbell's coffin and he was diplomatically moved 'upstairs' to make way for Ian Porterfield.

The arrival of Porterfield did not make much immediate improvement on the league front but in the FA Cup things were different. In the third round of the cup, a potential banana skin away to Hull City was easily dealt with when goals from Vinnie Jones and Dennis Wise saw Chelsea win 2-0. When Everton were beaten at Stamford Bridge in the fourth round in front of the watching millions on the BBC, the fans began to feel that this was going to be Chelsea's year. A full house at the Bridge for the fifth round saw Graham Stuart's first-half goal put Chelsea through to the quarter-finals. Second Division Sunderland came out of the hat to play the Blues at Stamford Bridge and cup fever was well and truly breaking out all over south-west London.

At Stamford Bridge another full house saw Clive Allen give Chelsea an early first-half lead and with the tie delayed till the Monday night, the fans knew that Norwich City were waiting for them in the semi-final if they won.

The longer the match went on though, the lower the noise of the crowd became. It was as if everyone was possessed by the same negative thoughts. Having seen Chelsea snatch defeat from the jaws of victory on so many occasions, there were a lot of worried faces at the Bridge. Not surprisingly, the fans worst fears came true when poor marking and bad goalkeeping allowed John Byrne to equalise thirteen minutes from time.

Still, with fans' optimism knowing no bounds, Chelsea sold out their allocation of tickets for Roker Park and everyone travelled up convinced that the Blues would repair the damage and get through to the semi-final and go onto Wembley.

It was Sunderland, though, who took the lead after twenty minutes. Byrne was put through with only Beasant to beat – the goalkeeper saved but the ball rebounded into the path of Peter Davenport, who took the simplest of chances to put the ball into an open net.

The 3,000 away fans sang for the whole game and continued to get behind their team but the longer the game wore on, the more it looked as if the game was slipping away. I remember looking at my watch and there were seven minutes to go. Come on Chelsea. I looked at my watch again. Six minutes to go. I looked at my watch. Five minutes to go. I looked at my watch. Four minutes to go. Then, it happened. Vinnie Jones crossed from the right and from the other end of the ground it was impossible to see who scored but it did not matter, Chelsea had equalised. Dennis Wise was the heroic goalscorer but the travelling Chelsea fans celebrated as if they had won the FA Cup. Many opposing fans have commented on that live BSkyB game since then and said they had never seen football fans celebrate a goal as wildly as the Chelsea fans did that night. The Chelsea end was going wild. Everyone was convinced that the game would go into extra time, everyone seemed convinced that the Blues were going to win the tie. You looked out on the pitch and the Sunderland players' heads and hearts were gone. You kept telling yourself, 'that's it, now extra time. We'll win this one now. Norwich in the semi-finals. Maybe this year we'll finally go to Wembley.'

Then the nightmare. With two minutes left, Sunderland got a corner. By now, Chelsea defender Jason Cundy had gone off so the defence was lacking height at the back. Sunderland, looking out of it, threw everyone forward in a last effort and when the ball came in, Jonah Townsend was beaten in the air by Gordon Armstrong, who headed the ball into the net. Cue scenes of mass Wearside hysteria and equal desperation in the away end. There was still time left for Chelsea to go straight back up the other end to grab an equaliser, but to no avail. Even worse than the semi-final defeat the previous year, Chelsea had spontaneously combusted once again. The twin towers of Wembley had appeared briefly, only to be taken from the Chelsea fans' view.

Whoever said football was a cruel game must have been a Chelsea supporter. I still dream of that Sunderland game to this day and it still feels like Bill Murray in *Groundhog Day*. Every time I wake up in a cold sweat it is still the 88th minute at Roker Park and Gordon Armstrong gets up every time to head the winning goal. Maybe one day when I awake we'll have taken the game to extra time, won by two clear goals and gone on to beat Liverpool at Wembley.

Ian Porterfield's managerial demise began that night as the inquests started among the thousands of Chelsea fans returning to London. Porterfield's Chelsea were unattractive and the fans were already disenchanted at watching the long-ball game with Tony Cascarino as a spearhead. Porterfield eventually got his cards in February 1993 and after David Webb had made sure that Chelsea avoided relegation, the Chelsea Revolution began in earnest with the arrival of Glenn Hoddle as manager.

The succession of Ruud Gullit finally brought Chelsea their first trophy in twenty-six years. Their victory in the 1997 FA Cup seemed to spell the end of the old days of self-inflicted wounds. However on 12 February 1998, with Chelsea in the quarter-finals of the European Cup Winners' Cup, second in the league and in the semi-finals of the Coca-Cola Cup, Chelsea did the unthinkable and sacked Gullit as manager. Almost to a man (and woman) when Chelsea fans heard the news, many were thinking, 'here we go again'.

The chain of events began on the afternoon of 5 February when Colin Hutchinson met with Gullit to talk about the future of the club and the plans for the following season. Also on Hutchinson's agenda was Gullit's new contract, which had been up for discussion since the previous October.

Matters were made more urgent because, under the Bosman ruling, clubs are allowed to speak to players who are soon to be out of contract from January 1 each year, in order to negotiate 'a pre-contract contract'. Because of the dispute over the manager's contract, Chelsea had already lost momentum by not knowing if Gullit was still going to be their manager the following season. Having learnt the hard way from losing Glenn Hoddle two years previously, the club were unwilling to allow lightning to strike twice and lose a manager at the end of his contract.

Gullit indicated a willingness to sign but when Hutchinson asked what figure Gullit had in mind for a yearly salary, the dreadlocked Dutchman told him he wanted £2 million a year.

'Is that gross or net?' came Hutchinson's reply.

When Gullit indicated 'netto', Hutchinson quickly dug out his calculator and worked out that Gullit was asking for the equivalent of £3.5 million a year. The amicable mood of the meeting changed as Hutchinson explained to Gullit that the club would not be able to afford that sort of money. The figure Hutchinson and Chelsea had in mind for team manager was £1 million a year. Although less than Gullit was earning as player, the figure would have made him the highest-paid manager in the country, dwarfing Alex Ferguson's salary at Manchester United. More importantly, Hutchinson also advised Gullit that he wanted him to be manager only during the following season, rather than be on the player-coach contract he currently had. If Gullit had any doubt in his mind about the implications of not agreeing a deal, Hutchinson spelled them out, telling Gullit that if they could not come to an agreement then Chelsea would have to look for another first team coach.

The two parties did not meet up again until the following Wednesday, 11 February, when Hutchinson called at the training ground. In Gullit's autobiography, he claims that Hutchinson told him that 'we have had talks with the board and have decided that we will not accept your demands. And the board have decided to look for a new coach.'

In Brian Woolnough's book about Ken Bates, *My Chelsea Dream*, the writer says that Hutchinson had gone to Harlington for one last meeting but the Dutchman had stormed out before Hutchinson could discuss matters with him.

To quote Ken Bates, 'Ruud protested that he didn't know the real reasons. Had he not walked out of a meeting with Colin Hutchinson, with Colin in mid-sentence, then he would have found out.'

What both versions of the story are clear on is that Gullit stormed out of the training ground, leaving Hutchinson behind, and went looking for Chelsea chairman Ken Bates. In the meantime word had already filtered through to the media that Gullit had been sacked and a hastily-arranged press conference that same afternoon went ahead. Sitting on the top table were Colin Hutchinson, Ken Bates and Gianluca Vialli, who was announced as Chelsea's new manager.

At 6.30, Bates and Gullit met at the Conrad Hotel. As hard as Gullit pushed Bates as to why he had been sacked, the Chelsea chairman advised him that the decision had been made by the board and not by an individual. The two men parted with Gullit's parting shot, 'I hope we stay friends, because this world is a very small one.'

The following day, Gullit held his press conference at the International Sportsman Club on Kensington High Street. Sitting on a sofa surrounding by the world's media, Gullit told the press he could not understand why he had been sacked. 'What I want to know is what are the real reasons they let me go. The money is only the stick they used to beat me with.'

From Chelsea's point of view, the main reason for getting rid of Gullit came down purely to money. As Bates said, 'We had to make a simple decision. Did we want a player-coach at £3.7 million a year or the opportunity, post-Bosman, to acquire another two or three world-class players?' Colin Hutchinson, Ken Bates and Chelsea Football Club took possibly the biggest gamble of their lives and decided that they wanted to acquire the world-class players, even if it risked losing their manager in the process. After Gullit's departure, Chelsea put the money towards buying Marcel Desailly, Albert Ferrer, Pierluigi Casiraghi, and Brian Laudrup. Some might say, particularly of the latter two, that Chelsea should have kept the money and given it to Gullit, but despite the risk, the decision to appoint Gianluca Vialli was vindicated and he became the most successful manager in Chelsea's history with five trophies won during his three-year spell in charge.

If that was not enough, on Tuesday 12 September 2000 news filtered through that following a meeting between Vialli, Ken Bates and Colin Hutchinson, the axe had fallen once again on a Chelsea manager, the eighth managerial casualty under Bates.

In his two and a half years as manager, Vialli had spent £57 million and had brought Chelsea five trophies in such a short space of time. Sadly this was still not enough to secure his future and with rumours circulating about whether his contract was about to be renewed the more shocking news broke just after 5pm that Vialli services were no longer required.

A rushed press release read, 'Following discussions with Ken Bates and Colin Hutchinson, Gianluca Vialli has been relieved from his duties. Chelsea have great admiration for his achievements in his two and a half years in charge of team affairs and would like to place on record our appreciation for his services. However the club feel that it is in our best interests to seek a change of direction.'

So have Chelsea pushed the self-destruct button once again? Within 24 hours fans were venting their feelings on the club's official website. A poll asked 'Are Chelsea right to replace Vialli?' Within a matter of hours, 5,000 fans had voted – an overwhelming 70% voting 'no'. In business, if 70% of your shareholders voted against a company decision, it would be quite likely that either the board would either be voted out or the decision reversed. Sadly the supporters of Chelsea Football Club are only emotional shareholders rather than financial ones, and their opinion would did not cause the slightest ripple in the higher echelons of the Club.

The one person to emerge with dignity from this sorry scenario was Vialli himself. Ever the gentlemen, he accepted the traumatic news in a dignified manner. 'There is never a happy time for a parting of the ways but the club is more important than any individual,' Hutchinson commented afterwards. 'We had various issues to consider, but the meeting was held in a dignified manner. We parted on pretty good terms and there were no raised voices.'

So why was Vialli sacked? Afterwards Vialli claimed he had not received enough support from someone at the club who seemed more concerned with their 'nice guy image' and Colin Hutchinson retaliated by suggesting that Vialli had spent too much time on holiday and Ken Bates chipped in suggesting that things had been decaying under the likeable Italian. With the exception of Manchester United and perhaps Arsenal there is not a club in the Premiership who would not swap places with Chelsea over the last two and a half years. Perhaps Ken Bates lackey David Mellor suggested the real reason for Vialli's dismissal in his newspaper column three days later. 'There's a new 7,000 seater 'lid' to the West Stand to fill come Easter, and some corporate boxes are being marketed at £1million a year. Fans won't pay that for mid- table mediocrity.'

In English, that means Ken Bates knows that to sell those pricey corporate boxes at a staggering £1m a year he has to guarantee success on the pitch. As a result Chelsea must challenge for the title every year and, like Manchester United, must play Champions League football each season. Last season Chelsea earned £12 million in TV revenue alone from being in the Champions League, irrespective of what they earned separately in terms of prize money for qualifying through the two group stages and reaching the quarter-final. Although Chelsea have now been knocked out of the UEFA Cup, even if they had won through to the final of that competition, they would get nowhere near the pot of riches they earned through their successful Champions League run.

However, what is so inexplicable is how Vialli has gone from being the chairman's hero (including being personally escorted around the pitch against Derby on the last home game of his last full season) to having to leave because the club was 'decaying' a matter of months later. After all, the club sanctioned Vialli's £25 million summer spending spree on the likes of Hasselbaink, Stanic and Gudjohnsen. If the club had been 'decaying' surely that would have been happening for some time and Vialli would have gone at the end of last season before being allowed to spend money on players that Claudio Ranieri might not want.

So what now for Chelsea? Despite winning five trophies, Vialli, like all his predecessors, had failed to emulate Ted Drake and bring the Championship to Chelsea. With a chairman impatient to win the Premiership, Vialli simply ran out of time. Ranieri will have the momentous task of delivering the title by next April.

Anything less and Chelsea supporters will be in an unforgiving mood.

Moreover, following Chelsea's premature exit from the UEFA Cup, Ranieri already has one less trophy to aim for and if he only finishes the season with the FA Cup, most fans will realise that this does not represent an improvement on Vialli's achievements. When Vialli took over he drew much of the sting from the criticism surrounding Gullit's dismissal as he was immediately successful. In the short term the Board's decision was vindicated. As Bates himself said a few days after Vialli's departure, 'All these dismissals were controversial at the time, but looking back, can anyone say any of them were wrong?'

Having succeeded Vialli, Ranieri must quickly manage to appease both a frantic board and supporters mourning the loss of one of the most successful and popular managers in the club's history. He has started promisingly but has a momentous task in front of him. His chairman is desperate to win the league before he retires, while the club continues to struggle with a £75 million loan that needs guaranteed success and regular Champions League football to finance it. I wish Ranieri well as he'll need all the luck in the world – for it seems it has fallen to the Italian to discover a cure for Chelsea's appetite for destruction.

REVOLUTION

When football scholars consider the Chelsea of the nineties, many will ask how years of under-achievement disappeared under an avalanche of trophies. When did the Chelsea revolution really begin? Was it the appointment of Glenn Hoddle or Ruud Gullit? The introduction of the Bosman ruling? Or the original £5 million donation by the late Matthew Harding that kicked off the ground improvements at Chelsea?

On reflection, I do not think it was any of these. The turning point for me was Saturday 13 February 1993. On that day Chelsea were at home to an Aston Villa side challenging Manchester United for the first-ever Premiership title. The Blues had not won a league game since their annual victory at 'Three Point Lane' on December 5 and had gone from second place in the league (and potential title contenders) to mid table obscurity. Indeed they seemed in serious danger of being caught by relegation candidates now only six points behind them.

A rather sterile game was heading for the second successive goal less draw at the Bridge in a matter of days (after an ordinary Liverpool side had scrambled a point three days earlier.)

Then an apparently innocuous ball into the Chelsea half managed to provide Villa with the only goal of the game. Question of Sport may feature this particular defensive shambles in their 'What happened next?' round. In a moment of high farce the ball floated toward Mal Donaghy and Frank Sinclair. Both attempted to clear, collided and with both central defenders prostrate, a delighted Ray Houghton strolled past them and beat an advancing Kevin Hitchcock with a firm shot. It was the final nail in manager Ian Porterfield's coffin. Within forty-eight hours Ken Bates brought his twenty-month reign to an abrupt end.

For years Bates had been promising the fans, through his regular programme column, that once the battle for the ground was won a new super stadium would be built. If his dream of a 40,000 all-seater stadium at Stamford Bridge was not to become an albatross around his neck (in the same way that the East Stand had crippled his predecessors) he had to have a successful Chelsea side competing at the highest level every week. There seemed little point in having a decent stadium without an attractive and competitive Premiership team, or worse having a super stadium in the First Division. There was no way Bates could hope to achieve his dream if the club found themselves outside the top flight once again. He knew he had to move quickly, so there was only one thing for it - Porterfield had to go!

Bates had never been keen on Porterfield in the first place but either through a lack of genuine alternatives or the popularity of Porterfield with the playing staff, he allowed himself to be persuaded into appointing the 1973 FA Cup final hero. It was a decision he now clearly regretted.

Way back in April 1991 a Chelsea season ticket holder, Mr Benjamin, wrote to Ken Bates to moan about the then incumbent Bobby Campbell.

'As I said earlier in my letter,' wrote Benjamin, 'the cause is bad management. It is obvious to all that the rot set in the day Mr Porterfield left the club. If you have an allegiance to Mr Campbell then promote him to the Board and appoint a new manager. In my view you should look no further than Mr Porterfield to fill this position. Surely with the right incentive, he would accept the challenge of such an important club.'

Bates was surprisingly dismissive in his reply, considering that within 12 months he had followed Mr Benjamin's advice and appointed Porterfield and moved Campbell 'upstairs'.

'I note what you say about Mr Porterfield,' Bates said in his reply, 'but quite honestly his performance at Reading as No. 1 is hardly a recommendation for promotion to a bigger club elsewhere.'

Fast forward to the time of Porterfield's dismissal and Bates was gracious toward the former manager in his programme column: 'To replace a manager is always a difficult and emotional thing. You consider the results, evaluate the moves in the transfer market and make allowances as best you can for luck and injuries. You then try to picture the club in two or three years time under the same leadership.

'Colin Hutchinson and I both had reservations as far back as October last, but the team continued winning and, as John Hollins once said, in the short term success papers over the cracks. Once the decision was taken it was right, it was implemented quickly. Ian Porterfield leaves with our best wishes.'

Unfortunately, all Chelsea supporters did not share Ken Bates' sentiments towards his departing manager. There were many fans surprised that he had taken so long to get rid of Porterfield, a fact that Bates was later to acknowledge many years later when Sun journalist Brian Woolnough wrote a book on the Chelsea chairman. 'Porterfield was a disaster. There were times, especially in his last six months, when I could not bear to talk to him.'

There were many fans, myself included, who thought Porterfield should have gone just under twelve months earlier following that harrowing cup defeat at Roker Park. In all my many years of following Chelsea through relegations, cup exits at the hand of lower league clubs and heart-breaking semi-final defeats, no one moment has ever been quite as bad as when Sunderland scored in the last minute to knock Chelsea out of the cup.

Then, at the beginning of the following season, the general mood went from everybody expecting Chelsea to be trophy contenders to the usual dose of cup heartbreak. The club went from second in the table and the quarter-finals of the League Cup, to relegation candidates in a matter of months. Porterfield had to go. Bates made the right decision but I still believe he should have done it six months earlier.

Not that Porterfield's reign was entirely barren. However a victory in the Middlesex Charity Cup (also known as the Cuddly Russell Cup after benefactor astrologer Russell Grant) and the Cross Channel Trophy was little to write home about. Can't win one of the three major trophies? I know, let's invent one we can win. Only two teams enter each year and, as one terrace wag in the Shed end was overhead saying, 'I see we have drawn Le Havre in the Cross Channel Trophy again this year!!'

Having rid the club of Porterfield, Bates had to find a replacement. Both Bates and Colin Hutchinson were keen on Glenn Hoddle, but with his Swindon side still well positioned in the First Division and potential promotion candidates, they were unwilling to play ball. Not one to make an illegal approach for a manager, Bates backed off but was determined to make another bid for Hoddle at the end of the season. In the interim Bates appointed former Chelsea Cup hero David Webb as manager to ensure that Glenn Hoddle would have the opportunity to manage a Premier League side the following season.

By May, Hoddle's Swindon had reached the play-off final at Wembley against Leicester City. Win or lose, the tabloids had already declared Bates' hand for him - Hoddle was definitely coming to Chelsea. In the event, Swindon won the play off and gained promotion to the Premier League for the first time in their history. Would Hoddle have a change of heart and finish the job he had started at the County Ground? Within 48 hours, Swindon had their answer. Hoddle resigned and became the seventeenth manager in Chelsea's history.

Before he signed on the dotted line with Chelsea however, Hoddle had the tempting carrot of his old club Spurs dangled in front of him. Tottenham chairman Alan Sugar was keen for a high profile manager following the acrimonious departure of Terry Venables. Hoddle met with Sugar for four hours the day he was scheduled to sign with Chelsea but chose to plump for the Stamford Bridge hot seat instead.

Even Ceefax viewers thought Hoddle had lost his marbles by taking Chelsea's poisoned chalice. On the day of his appointment, Ceefax viewers found a telephone poll claiming that 79% of callers thought Glenn Hoddle was wrong to leave Swindon.

Matters did not start well for Hoddle. Shortly after reporting back for pre-season training Dave Beasant somehow managed to drop a salad cream jar on his foot, breaking it in the process and Hoddle found himself minus one goalkeeper for the coming campaign. But larger problems awaited the new manager at the training ground.

On his arrival Hoddle was clearly shocked at what he found. For a man who had come from a side a division below Chelsea, he was surprised that the training ground had few facilities for treating injured players; there was no gymnasium and Hoddle himself had no office where he could speak privately.

He wasted no time in installing his own office, upgrading the training facilities at Harlington, recruiting a chef to cook the players' meals and a dietician to make sure the players were eating the right kind of food. Masseurs and reflexologists soon followed as Hoddle looked to change the club completely both on and off the pitch. His arrival at the Bridge created a stir not seen for many a year but one setback for Hoddle was the rumoured departure of Andy Townsend.

For many Townsend had never quite been the same after the Sunderland defeat the previous season. Yes, he still turned it on in the green shirt of Ireland, especially with the incentive of a World Cup trip to the USA on the horizon but perhaps one of the biggest criticisms levelled at the Chelsea captain was his lack of motivation and commitment in the more mundane Premier League games. The rumours of Townsend's departure had started before the players reported back for pre-season training. Aston

Villa and Manchester City were first in with bids of £1.7 million. In the end £2million for a player the wrong side of thirty, and a bad luck charm to boot, was good business. The year before he was on the verge of joining Arsenal but Chelsea increased his salary and he stayed on. Most supporters' money had been on Townsend joining Tottenham but the fiasco at Three Point Lane between Terry Venables and Alan Sugar meant that the proposed deal fell through.

Townsend made 138 appearances and scored 19 goals for Chelsea and, although he will be remembered with affection by some, he managed to alienate many Chelsea fans on his departure, saying of his move to Villa, 'I have waited all my life for a chance to land a major trophy, now I know that target could be within my grasp.' With this statement Andy Townsend indicated his complete disdain for Chelsea fans. Like many modern players he showed no loyalty to the club at all. Like many other modern players he felt compelled to move on every two or three years, with healthy transfer bonuses to follow. All of which engendered further hatred among a group of supporters who stupidly believed the age-old yarn 'I have always wanted to play for this club since I supported them as a boy.'

Andy Townsend had spun that line when he had joined the club from Norwich in 1990 and then kicked those same fans in the teeth three seasons later. During his time at Chelsea, Townsend's reputation of being a bad luck charm had grown as the club left cup competitions at both the quarter-final and semi-final stages. Not long after leaving Chelsea, he enjoyed Coca-Cola Cup success with Aston Villa, so he has since lost that Jonah tag. And although he now has a Cup winners' medal to sit on his mantelpiece, he may look back on his years at the Bridge with affection – whether the supporters feel the same way is doubtful.

Hoddle's troubles continued. Graham Stuart knocked on his door demanding four thousand a week plus bonuses for goals scored. Chelsea were not prepared to pay and Colin Hutchinson wasted no time in telling the national press how greedy he thought

Stuart was. Everton thought differently and with neither club able to agree a fee, the deal was decided by tribunal.

One of the first things Hoddle did when he became manager was to make Dennis Wise captain. He wanted to give Wise extra responsibility but told his new captain he had to cool his temper and be more disciplined on the field. He also asked Wise to play in central midfield rather than out on the right where both Campbell and Porterfield had used him. Hoddle instilled in Wise the need for him to have only three touches before he passed the ball. Practice matches would see all the other first teamers have as many touches as they wanted but Wise was only allowed three. As a result, most of Wise's football these days sees him use three touches or less, but he is in the more fortunate position that he has the likes of Zola, Poyet, Di Matteo and Stanic around him. If he gave the ball to one of his teammates after three touches in 1993 there was a strong chance he would not get it back.

The first chance many fans got to see Hoddle's Chelsea was the traditional curtain-raiser at Kingstonian. The friendly revealed little as Hoddle used two completely different line-ups for each half and gave Andy Townsend his farewell forty-five minutes in a blue shirt. Townsend signed off with a goal but, although the transfer speculation was rife at the time, it surprised many when he actually left the club a few days later.

Soon after, Hoddle took his players away on a two game tour of Denmark but not before he had signed Gavin Peacock from Newcastle. Peacock got a brace on his first appearance in a blue shirt in a 2-0 Chelsea win against Ikast FS. Forty-eight hours later a 2-2 draw with Viborg FF brought the brief tour to an end but the 25 die-hard Chelsea fans that had made the journey over to Denmark were not even acknowledged by Hoddle or his players, despite travelling all that way for two meaningless friendlies. To get their own back, two of the travelling Chelsea fans boarded the team coach after the game and doing their best terrorist impersonations, told the players that they were hijacking the bus. Fortunately they saw the funny side.

In the weeks to come, despite the club's claim they were penniless, Hoddle managed to sign Jakob Kjeldbjerg, Andy Dow on the recommendation of Graham Rix, and a little later Mark Stein for £1.5 million from Stoke City, to add to the earlier arrival of Gavin Peacock. Hoddle reintroduced the sweeper system that coach Don Howe had experimented with two years earlier and all the Chelsea teams from first team down to youth and schoolboy level soon found themselves playing in a similar style and formation. The long ball game of Porterfield had gone and traditional Chelsea football had returned.

Although the revolution had begun, success was not instant and the first half of the season saw an early exit from the League Cup and a failure to win a single away game. Hoddle also had to contend with unrest in the dressing room caused by goalkeeper Dmitri Kharine telling a Moscow journalist that his team mates were 'not intelligent enough to adapt to Hoddle's ideas, only Peacock is playing adequately.' Russian goalkeepers, you just can't trust them can you?

Hoddle's nadir came on Boxing Day 1993. Chelsea travelled to the Dell and lost 3-1 leaving them one place off the bottom of the table. After the match Hoddle locked his players in the dressing room for 'clear the air' talks. Every player was given the opportunity to have his say before the crucial home game against highflying Newcastle the following day. The meeting seemed to do the trick. A solitary goal from Mark Stein gave Chelsea a 1-0 victory, and quick wins followed at Swindon (3-1) and at home to Everton (4-2). Chelsea entered 1994 unbeaten in three games.

If Southampton was the low point of Hoddle's first season, then the real turning point probably came at Hillsborough in 1994. Having struggled to beat Barnet (and Hoddle's brother Carl) in the third round of the FA Cup, Chelsea drew 1-1 at home to Sheffield Wednesday in the fourth round and with bad memories of the League Cup semi-final defeat by Wednesday a couple of years before, few fancied Chelsea's chances in the replay.

But Hoddle gambled, putting together the smallest strike force in the Premier League, pairing Mark Stein and John Spencer for the first time. The gamble paid off. Spencer scored after seven minutes and although Wednesday equalised and took the game into extra time, Chelsea ran out comfortable 3-1 winners with goals from Gavin Peacock and Craig Burley.

The fifth round saw Hoddle keep faith with Stein and Spencer. Spencer scored again while Burley also got on the score sheet in a 2-1 win against Oxford United at the Manor Ground. They even survived a last-minute penalty miss to reach the quarter-finals. Gavin Peacock's goals against Wolves (1-0) in the sixth round and Luton (2-0) in the semi-final helped Chelsea reach their first cup final in 23 years.

However Chelsea's league form remained as inconsistent as ever. Good performances, such as the win at Old Trafford against Manchester United and the 4-3 win over Tottenham at Stamford Bridge after being 2-0 down, were followed with poor results and although Chelsea did the double over eventual double-winners Manchester United, they still lost to five of the bottom six clubs in the table that season.

In his first season in charge, Hoddle took Chelsea to fourteenth, two points fewer than the total of the previous season. It was not quite the outcome most Chelsea fans had hoped for but what Hoddle and Chelsea did have was the small matter of an FA Cup final against double-chasing Manchester United to look forward to.

However, having waited so long to see Chelsea play at Wembley in the most prestigious cup tournament in the world, the manner of Chelsea's defeat was cruel beyond belief. Chelsea were the better side in the first-half. A long range Gavin Peacock effort shaved Peter Schmeichel's cross-bar and most fans in the bars and toilets at half time were optimistic that the Blues would win the cup in the second half. But during the torrential downpour that lashed Wembley during the second forty-five minutes, Chelsea's cup dreams sank without trace. A reckless challenge by Eddie Newton on Dennis Irwin enabled pompous Harrow referee David Elleray to award Man United a penalty. A side bet of £100 from Dennis Wise could not distract Frenchman Eric Cantona from sending Kharine the wrong way.

Minutes later, we witnessed the worst refereeing decision at Wembley since Willie Young's professional foul on Paul Allen failed to receive a red card in the 1980 final. A 50/50 challenge outside the area between Frank Sinclair and Andrei Kanchelskis saw the Ukrainian tumble over and skid into the box. Elleray gave a penalty and ensured that all future appearances at Stamford Bridge would guarantee the official a 'warm' reception from the Chelsea faithful.

Perhaps the only way David Elleray will ever manage to redeem himself is by giving us a dubious last-minute penalty at Old Trafford in a Premiership title decider that gives the trophy to Chelsea. However since Alex Ferguson has somehow secured a ban on Elleray refereeing any Old Trafford game, it seems unlikely that will ever happen. When the dust had settled and Elleray had dismissed all the Chelsea appeals, Cantona offered Wise 'double or quits' on him missing the second penalty but the Chelsea midfielder wisely kept his money in his pocket. Cantona scored, United got two more and Chelsea's cup dreams were shattered.

Hoddle was philosophical in defeat, 'to actually lose 4-0 did not justify the performance. At half time, anybody who knows anything about football would have said Chelsea had a good chance of winning. Games change on little bits of fortune and if Gavin's shot, which hit the bar, had gone in it might have been different.' After the medals had been awarded the Chelsea players walked round the Wembley pitch to stunning applause from the Chelsea end with many fans, like players such as John Spencer, reduced to tears.

After the game, Hoddle addressed a dressing room full of players shell-shocked by what had happened to them in the second half. With such a negative atmosphere Hoddle did his best to lift their morale. He reminded the defeated Blues that on Christmas Day they had been second from bottom in the table and staring relegation in the face. He told them, 'If someone had said then: "You will end up fourteenth and there is a cup final at the end of it and European football to look forward to next year" you would have settled for it, wouldn't you?'

Indeed. The silver lining on a rainy, miserable day at Wembley was a return to Europe.

During the close season Hoddle strengthened his squad, signing Paul Furlong, David Rocastle and Scott Minto from Charlton. The Minto transfer was particularly amusing as two years earlier, as the story goes, a Chelsea representative had been sent to watch a Charlton game at Upton Park with a view to signing the left back. Unfortunately on the day, Minto was injured and a young lad called Anthony Barness, with only a handful of first team appearances behind him, suddenly found himself in Chelsea's first team!

Chelsea's opening day opponents were Norwich City, who had recently sold their young striker Chris Sutton to Jack Walker's chequebook-busting Blackburn Rovers. In the first programme of the season, Colin Hutchinson remarked that the transfer market had gone bonkers if Sutton was worth £5 million. Safe to say that five years later Hutchinson would pay double the amount for the same player. Around Stamford Bridge the streets were buzzing and with a restricted capacity of 23,000, due to the demolition of the Shed and the hasty construction of a temporary South stand, several thousand fans were locked out and missed new signing Furlong and Frank Sinclair grab the goals in a Chelsea victory.

A week later, Chelsea came back from 2-0 down at Elland Road with two goals from John Spencer and a penalty from Dennis Wise to win 3-2. Then four days later, in a downpour at Stamford Bridge, Chelsea beat Manchester City 3-0 and Hoddle had started with a 100% record. Unfortunately it was the only time that season that the side won three games in a row. Distracted by a run to the semi-finals in the Cup Winners' Cup, Chelsea's league form displayed all the inconsistencies of the past. The highest position in the table all season had been the 5th place achieved at the start and although there were no relegation worries, Chelsea dropped out of the top ten on the last day of the year and spent the second half of the season in mid-table.

When he first took the job, Hoddle had told the press that he would build a championship-challenging side within three years. After two years it appeared he had made little progress in that direction, although the football had certainly improved, Hoddle was still a young manager learning his trade the hard way. However, as Chelsea had been starved of success for so long he was fortunate in that most fans remained patient. They were also clearly impressed at the rebuilding job Hoddle had started at the club and largely supported what he was trying to achieve. They were prepared to see the job through.

Little did anyone expect what season 1995/6 would end up having in store for Glenn Hoddle and Chelsea. Hoddle's reign changed dramatically in his favour with the double signing of Ruud Gullit and Mark Hughes in the summer of 1995. Back then the Chelsea board had taken a long-term strategic decision to really put their name back amongst the top clubs in the country and look to conquer Europe. Although Hoddle takes the credit for bringing the dreadlocked one to Stamford Bridge, it could easily have not been the case as his first choice that year was to bring Paul Gascoigne back to England from Lazio. Hoddle and Colin Hutchinson had talks in Italy with the fat boy but he failed to endear himself to the Chelsea hierarchy when all he seemed interested in was how much money he would be earning. The subject of football hardly entered into the conversation. Gascoigne's salary demands were finally met by Glasgow Rangers.

Ken Bates has reminded supporters since how close Chelsea came to missing out on Gullit. 'Look, under Hoddle, Gascoigne was his first choice. Gullit was second,' says Bates. 'Our managing director Colin Hutchinson jokes about it and says: "Just think about it, Ken, we could have had Gascoigne as player-manager now!" Can you imagine?'

Fortunately Gullit was a different proposition altogether. Perhaps Hoddle's initial leaning towards Gascoigne might have been because the Chelsea manager had been warned that the Dutchman would create trouble in the dressing room. I imagine whoever gave Hoddle that ill-informed piece of advice must have mixed Gullit up with Gascoigne. Hoddle and Gullit took to each other immediately. The talk at their first meeting was all about football, unlike the money obsessed Gascoigne and to this day Hoddle describes the Gullit deal as the easiest he has ever done.

Gullit was the first piece in a five-year strategy that Chelsea hoped would eventually see them challenging regularly for honours and eventually, lead to qualification for the Champions League but the second piece in the jigsaw was a different matter altogether.

Mark Hughes and Hoddle shared the same agent, Dennis Roach, and when Hoddle got wind that Hughes had not been offered a new contract at Old Trafford he bought the Welshman for £1.2 million. Of the two transfers, the Hughes one made Chelsea fans finally realise that the club meant business. Gullit was the glamorous, sexy signing that captured all the headlines but Hughes was high on the list of players Chelsea fans loved to hate and exactly the type of player Chelsea needed. Hughes was a winner, no question about it and if Chelsea were serious about becoming contenders, they needed quality signings like Mark Hughes.

Some sections of the press were cynical about Chelsea signing two players apparently in the twilight of their careers. If you believed everything you read, Gullit was only at Chelsea for the money, his knees were knackered and he'd be gone by Christmas. The criticism aimed at Hughes suggested that if such an astute judge as Alex Ferguson was prepared to sell him then he must be past it!

The first chance Chelsea fans got to see the two new signings at Stamford Bridge was on 30 July at Paul Elliott's testimonial against Bobby Robson's FC Porto. Two weeks later, at the start of the new Premier League season, 30,189 packed into Stamford Bridge to see Gullit and co take on Everton. During a goalless draw Gullit showed enough skill at sweeper to suggest that Hoddle's purchase was inspired.

During the first few months of the season Gullit remained in inspired form but it soon became clear that some of the Chelsea players were either in awe of the Dutchman or incapable of understanding his wavelength. An early Coca-Cola Cup exit against Stoke City was followed by a 4-1 demolition by Manchester United and then a 3-0 defeat by Blackburn Rovers.

Gullit's frustration was there for all to see at Ewood Park, where a rather ordinary Blackburn side were 3-0 up within an hour; Gullit pushed himself into attack for the last half of the game to try and make the score more creditable. It did not happen and Gullit took his frustration out on Paul Furlong and then his replacement Mark Stein, both of whom spurned good chances to get Chelsea back into the game. It was perhaps no coincidence that when Gullit became manager two of the first things he organised was the sale of Furlong and a refusal to give Stein a squad number.

The following week Gullit was injured in a home game against Sheffield Wednesday. In his absence, Hoddle's fortunes improved, with a couple of key signings and a change in tactics. He moved David Lee to Gullit's position at sweeper, brought in Michael Duberry beside him, signed Dan Petrescu from Sheffield Wednesday for £2.3 million and soon after bought Terry Phelan from Manchester City for £750,000. For the first time since becoming manager, Hoddle had the players who would allow him to play three at the back and two wingbacks. In Gullit's absence, Chelsea's form improved and other than an unlucky 1-0 defeat at Elland Road, they remained unbeaten for five games before he returned to the side in a midfield berth rather than at sweeper.

The signing of Petrescu in particular proved to be an inspiration. There was no doubt that Petrescu and Hoddle mutually benefited from his arrival, a fact the Romanian is quick to acknowledge: 'I have had a lot of managers and I have learned a lot from all of them, but Glenn is the one that really stands out. He helped my career. He has also impressed me with his tactics.'

Hoddle was beginning to shine and an eight-match unbeaten run into February included an historic FA Cup replay win at

Newcastle and the live on television 5-0 thrashing of Bryan Robson's Middlesbrough. The records tumbled: Gavin Peacock scored Chelsea's first hat-trick since Kerry Dixon in 1990 and it was Chelsea's biggest win in the top flight for over 30 years since they beat Birmingham City 6-1 in 1964. With Gullit now back and in inspirational form, Chelsea destroyed Middlesbrough with probably the best exhibition of football seen at Stamford Bridge since the days of Alan Hudson and Charlie Cooke. Gullit was rewarded with the *Evening Standard* Player of the Month award for February but insisted on the day of the photo-call that his teammates appeared with him, as without them, he could not have won it.

Chelsea once again reached an FA Cup semi-final, this time against their nemesis Manchester United at Villa Park. After Gullit had scored in the first half, goals from Andy Cole and David Beckham frustrated his ambition to play at the home of English football. The cup run to the semi-final had produced many good headlines but by now it was not Gullit the press were talking about, but manager Glenn Hoddle.

England manager Terry Venables had been told that his contract would not be renewed after Euro 96 and Hoddle had leapt to the front of the queue to be his successor in the eyes of the press and on the back of the mauling of Middlesbrough. It became a game of 'will he, won't he' and by the time of the last game of the season, at home to Blackburn Rovers, Hoddle had all but accepted the England job. Matthew Harding, by now a close friend of Hoddle, attempted to persuade Hoddle to stay but despite a four-hour meeting at the Royal Berkshire Hotel, Hoddle took the England job.

As far as Chelsea were concerned, if the revolution had been started by Hoddle, it was essential the baton was passed to an appropriate successor. Hoddle had been at the club three years and on the face of it, final league positions of fourteenth, eleventh and eleventh represented little improvement on Porterfield's record. And although Hoddle's Chelsea had been a good cup side, they remained inconsistent in the league as Hoddle himself admitted.

'We are three years down the road from me coming here, and we haven't stamped out this inconsistency yet. It seems to have been a club disease for so long. We need to find the right antibiotic very quickly.'

Within the club however, Hoddle had initiated a culture change. He made Chelsea more professional, they played good football once more and were threatening to become a big name in Europe once again. Although Chelsea failed to win anything under Hoddle, his reign certainly got the fans excited. In his first year Chelsea had reached the FA Cup final, the second year saw a memorable Cup Winners' Cup run and in his third year there was an FA Cup run to the semi-final and the arrival of Ruud Gullit and Mark Hughes.

So to what extent did Hoddle lay the foundations for the Chelsea of today?

Without Hoddle there would have been no Gullit and without Gullit there would have been no Vialli and without Vialli we would probably still be finishing between eleventh and fourteenth each season with an occasional cup run to keep the fans happy. An example of the progression of the club came following Vialli's shock dismissal in September 2000.

It was clear from the start that Chelsea would look to the continent to appoint a successor. Colin Hutchinson claimed at the first press conference after Vialli's dismissal that the Stamford Bridge hotseat was no poisoned chalice but that he had received 'at least 30 telephone calls from people in and out of work and a number of faxes from Europe.' One name immediately put forward was Lazio chief Sven Goran Eriksson, ironically the same man considered by Chelsea when Hoddle departed in 1996.

On announcing his departure, Hoddle was asked about possible contenders for his successor and straightaway he suggested Eriksson, then coach of Sampdoria. Hoddle believed Eriksson would be a good appointment but when Chelsea tried to lure the Swede from Genoa they found he was tied to his contract. George Graham was touted as a possible successor but there was only one man the fans wanted and that was Gullit.

Hoddle's last match in charge was an emotionally-charged affair. The Chelsea fans turned up in their thousands to wish him well, with banners scattered around the ground simply reading 'thank you'. A 3-2 defeat by Blackburn Rovers meant little in the end. After Hoddle was given a hero's send off, the cult of Gullit took over. For ninety minutes the Chelsea fans sang the Dutchman's name and with the rumours that George Graham may be replacing Hoddle, they quite rightly let the board know how they felt as 'You can stick George Graham up your arse' rang round the ground. The Chelsea public had vivid memories of the boring, unattractive football played under Porterfield, had enjoyed Hoddle's reign as manager and wanted the revolution to continue. The general sentiment seemed to be 'The king is dead. Long live the king' – this was effectively Gullit's coronation.

The dreadlocked one was flattered by the adoration of the fans, 'I am honoured by what the Chelsea players and fans have said about me. If I am offered the job I would seriously think about taking it.' Managing Director Colin Hutchinson needed no more persuasion, saw Gullit a few days later and offered him the job. Gullit wanted time to think about it and wanted to know if the board at Chelsea matched his desire to see Chelsea dominate English and European football. Gullit wanted to win the cup with 'the big ears.' The board at Chelsea shared his ambition and the Dutchman succeeded Hoddle. The second stage of the Chelsea revolution was about to begin.

He wasted little time in bringing in his own players. His first three signings demonstrated he meant business. All great sides have a great spine and Gullit signed a centre half, a central midfield player and a centre forward. Gianluca Vialli came first on a free transfer from Juventus. Like the arrival of Gullit, certain sections of the media regarded Vialli as another player who had seen better days, especially if Champions League winners Juventus were letting him go on a free transfer. However, on his arrival Vialli laughed off the charge that he was too old to give his best to the club, 'Age? That is something written in a passport or one of our Italian identity cards. You tell the Chelsea supporters that I am coming with all my ability still intact and I am going to score plenty of goals for them. Someone said that when you are tired of London, you are tired of life. Well I am not tired, I am coming to London with the enthusiasm of a kid.'

Vialli dispelled the idea that he was taking easy money - about £3 million over three years – or that the club offered less of a challenge than that offered by Juventus or indeed Rangers. 'This is no holiday,' he told journalists at his first press conference, 'I will stop playing when I want to go on holiday. I know just how demanding the Premiership is. It is all about total commitment, it's very physical but also sporting. I reckon I'll fit in just fine.'

Following the Vialli deal, Frank Leboeuf was signed for a then club record fee of £2.5 million and within a matter of weeks Gullit had broken the transfer record again, paying £4.9 million for Lazio midfielder Roberto Di Matteo. The Di Matteo transfer proved particularly controversial, as Lazio fans were so angry that the club had sold one of their star players that they wrecked the club's offices!

With his new stars in place, the season began well and Chelsea went unbeaten in their first five games until they received a surprise 5-1 hammering at Anfield. Things were quickly back on track however, and Chelsea were never out of the top eight all season.

Gullit made further ventures into the transfer market, signing Norwegian keeper Frode Grodas before bringing one of the greatest (if not the greatest) Chelsea players of all time, Gianfranco Zola. Zola had that good a season that he became the first Chelsea player to win the prestigious Footballer of the Year award in his first season and he did not join the club until November.

Zola's arrival in November gave him enough time to settle into the side before the start of the FA Cup when Chelsea's season really took off. In the third round at Stamford Bridge Zola, scored in a 3-0 victory but it was the events of the fourth round tie at home to Liverpool that will be best remembered. After 45 minutes Chelsea were 2-0 down in front of a full house at Stamford Bridge, and millions watching on the BBC at home. They looked out of the cup. It could have been a great deal worse had Steve McManaman not missed an absolute sitter on the stroke of half time that would surely have put the tie beyond the Blues.

In the dressing room, a desperate Gullit went took a huge gamble. He took off Scott Minto, went with three at the back and pushed Mark Hughes up front with Vialli and Zola. His 3-3-1-3 formation was unusual to say the least but Chelsea had to make a go of it and Gullit's natural attacking style suggested he would rather go out and have a go than meekly surrender. Gullit later confirmed this instinct in his autobiography when he wrote 'If I'm 2-0 down, I'd rather lose 5-0 than mount a damage limitation exercise.'

Hughes, having twiddled his thumbs on the bench for 45 minutes, was about to explode and it was the Liverpool defence that was on the receiving end. No matter what Mark Wright and co tried to do they could not stop or control Hughes. When he scored Chelsea's first goal to put the Blues back in the game there was then no stopping him or Chelsea.

When Zola equalised with a shot from 25 yards out, Stamford Bridge exploded and moments later, when Vialli beat Liverpool's offside trap to make it 3-2, there was a real danger that the hearts of some of the older fans might give up. Vialli completed the dream comeback with a header from a Zola free kick and ensured that this game went straight into the top ten, if not the top five, of every Chelsea fan's games of all time.

Afterwards, Gullit warned against repeating the mistakes of Chelsea sides past in being knocked out in the next round. 'I made the changes against Liverpool,' said Gullit, 'and you hope they can respond the way you want them to. But that game has now gone and there is the next one to think about.' He then fired a warning to his players: 'The Liverpool game will have no relevance if we lose the next cup-tie at Leicester.'

The players appeared to have heeded Gullit's warning in the fifth round at Filbert Street as they raced into a 2-0 lead with goals from Mark Hughes and Di Matteo complete with his new Roman Emperor goal celebration. Foolishly, Chelsea let Leicester back into the game, and after Steve Walsh had pulled a goal back, a late Eddie Newton own goal gave Leicester an undeserved draw. The replay at Stamford Bridge ended in controversy when, with a couple of minutes left in extra time, Norwegian 'Moonman' Erland Johnsen was apparently brought down by Spencer Prior who accused him of cheating. When the brouhaha died down, up stepped Frank Leboeuf to put Chelsea into the quarter-finals.

With Chelsea through, Leboeuf revealed how he coped with the pressure of taking such a vital penalty so late in the game: 'As I walked up to take the penalty, I kept repeating the words "SCORE, SCORE, SCORE" in my head. I painted a picture of the net in my mind and decided where I would shoot the ball.' When asked by a journalist afterwards whether Leicester must have been disappointed, Leboeuf replied in a manner that he would repeat again after he played in the 1998 World Cup Final. 'Yes, they would have been disappointed, but I don't play for Leicester so I don't care.' In the quarter-finals, in the fog of Fratton Park, goals from Hughes, Wise (2) and Zola made sure Chelsea had an easy ride to their fourth successive FA Cup semi-final.

And so to Highbury, where Chelsea faced Wimbledon in an all London semi-final. Gullit had experienced the Dons first hand when Vinnie Jones was dismissed at Stamford Bridge on Boxing Day 1995 after kicking several lumps out of the Dutchman. Gullit had fallen out with Hoddle over tactics when Chelsea had played Wimbledon in the FA Cup the previous season. Hoddle wanted his side to concentrate on defending high balls into the area so they would be ready for the Don's long ball game.

'All we have done is concentrate on what Wimbledon can do,' he told Hoddle. 'We are a far better team than Wimbledon, let them worry about us for a change.'

With Gullit now in charge, Chelsea would take on Wimbledon his way. Two goals from Mark Hughes and a tremendous finish from Zola saw Chelsea comfortably through to Wembley once again. There were many heroes on the day but Zola stole the show, as Oliver Holt in *the Times* described his performance:

'Zola provided the original star turn of the afternoon. His was a virtuoso performance, full of twists and turns that bamboozled the Wimbledon defenders who were supposed to strike fear into him, dotted with darting runs and stinging shots and capped by a story-book goal.'

So Chelsea lined up against Middlesbrough at Wembley, and with players like Steve Clarke and Dennis Wise determined to be on the winning side after the disappointment of 1994, there was only going to be one winner. Clarke and Wise had more than the ghost of 1994 they wished to bury. Before the kick-off Clarke turned to Dennis Wise and said, 'Let's make sure after this game they are all talking about the team of the 1990s and not the 1970s'

It took all of 43 seconds for Clarke's wish to come true and for Chelsea to win the FA Cup. Roberto Di Matteo's stunning effort was remarkable and seemed to break the hearts of an already relegated Middlesbrough. It took another 82 minutes for Chelsea to make the game safe but when Eddie Newton made it 2-0, the biggest party SW6 had seen for many a year sprung into action.

There was only one place to be on cup final night. You had to be in one of the many packed pubs around the Fulham Road to savour the atmosphere of waiting 27 years for a trophy. An impromptu street party started on the Kings Road as Chelsea fans celebrated long into the night and forgot all about the gloomy years, countless relegations, poor Chelsea sides and even worse managers. As the song goes: 'CHELSEA ARE BACK, CHELSEA ARE BACK'. Thanks to Ruud Gullit, by 17 May 1997 Chelsea truly were.

Although Chelsea had won the cup and buried the ghosts of 1970 forever, Gullit was still far from happy. If the measure of a successful season is a trophy in the cabinet then his first season had been a successful one. However, despite Chelsea finishing a very respectable sixth in the table, Gullit knew that Chelsea could do a great deal better. 'There is no doubt I will demand much more of my team next season. I want us to improve and kill off teams who are worse than us. Chelsea have made giant steps this season by winning the FA Cup but we must make even more progress. This is vital for the club. I also need a new challenge in my life. I don't want to sit back and be satisfied. That's being lazy and sloppy.'

As a sign of his not wishing to sit back during his second season in charge, he strengthened his squad even further. Goalkeeper Ed de Goey was signed for £2.25 million from Feyenoord, Celestine Babayaro from Anderlecht for £2.25 million, Graham Le Saux re-signed for £5 million and Gus Poyet arrived on a free transfer from Real Zaragosa. Rounding it off, Bernard Lambourde was bought for £1.5 million and Tore Andre Flo arrived from Brann Bergen for a paltry £300,000. Going in the opposite direction were Scott Minto and Erland Johnsen on free transfers and the desperately unhappy Craig Burley who, upset at not making the FA Cup final team or even the bench, left to go to Celtic for a club record £2.5 million.

Gullit wanted to win the Premier League but on the first day of the new season he had to watch his side beaten 3-2 at Coventry. A run of four wins followed, with the highlight a 6-0 win at Barnsley when the long overlooked Vialli scored four. A defeat at home to Arsenal saw Chelsea slip to fifth in the table on September 21st but after that Chelsea never dropped out of the top five all season. Three successive wins at the end of November - at home to Everton (2-0) and Derby (4-0) and a memorable 6-1 thrashing of Tottenham at 'Three Point Lane' against Tottenham saw Chelsea rise to second in the table. For the first time in many, many years Chelsea were serious Championship challengers.

While all seemed well on the pitch, things did not go well off it. It was hardly a secret that Vialli and Gullit did not get on but some of Gullit's methods were beginning to cause disharmony in the dressing room and by Christmas the first cracks began to show. Chelsea travelled to the Dell having failed to beat a below-par Wimbledon on Boxing Day. Chelsea were hot favourites but lost to a Kevin Davies goal in front of the BSkyB cameras

Gullit's rotation system caused unrest in the camp but whenever challenged, the Dutchman defended his policy, 'I know that people, the press particularly, find it hard to understand that the rotation system works. No one can play 40 league games in a season any more and stay as fit as they need to be if you want to win things. I know that I can never keep all my players happy all of the time - it's impossible. There are unhappy players at every club. But the difference here is that my players are only unhappy for a week or two - then they're back in the team again. At most other clubs the unhappy ones stay unhappy for weeks and months.'

He even found an ally in Vialli who, although suffering more than most at the hands of Gullit's rotation system, diplomatically spoke out in support of his manager. 'The changes do not cause any problems. We are all friends and no one moans about the situation. The most important thing is that Chelsea win. The team has some faults but we have a lot of qualities and our biggest quality is the team spirit and support we have for each other.'

A few days later Manchester United visited Stamford Bridge in the tie of the FA Cup third round. Unfortunately Gullit made some basic errors on the day. He chose to play Mark Nicholls ahead of Vialli and put Mark Hughes in midfield where United's whippersnappers Butt and Scholes had a field day. By the time Vialli was introduced Chelsea were a staggering 5-0 down and despite two Vialli consolation strikes and one from Graham Le Saux, Man United had already eased up. Fergie had blitzed Gullit.

Three days later Gullit himself came off the bench in the Coca-Cola quarter-final at Portman Road. He clearly looked unfit and struggled against the pace of Ipswich's Kieron Dyer. Fortunately two penalty saves from Ed de Goey in a penalty shootout saw Chelsea through to the semi-finals against Arsenal.

However, unrest continued behind the scenes and Zola and Wise were surprisingly dropped for the visit to Everton. Chelsea deservedly lost 3-1. Two quick defeats in quick succession at Highbury and Gullit was sensationally sacked and replaced by the spurned Gianluca Vialli.

A hastily arranged press conference on Thursday 12 February confirmed that Gullit was to be replaced by Vialli: 'Once it became clear Ruud would not be with us next season we had to act quickly for the good of the club. We decided to relieve Ruud of his duties forthwith and in order to maintain continuity, appoint from within, so Gianluca Vialli is the new player-manager of Chelsea with immediate effect.

'We believe Gianluca is destined to become an outstanding coach. Over the last 18 months we have had the opportunity to get to know him and appreciate his deep thinking about football. We had him marked down as a future possible successor. His chance, because of circumstances, has come earlier than expected at Chelsea.

'Gianluca was surprised we considered him as the successor to Ruud and took all of five minutes to accept the position of player-manager. He will continue to be a player until June 1999 and after that, for a period of two years, a deal is in place for him to continue with the emphasis on a managerial role - although he will still be registered as a player.

'Gianluca wants to retain the present backroom staff including coach Graham Rix and assistant manager Gwyn Williams. Once it was clear Ruud was not going to be with us next season we had to act swiftly. We have made tremendous progress under Ruud and thank him for his contribution to Chelsea. His place in club history is assured and we wish him well for the future. For our part, we are pleased we recognised his coaching potential and gave him a start in management at Premiership level.'

When Vialli became Gullit's first signing he said he wanted to become a Chelsea legend. As a player under Gullit he had had little chance to do that. The relationship had started well enough and as first choice at the start of the 1996/7 season the Italian had scored 6 goals from 13 starts before the arrival of Zola. Gullit tried playing a 4-3-3 formation to accommodate all three strikers but three into two did not go so he reverted back to two strikers and Vialli lost out to Hughes and Zola. Vialli and Gullit fell out as a result and for the remainder of the season the

Italian only started a further twelve games. When Vialli told the Italian press of the personal humiliation he had suffered and suggested betrayal and bad vibes between with his manager, Gullit did not deny it. In fact, he went along with it, insisting, 'I try to get confrontation into my camp. Sometimes you look for a confrontation and sometimes it is also good to have that before important matches. The good players will always react in the way you want, because they get angry, their pride is hurt and they want to show everything they have.' The worst humiliation Vialli experienced was only being given two minutes in the 1997 FA Cup final and most Chelsea fans would have bet that Vialli would have left that summer but he stayed.

Despite this, Gullit's reign took the club onto a higher level. He not only made Chelsea great again but turned them into credible championship challengers. However, he never allowed himself the chance to finish the job he had started. Gullit's reign at Chelsea was memorable and while Hoddle's began something of a revolution, Gullit's tenure saw evolution. Now it was up to Vialli to keep up the good work of Hoddle and Gullit.

Back in 1997, not long after the Italian had joined Chelsea, Vialli was asked in an interview with *Chelsea Magazine* what his ambitions were. 'I think I will finish my playing career at Chelsea, because the rest of my career won't be very long. After that I want to be manager - in fact I would like to have Ruud's job. I will be manager, Steve Clarke will be my assistant, and Mark Hughes can be...the kit man.' Spookily, his ambition came true, although a lot sooner than most imagined. As for Steve Clarke being assistant, do not rule out the possibility of Clarke returning to Chelsea, to work short term with Ranieri. In the longer term he may become Chelsea manager. The dream ticket for Chelsea in a few years time may see old room mates Dennis Wise and Clarke as a joint management team, that is after Ken Bates has called time on his ninth managerial appointment - 'Come in number nine, your time is up!'

Vialli did not get an easy ride in his first match as manager. He had to prepare his players for the second leg of the Coca-Cola Cup semi-final against Arsenal. Chelsea were 2-1 down on aggregate and a place at Wembley was at stake for the winner. Before the match, Vialli handed paper cups filled with champagne to toast what he hoped would be a glorious new future for Chelsea. Even he must have been surprised how well his players responded. Goals from Hughes, Di Matteo and Petrescu saw Chelsea turn the one goal deficit into a fine 3-1 victory. There were many who believed that Chelsea had gambled by getting rid of Gullit but the club received an immediate dividend, as in only 90 minutes in charge, he got his team to Wembley.

If the players thought they would get champagne before every game the new manager swiftly shattered the illusion, 'There is no more champagne before the kick off – I can't afford it. Giving the players a glass before playing Arsenal in my first game in charge was just a way to begin the new adventure. But from now on its tea and coffee and we have to play well every week if we want to win trophies. Chelsea have improved dramatically since Glenn Hoddle came here, and then Ruudy took it on. But we have to go one more step. We have to show that we can be consistent and handle the pressure of being considered one of the best teams in England and Europe.'

Perhaps with his own experience in mind, Vialli was at pains to make all the right noises following his successful managerial debut: 'Of course I will listen to what the players think and say and share views and opinions with them, but I make the decision. By appointing me Chelsea have shown complete faith in me and are confident I will make the right decisions as the new boss. I am friendly with the players and trust that will not change. But above all I must be honest and direct with them. I now have to work twice as hard for the club and supporters and I want to convince the players they can always improve. But the most important thing is to defend the team spirit.'

Within a matter of weeks, Chelsea defeated Middlesbrough 2-0 (again) at Wembley with goals from Frank Sinclair and Roberto Di Matteo (again). When the players were ready to walk up to the royal box to collect the trophy, Wise and Clarke ushered Vialli forward and told him that he would be collecting the trophy, instead of the captain. Having left himself out of the side to ensure one of his players would get a medal instead, Vialli had already won the respect of his players and this was their way of acknowledging it.

In the remaining thirteen games Chelsea's league form was mixed (six wins, seven defeats) but they were still in the quarter-finals of the Cup Winners' Cup. Vialli steered Chelsea through two tough ties against Real Betis of Spain and Italian club Vicenza and the Blues were in their first European final since Athens in 1971. Facing them were VFB Stuttgart and on a memorable night in Stockholm, a stunning Gianfranco Zola goal 20 minutes from time won the cup. It was a dramatic end to a memorable season for both Vialli and Chelsea Football Club.

In preparation for his first full season in charge, Vialli was quick to add to his squad. In came Albert Ferrer, Marcel Desailly, Pierluighi Casiraghi and Brian Laudrup and out went Cup Winners' Cup heroes Danny Granville, Frank Sinclair and Mark Hughes. At the start of the season he made his ambitions crystal clear. He wanted Chelsea to do better in the Premiership and to qualify for the Champions League.

Once again, as tradition dictates, Chelsea lost their opening game away at Coventry but then embarked on a 21-match unbeaten run before losing to Arsenal at Highbury in January. Remarkably, the Blues only lost one further game that year and reached the quarter-finals of the FA Cup where they were once again knocked out of the competition by Manchester United. They reached the Cup Winners' Cup semi-final but were beaten by Real Mallorca while a Gus Poyet goal in Monaco against Champions League winners Real Madrid secured the European Super Cup. Overall Chelsea played 56 matches, won 30, drew 20 and lost only 6. They scored 86 goals and conceded 44.

It was in the league though that Chelsea had their most successful campaign for decades. From December onwards Chelsea were never out of the top three and actually went into 1999 top of the league. Vialli had taken Chelsea to the next level, they were a championship-challenging side. In the run-in however Chelsea ran out of steam and dropped crucial points at home to Blackburn Rovers, Leicester City and West Ham United. These dropped points would have been enough to give Chelsea their first title since1955.

Nevertheless, it had been a successful season and Chelsea's interest only faded in the penultimate game when for once they failed to earn their traditional victory at Three Point Lane. Their final position of third place with 75 points ensured qualification for the Champions League for the first time but only four points separated them from eventual Premier League winners Manchester United. So near and yet so far.

The 1999/2000 season is covered as a separate chapter later in this book so I will not dwell too much on it other than to say that despite all the criticism levelled at Vialli and his so-called foreign mercenaries, Chelsea once again finished the season with a trophy – winning the FA Cup for the third time in the club's history. As a result they also ensured another year of European football at Stamford Bridge. The only disappointment was that following a successful Champions League campaign Chelsea will not be taking part in it this season. Their failure to finish in the top three in the Premier League has meant that they will be forced to watch Leeds and Arsenal attempt to emulate their run to the quarter-finals.

Sadly, Vialli's part in the revolution came to end with his dismissal by Chelsea and Claudio Ranieri will now have to ensure the continuation of the revolution that Hoddle began back in 1993. Vialli had often said he would not leave until Chelsea won the Premier League and the Champions League and he had given himself five years to do it in.

So where to now for Vialli? He has said he plans to return to Italy eventually but only a few months ago admitted he was not yet ready for Serie A management.

'I don't like the way managers in Serie A are put up against the wall by a firing squad. Some Italian teams keep changing their teams and their managers to chase success. One day Chelsea might sack me and then I might consider a move to Italy. I want to be the best. I want to prove that I did not just come here for the money.'

Vialli prophetically predicted his own demise and was not allowed the five years he had asked to fulfil his ambition. He has spoken of taking time out if ever his stint at Chelsea came to an abrupt end. Meanwhile he has returned to his native Italy and could be a potential future manager of the Italian national side but at present, like his predecessor Gullit, he will probably stay away from the game for a while.

Chelsea will be poorer for Vialli's absence. The first time I met Gianluca Vialli was on Chelsea's pre-season tour of Devon in the summer of 1996. Although he did not play he had travelled to Exeter with the first team squad and due to the excitement of him actually being there, Chelsea had tried to sneak him out of the ground after the game. I had been drinking in the rather tiny overcrowded bar in Exeter's executive club area and on a hot evening I had gone into the main stand to sit in the cool Devon night breeze when Vialli came up the stairs with Eddie Niedzwicki. He stopped to talk and seemed excited to be at Chelsea and looked forward, in his words, to the 'adventure ahead'. The last time I saw and spoke to Vialli was at Hammersmith Town Hall, at the civic reception the day after Chelsea's FA Cup final victory. Despite Chelsea's victory, he was almost unrecognisable from our first meeting four years earlier. The pressure of managing Chelsea had left him drained and exhausted. My memory of Luca will be that first meeting at the start of his Chelsea adventure. He wanted to be a Chelsea legend and as the most successful manager in Chelsea's history he has achieved that ambition.

I've little doubt that Vialli will return somewhere in Europe and as his agent Athole Still said on the day of his departure, 'if I know Luca he will come back bigger than ever.' I think the majority of Chelsea fans share that hope.

Finally, despite Vialli's abrupt departure it is hard to believe that it has only been seven years since Ken Bates contemplated David Webb as an appropriate manager to keep his Chelsea dream alive. In that short time Chelsea have won six trophies and been knocked out at the semi-final stage on three separate occasions. It has been a tremendous time to be a Chelsea supporter. All the fans who have followed the club over land and sea over the years have earned the right to enjoy the most successful era in Chelsea's history.

So, to return to my original question, what's been behind Chelsea's success in recent years? Clearly, Hoddle started the revolution and Gullit and Vialli built on it but a Belgian footballer and an Australian media mogul have helped.

Pre-Bosman and Murdoch, Chelsea always seemed to miss out on the top players who would either join Manchester United, Arsenal, Liverpool or Tottenham. The Bosman ruling and Murdoch's millions changed all that. Suddenly, with the attraction of living in London, Chelsea found popularity with players all over Europe, eager to play for the higher wages offered after the formation of the Premier League.

Chelsea have made better use of the Bosman rule than any other club in the Premier League. As Colin Hutchinson has said on more than one occasion, the greatest benefit Bosman has brought Chelsea is that without it Chelsea would not have been able to achieve their planned five-year strategy. With transfer prices in this country going through the roof and silly prices being quoted regularly for average players, Chelsea would not have been able to buy the quality of player needed to establish themselves as one of the top clubs in the country and in Europe.

Blackburn Rovers are perhaps a classic case in point. With the late Jack Walker still putting his hand in his pocket long after their title-winning days, Blackburn were unable to compete in the transfer market but regularly paid over the odds for players which could best be described as average. When players such as Lee Carsley, Matt Jansen, Nathan Blake and Ashley Ward are costing £3-£4 million each and Christian Dailly £5 million, while the likes of Gullit, Zola and Hughes cost the same, and in some cases much less, the British transfer market clearly needs some form of overhaul.

Revolution

The Bosman law arrived at just the right time for Chelsea and although they have lost players such as Eddie Newton, Erland Johnsen and Scott Minto through the same system, the club has gained far more on the swings than they have lost on the roundabouts. Chelsea have also learned to play the transfer game, so when Craig Burley and Michael Duberry's contracts were beginning to run down they sold them each for a healthy sum rather than lose them as free agents when their contracts expired.

In the past, any up-and-coming player in this country would probably have gone to Manchester United, Liverpool or Arsenal and only a few years ago they might have chosen Tottenham ahead of Chelsea. Bosman opened up the European market place and Gullit's signing was crucial in demonstrating how serious Chelsea were in establishing themselves in the top tier of European football. Without Bosman, Chelsea would never have been able to sign Gullit, Gullit would never have been able to sign Vialli and Chelsea would probably still be a mid-table side content to avoid relegation. Thanks to a Belgian and an Australian, Chelsea's revolution was made possible and now there's little doubt that Chelsea are truly a force in Europe.

One team in Europe

Despite the disappointment of losing on Spanish soil in successive seasons at the semi-final and quarter-final stage, Chelsea have been an almost permanent fixture in European football. Although the manner of defeat in the Nou Camp last year was hard for many to take, there were still many fans grateful that the Blues were in the Champions League at all, especially as they had had to wait forty-four years for the opportunity. For a club whose recent history has seen them regularly competing against the best sides in Europe it is surprising that, up until recently, the number of times Chelsea had successfully qualified for Europe could almost be counted on one hand.

However, things could have been very different had Chelsea accepted an invitation to become the first English club to enter the European Cup 45 years ago. In the same way that Manchester United's history is forever linked with their countless exploits in Europe, who knows what would have happened many years ago if Chelsea had had shared their conviction.

The European Cup was the brainchild of French football journalist Gabriel Hanot who wrote for the leading sports newspaper *L'Equipe*. In 1955 he suggested a new competition to UEFA to find the best club side in Europe and from this notion the European Cup was born.

As First Division Champions, Chelsea had been invited to compete in the first tournament and were automatically entered into the first round draw against those giants of Swedish football, Djurgardens. Behind the scenes, the grey men of the Football Association had been applying pressure on Chelsea not to enter the competition from the moment it was known that they would be England's first entrants in this new competition.

The FA, having given the beautiful game to the world, still believed English football to be the best and looked down on what they perceived would be an inferior competition. They also believed that if an English club entered, it would cause havoc to the First Division fixture list.

Chelsea chairman Joe Mears was a member of the FA at the time and well respected in the game but he was somehow persuaded by his colleagues that Chelsea taking part in this competition would bode ill for the English game. Whatever skulduggery took place within the corridors of Lancaster Gate, the grey men won and Chelsea declined UEFA's invitation, being replaced by Polish side Gwardia Warsaw. In declining the invitation to enter the European Cup, the club and its supporters would have a 44-year wait for a similar opportunity.

The inaugural competition was an amazing success and Chelsea could only console themselves with the day-to-day domesticity of the First Division when they could have been testing themselves against some of the giants in European Football.

Some of the entrants in that first year included AC Milan, Real Madrid and PSV Eindhoven. Real were the eventual first winners of the competition beating Stade de Rheims in Paris in June the following year. The following season, the First Division title was won by Matt Busby's young Manchester United side and once again, UEFA came with their invitation card.

Soon after, the grey men at the Football Association put a call in to Old Trafford but were told where to go. Strong-willed as he was, Busby saw how successful the first competition had been and wanted his young 'Babes' to be tested against the best sides in Europe. Manchester United entered the competition and never looked back, while the club's reputation grew as the name of Manchester United spread around the cities of Europe.

A further competition was soon introduced on the back of the European Cup called the Inter-Cities Fairs Cup whose object was to 'further international sporting relations, particularly between cities who annually hold Industry Fairs'. The early years of the competition saw England's representatives come from cities such as Birmingham and London, and it was not until 1958 that the competition was changed to a knockout tournament.

Surprisingly Chelsea were invited to represent London in the new look competition and on September 30 1958 the club took their first tentative steps into the European theatre with a first round, first leg tie away in Copenhagen against Danish representatives BK Frem.

Chelsea won, 3-1, with two eighteen-year-olds grabbing a goal apiece and all the congratulations. Michael Harrison had made his debut for Chelsea in 1957 just days before his 17th birthday. He'd made only a handful of appearances but manager Ted Drake put him into the side to face the Danes alongside Jimmy Greaves, who had made his first team debut a year earlier. It was a promising baptism for Drake's side but instead of today's two-week gap between ties, his players had to wait five weeks for the return leg at Stamford Bridge.

Unfortunately, the new competition had yet to fire the Chelsea fan's imaginations and only 13,104 people turned up on 4 November to see Greaves grab two goals in an easy 4-1 victory for Chelsea, 7-2 on aggregate.

Amazingly, Chelsea had to wait until after the football season was over to play in the next round when they were drawn against Ville De Belgrade. This time a more respectable 25,771 turned up at Stamford Bridge to see Peter Brabrook score Chelsea's only goal in a 1-0 victory. In the return leg two weeks later in Belgrade, Brabrook scored again but Chelsea were easily beaten 4-1. Their first European campaign had ended and they would wait another seven years before opportunity knocked again.

Chelsea's third place in the 1964/65 season automatically qualified them for the Fairs Cup the following season. Chelsea's first opponents were Roma and having easily beaten the Italians at the Bridge with a Terry Venables hat-trick, all hell broke loose in Rome for the return leg. Former Chelsea player and manager, John Hollins, remembers the events of October 1965 well. 'We beat them 4-1 at the Bridge,' recalls Holly 'but we went over there for the second leg and when we went out on the pitch everything rained down on top of us; rotten fruit, tomatoes, the lot. Peter Bonetti got the worst of it; he got hit with apples, oranges and tomatoes. They threw cups of piss, bottles and bricks. Apparently Eddie McCreadie had thumped a Roma player behind the referee's back in the first game and the referee missed it. But by the time Chelsea arrived in the Italian capital two weeks later the whole ground knew about it.'

Chelsea managed to survive what became known as the 'Battle of Rome', drawing 0-0, and went into the hat for the second round where they were drawn against Wiener Sport Club of Austria. Despite losing the first leg in Vienna 1-0, Chelsea won the second 2-0 but the game is best remembered for the goal scored by a young eighteen-year-old called Peter Osgood, who had only played seven first team games before Docherty threw him in at the deep end against the Austrians. After Bert Murray had levelled the scores on aggregate, the teenager won the tie with a sensational diving header and a new star was born.

The competition shut down until the new year when the mighty AC Milan were Chelsea's third round opponents. The first leg in Milan took place in early afternoon and with most Milanese hard at work the San Siro was almost empty. With seconds left and Chelsea 2-0 down, the Blues looked out of the competition until George Graham scored a vital away goal from a John Boyle cross. That goal turned the tie on its head and the sixteen strong Chelsea support in the San Siro were rewarded for their efforts by being allowed to carry the players' kit onto the team bus!

Two weeks later, 59,541 fans crammed into Stamford Bridge for one of the most memorable nights in Chelsea history. Graham scored again, heading home a Bobby Tambling corner to level the scores on aggregate. Then, enter Osgood to put Chelsea 2-0 up with a goal that is still talked of today. A loose ball cleared from the Milan area landed at Osgood's feet. Osgood slipped past West German international Schellinger and let fly with a shot into the top corner of the net. Milan spoilt the premature celebrations when a second half goal levelled the tie once again on aggregate and when Ron Harris lost the toss after the game to decide where the third play-off game would be played, gloom descended over Stamford Bridge. Most Chelsea fans presumed their European adventure was over for another year.

Little did they realise what lay in store on March 2 1966 in Milan. Docherty's diamonds played out of their skin in the San Siro and managed to hold the Italians to a 1-1 draw after extra time. In those days, matches were decided on the toss of a coin and skipper Ron Harris managed to call correctly and Chelsea had won through to the fourth round of the competition.

Two valuable Bobby Tambling away goals in Munich saw Chelsea grab a 2-2 draw with their next opponents TSV Munchen 1860. The Germans had been beaten at Wembley by West Ham a year earlier in the Cup Winners' Cup final and were fancied by many to reach the Fairs Cup final that year. The young Osgood scored another wonder goal in the second leg to make sure that Chelsea made the semi-final at only their second attempt in European competition.

Chelsea had surprised most people, but the opportunity to play against the best in Europe had clearly benefited Tommy Docherty's young side. 'Participation in European competitive football is a must for any top level British club today.' said the Doc. 'This has been shown to us by the Inter-Cities Fairs Cup tournament this season. For the club it has meant a growing reputation throughout world soccer; big money, too, with receipts at a record level and greater than any domestic competition. Going into Europe has enabled our players to improve and mature more quickly than would otherwise have been possible. I would say, for instance, that our three games against Milan were equal to a whole season's Football League experience for youngsters like John Boyle and Peter Osgood.'

The semi-final saw the mighty Barcelona stand in the way of Chelsea and a place in the final of the competition. Chelsea were drawn at home in the first leg but Docherty was experiencing his worst injury crisis at the club so a bit of skulduggery was required to turn the tables in Chelsea's favour. The night before the game Docherty arranged for the local fire brigade to flood the Stamford Bridge pitch. When the Spaniards arrived they could not work out how the weather had changed so dramatically overnight from a bright sunny day in London to such torrential rain leaving the referee with no choice but to call off the game.

Years later, Docherty confessed to his crime. 'We were due to play them at the Bridge but I had two or three players missing through injury. It was raining, but not that heavy, so I arranged for the fire brigade to come in the night before and flood the pitch even more. The referee came on to examine the pitch in his Wellingtons. He said it was unplayable but no one could fathom where the rain had come from. I had arranged that with the local fire brigade.'

The return leg in Barcelona now became the first leg but with things not going well between Docherty and some of his players, Chelsea lost the Nou Camp leg 2-0.

Two weeks later, all seemed lost when, despite Barcelona having a man sent off, time was ticking away and with twenty minutes left Chelsea still needed three goals to win the tie. Then, the Spaniards pushed the self-destruct button and conceded two own goals in the closing stages of the game.

With 40,000 Chelsea fans roaring the Blues home, Docherty's men could not get the all-important winner and Ron Harris once again lost the toss for the play-off game. Two weeks later in Barcelona, the Spaniards gave Chelsea no second chances and romped home 5-0 winners. The European dream was over for at least three seasons.

Chelsea's next chance to sample the delights of Europe came courtesy of a Tommy Baldwin goal on the last day of the 1967/8 which saw new manager Dave Sexton steer Chelsea to sixth in the table. Since Chelsea's previous excursion in the Fairs Cup, the competition had been expanded to 64 clubs. Sixth position was enough to enable the Blues to take their place once more. When the first round draw was made in August they were paired with Scottish club Morton with the first leg at Stamford Bridge. The tie was over by the end of the first game with goals from Peter Osgood, Alan Birchenall, John Boyle, Charlie Cooke and John Hollins sealing a 5-0 home win.

In most people's eyes, the tie was over, yet the return leg managed to capture the imagination of the Scottish club's fans and 8,000 fans crammed into the tiny ground at Cappielow Park. However, when Tommy Baldwin scored in the first minute to make the tie 6-0 on aggregate the temptation must have been for everyone to go home, Morton proceeded to make a game of it and quickly ran into a 3-1 lead as Chelsea complacently sat back. Dave Sexton's half time speech woke his players from their slumber and Alan Birchenall and Peter Houseman scored in quick succession to send the teams in level at half time. A second half Bobby Tambling goal gave Chelsea a flattering 9-3 aggregate victory.

In the second round, DWS Amsterdam were the Blues' opponents and the 28,428 fans in the first leg at the Bridge endured a frustrating evening as Chelsea failed to break a resolute Dutch defence. Two weeks later, in the return leg, despite Peter Osgood's return from injury, they could not get the valuable goal and the game ended goalless. Once again Ron Harris had to face the toss of a coin, this time for a place in the next round. The toss went against Harris and Chelsea were out.

Following their success in the 1970 FA Cup, Chelsea's fourth campaign in Europe commenced in September in Greece with a first round tie against the Greek cup-winners Aris Salonika. Before the match the Greek press hyped the game and on reaching the stadium the Blues discovered 50,000 fevered locals waiting for them.

During the Sixties and early Seventies Chelsea earned a glamorous reputation. But while they may have welcomed Hollywood actresses and heads of state they were not always as accommadating to visiting teams as this shot shows.

Clive Walker's 35-yard piledriver staves off relegation to the Third Division for the Blues in 1983.

John Hollins, Ken Bates and John Neal in happier times, celebrate Chelsea's promotion to Division One in 1984...

...Ken Bates celebrates in the dressing room alongside Joe McLaugh Keith Dublin, Colin Pates and Paul Canoville after Chelsea had beaten Leeds to win promotion.

Pat Nevin. The greatest compliment I can pay to the former Blue maestro is that, despite seeing Gullit, Zola, Vialli and Poyet grace the Stamford Bridge pitch in recent years, for me Nevin remains the most talented player to ever pull on the famous blue.

Chelsea's most recent former managers:
Hoddle (left) is widely credited with bringing a new attitude to the club which Gullit (centre) brought to fruition with victory in the 1997 FA Cup Final (below).
Vialli (right) became Chelsea's most successful manager winning five trophies in three years until his dismissal after just six games of the 2000/01 season.

Chelsea march back into Europe to face Czech team Viktoria Zizkov.

This memorable John Spencer effort against Austria Memphis sealed Chelsea's semi-final place in the same campaign.

Chelsea's semi-final against Real Zaragosa (above) and things went wrong both on and off the pitch for the Blues as Chelsea's reputation ensured a hostile reception from both fans and police. The Spaniards eventually triumphed 4-3 on aggregate.

The Glory Days return to the Bridge: Avid Chelsea fan Tony Banks celebrates the 1997 FA Cup triumph with latter-day heroes Peter Osgood, Alan Hudson Ian Hutchinson and Ron Harris.

In the late 90s Chelsea made a decision to recruit top quality European players. In the summer of 1995 Glenn Hoddle signed Mark Hughes and Ruud Gullit. Gianfranco Zola and Gianluca Vialli swiftly followed the following winter. Within 6 months Chelsea's foreign legion had expanded the club's horizons. Success was now not a bonus - it was a requirement.

Ken Bates and partner Suzannah Dwyer relax before Chelsea's 1998 semi-final against Vicenza in Verona.

A different kind of preparation: Chelsea supporters refresh themselves in Seville.

Right: the Blues line-up ahead of the 1998 Cup Winners' Cup Final against Stuttgart in Stockholm.

Left: Zola comes off the bench to fire Chelsea's 72nd minute winner giving Vialli his second trophy as manager.

Gianluca Vialli shows the FA Cup to Chelsea fans at Fulham Town Hall civic reception following Chelsea's 2000 FA Cup win.

Vialli with Frank LeBoeuf, the player some claim was the architect of the Italian's demise.

With memories of Rome still fresh in some player's minds, Peter Osgood inspirationally defused a volatile situation and at the same time won the admiration of the locals. On inspecting the pitch before the match, Osgood noticed the disabled spectators in wheelchairs at the pitch perimeter and he took his teammates over to shake hands with each of them to the applause of the home fans.

With tempers now cooled, the first half contained little goalmouth incident until Chelsea were awarded a penalty following a run by Paddy Mulligan, which was terminated by a crunching tackle by Aris's centre half. The Greek players and home fans were incensed at Hungarian referee Emsberger's decision. A combined effort by fans and players succeeded in putting Osgood off and keeper Christidis saved, temporarily making him a local hero. Five minutes before half time Chelsea were stunned when Emsberger seemed to be the only person in the ground who saw John Dempsey strike one of the Salonika forward line. Despite the sending off, the crowd gave Chelsea a good reception as they left the pitch at half time.

However, the poor pitch continued to frustrate in the second half and with the Greeks content to play a spoiling game, they surprising took the lead. They looked likely to take their one-goal advantage to Stamford Bridge when, with time running out, Osgood grabbed a vital away goal and effectively killed off what little chance the Greeks had of winning the tie.

The British press were quick to praise Chelsea for a good away performance in the face of early intimidation from the Greeks and the first half sending-off of Dempsey. Desmond Hackett of the *Daily Express* was quick to offer praise. 'Chelsea are to be cheered for their determination to avoid a pitched battle in a petulant second half. This tolerance finally rubbed off onto the players of Aris. The good sense and good manners of Chelsea ended with them being applauded off the field. If British teams follow the example of Chelsea, sanity can be restored and these exciting contests will continue to command attention for great football, and not ugly punch-ups.'

It was a happy Chelsea camp that flew home to London but Dave Sexton knew that the job was only half-done, despite the likes of Bernard Joy of the *Evening Standard* predicting a massacre at Stamford Bridge two weeks later. With the Dempsey sending off, the poor pitch and the spoiling tactics of the Greeks, the Chelsea manager had little to do in terms of motivation. His players were determined to finish the job. Hollins started the rout with less than ten minutes gone, Hutchinson made it 2-0 with a trademark header on seventeen minutes and Hollins again on the half hour put the game well beyond Aris Salonika's reach with a 35-yard piledriver. The second half was then a matter of how many Chelsea would score, but the least likely scorer, other than Peter Bonetti, grabbed the fourth. Marvin Hinton, who was only playing because John Dempsey was suspended, scored his first goal in five years before Ian Hutchinson chipped in Chelsea's fifth and his second of the game. With half an hour to go and both Hollins and Hutchinson chasing their hat tricks, the 40,425 Chelsea fans expected more goals but they never came and with five minutes left the Greeks scored a consolation goal.

The Blues' next opponents were CSKA Sofia from Bulgaria. The Bulgarians were unbeaten at home in Europe and even giants of European football such as Barcelona, Inter Milan and Juventus had failed to beat them there. Juventus had more reason than most to forget their visit to Sofia, as they were surprisingly beaten 4-0! Milan were also taken to a third game by the Bulgarians in the 1967 European Cup quarter-final after a draw in Sofia and Milan, so CSKA clearly had some European pedigree. Along with Levski Sofia, CSKA were the biggest club in Bulgaria. CSKA were the Bulgarian army team with most of their players recruited to the ranks after carrying out their national service. They had done the league and cup double six times before Chelsea's visit in 1970. The Bulgarians also had greater experience in European football, having played in eleven campaigns while Chelsea were in only their fourth continental campaign. Clearly they were going to be formidable opponents and a sterner test of Chelsea's ambitions than the Greeks of Salonika.

The first leg was away in Sofia and following on from their goodwill gesture in Salonika, Chelsea repeated the gesture when they walked out on the pitch and threw bouquets of flowers to the home crowd. The all-important goal came on the stroke of half time. Keith Weller got down the line and sent over an inch-perfect cross that Baldwin steered home. Chelsea held on to the valuable away goal and after twenty matches and eleven seasons of European compeition, CSKA Sofia had lost their first ever home game.

After the game, the Chelsea players and the fans who had ventured behind the Iron Curtain with 4S Travel met up in the players' hotel disco after the match and partied together. The highlight of the night was David Webb's rendition of the old French tune 'Allouette' with fans and teammates joining in.

One unusual tale to come out of the Sofia trip concerned a blind Chelsea fan who used to watch the Blues home and away with a couple of mates who provided him with a commentary of the game. While drinking with the players, his mates somehow lost him in the hotel disco and the term 'blind drunk' may have been never more appropriate as the visually-impaired supporter managed to walk the three miles back to his hotel on the outskirts of Sofia, despite never having been to the city before. Who said Chelsea fans are not resilient?

The second leg was pretty straightforward. The Bulgarians never looked likely to manage the two-goal victory they needed to steal a quarter-final place and when Dave Webb scored just before half time the tie was as good as over. In Zurich the following day, Chelsea were drawn against Bruges of Belgium in the last eight.

It seems surprising today but only thirty years ago most of Belgium's footballers were part-timers with only a handful of professional players at the top clubs such as Anderlecht and Standard Liege. Indeed only three of the Belgians were professional: Kurt Axelsson who played in defence for Sweden in the 1970 World Cup finals, Hendrik Houwaart and Pieter Rensenbrink who were both Dutch internationals. Rensenbrink is probably better known as Robbie Rensenbrink's brother to most football fans and in particular those West Ham fans who remember, or may wish to forget, his exploits against them in the Cup Winners' Cup in 1976. The remaining Belgians all had day jobs with most having to start work at the crack of dawn as the players trained four afternoons a week between 3pm and 5pm.

A variety of occupations were represented by the Belgians: goalkeeper Luc Sanders worked in a laboratory, Norbert Denaeghel, Raoul Lambert and Freddy Hinderyckx were all metalworkers, and Pierre Carteus and John Moelart worked in a massage parlour.

Bruges were unbeaten at home for three years and the Chelsea players who played on the night could see why. Steve Curry, then working for the Daily Express, was overwhelmed by the noise in De Klokke Stadium. 'I cannot recall such a small crowd producing such an awesome sound,' he wrote in his match report the next day. Despite only 23,000 fans being present they made a noise on the night that was deafening and after four minutes they got the start they wanted. Despite the presence of Webb, Raoul Lambert was first to Johnny Thio's corner and he headed the ball past the helpless John Phillips. Just before half time another Thio corner had Chelsea's Cup Winners' Cup ambitions in serious danger. Rensenbrink was first to the ball and his goal bound header was deflected past Phillips by midfielder Gilbert Maemenout.

The second half followed a similar pattern to the first and only an outstanding second-half performance by John Phillips prevented Chelsea from being knocked out of the tournament in the first leg. One particular save from Hendrik Houwaart on seventy-eight minutes had Brian Scovell, of the now defunct *Daily Sketch*, seeing it as the turning point in the tie. 'Chelsea lost a punishing battle but refuse to accept they had lost the war,' wrote Scovell. 'John Phillips made a vital save from Houwaart after 78 minutes. Another goal then and that would have been that'.

Despite being unbeaten at home for three years the Belgians were poor travellers and had lost all their six previous European ties away from home. In one tie they had embarrassingly managed to throw away a four-goal lead from the home leg, so the tie was far from over and Chelsea still had a chance.

Another black mark on a disappointing evening was the behaviour of some of the Chelsea fans who travelled to Belgium for the first leg. The trouble did not go unnoticed within Stamford Bridge and for the return leg two weeks later the lead article in the match programme criticised travelling fans for giving the club a bad name. 'On the field, the first leg in Belgium belonged amongst the most sporting matches we have encountered on our travels in European football, and it was a pity that Chelsea's - indeed Britain's – reputation in Belgian eyes should have been besmirched by the hooligan element (small but lamentably noticeable) among the 1,500 or so who followed us to Bruges.' Sadly, it wasn't the last time a Chelsea match programme would devote space to comment on fan behaviour in Europe.

In the days leading up to the second leg the main talking point concerned Dave Sexton's selection. Would he stick with the side which had played out a sterile 0-0 draw at home to Huddersfield the previous Saturday? Or would he recall Peter Osgood, who had just come to the end of an eight-match suspension, one of the longest the FA had ever imposed?

Osgood had been summoned to the FA in January following three bookings during the season. He had expected a small fine or perhaps a short suspension but was shocked at the severity of the punishment.

For a player who was my idol when I was growing up I had the fortunate opportunity to interview Osgood last year and we talked about the Bruges game and everything that led up to that memorable night on March 24 1971.

'I was called up before the FA for three bookings, and they gave me a six week suspension,' recalled the great man. 'Can you believe that, six weeks for three bookings! Apparently Bestie had been up before them the previous week and the FA had warned that the next person up after him would be made an example of. Unfortunately, it was me. So anyway, Brian Mears says to me that we would appeal as "my father is well respected at the Football Association" or so he told me – "that should count for something". Joe Mears must have made a few enemies in his time at the FA as his son's top striker had his ban increased from six weeks to eight weeks. I kept myself fit during that eight-week period. I did the long distance runs, the doggies, and I played in practice games. My ban finished on the Monday before the game and the day before the match I went on a cross-country run with Ron Suart. When we got back Dave Sexton was waiting for me and told me he thought he was going to start with me on the bench, "Look Dave," I replied, "I have done the training, the runs, everything, we are 2-0 down for Christ's sake, I want to play!"

On the night, the match programme editor clearly thought Osgood was not in the team line-up: Tommy Baldwin's name was printed alongside the number 9 slot.

The second leg at the Bridge was make or break for Chelsea. They needed a 3-0 win to go through to the semi-finals and despite the eight-week ban, Sexton went with his instincts and put Osgood straight back into the side at the expense of leading scorer Keith Weller.

Houseman stroked in the first goal on 22 minutes following Osgood's header from a Baldwin cross. Two minutes before half time Harris, back after a four match absence through injury, smashed a low 30-yarder shot against a post. With Boyle substituted at half time for Dempsey (slight concussion and two stitches in a cut forehead) and Bruges resisting all Chelsea's attacks we still needed a goal to draw level on aggregate with only nine minutes left. To everyone's relief Osgood then shot in from Cooke's pass. After leaping the advertising hoardings, Osgood ran to the Chelsea fans behind the goal and in a never to be repeated goal celebration, dived on top of a hot dog trolley and sent the buns, hot dogs and burgers flying as the Chelsea fans engulfed him.

After two minutes of extra time, Baldwin hit the bar from close range, and three minutes into the second half of extra time Boyle cleared off the line from Rensenbrink. Then came two goals in three minutes (114th and 117th) to take us through to the semi-finals - both made by Hudson, with Osgood shooting his second of the night (in his first match for eight weeks) and Baldwin completing the scoring.

Of all the games that Peter Osgood played in his illustrious Chelsea career this one holds great memories for him: 'There were 45,000 fans there that night and it was a tremendous atmosphere and a great game to play in. I will never forget that night. I imagine the 45,558 lucky individuals there that night feel the same way.'

With that mammoth hurdle overcome Chelsea were now in the last four. It was a strong quartet. Chelsea were joined by Cup Winners' Cup holders Manchester City, PSV Eindhoven who had seen off Steau Bucharest in the second round and favourites Real Madrid. Many English football fans were hoping for an all-English final but the draw in Zurich put paid to that, as Chelsea were drawn at home to Manchester City. Psychologically it was not the best draw for Chelsea as memories remained fresh from City's 3-0 FA Cup victory at the Bridge in January.

With Osgood injured and Tommy Baldwin and Keith Weller seemingly out of favour with Dave Sexton, Chelsea started the first leg of the semi-final with a very makeshift forward line. Derek Smethurst was given his European baptism and David Webb was pushed up front to play beside him. Sexton's gamble appeared to pay off as the South African scored the only goal of the game to give Chelsea the slenderest of margins to take to Maine Road in a fortnight's time.

Sandwiched in between was the small matter of a league game at Maine Road and the psychological pendulum swung Chelsea's way when a Keith Weller second half goal gained Chelsea a point and set them up nicely for the semi-final second leg just four days later. Despite a lengthening injury list that now included Baldwin, Hollins, Hutchinson, McCreadie and the still injured Osgood, City were no better off with six key players out including giant goalkeeper Joe Corrigan who pulled out of the game after failing a late fitness test.

However, if Chelsea scored a valuable away goal, City would need to score three to win and just before half time Keith Weller put the tie out of City's reach. Well, not quite. When Chelsea were awarded an indirect free kick by the corner flag, Weller took it quickly and went for goal. Had his shot gone straight in it would have been disallowed but City reserve goalkeeper Ron Healey, in trying to stop the shot, only succeeded in helping the ball into his own net and Chelsea went 3-0 up on aggregate.

Despite their best efforts in the second half, City could not break the Chelsea defence and the 10,000 fans who had made the midweek trip to Manchester were richly rewarded with not only the club's first European final but also the chance of a few days in the sun with a trip to Athens for the final. Waiting for them would be perhaps the greatest name in European football - the mighty Real Madrid. It could so easily have been PSV Eindhoven however as the Dutch side had been eight minutes from beating the nine times European finalists on away goals in the Bernabeu Stadium.

So Wednesday, May 19 1971 and Chelsea returned to Greece where they had begun their Cup Winners' Cup campaign back in September. The final was to be held in the Karaiskaki stadium in Athens, near the port of Piraeus which was renowned among the locals as an area of ill repute where prostitution and robbery were commonplace. From Chelsea's point of view the only robbery they experienced on the night was a Madrid equaliser in the last minute of normal time to deny them their first European trophy.

With the clock ticking down and the Spaniards a goal down to a 55th minute Peter Osgood effort, a last ditch assault was made on the Chelsea goal and John Dempsey was the unlucky villain of the hour. In trying to clear a cross he only succeeded in deflecting the ball into the path of Zoco who blasted the ball past Peter Bonetti. Seconds later, Swiss referee Buchelli blew for the end of normal time.

Two nights later the teams reconvened again but without the majority of Chelsea fans, who made the first trip but had to return home. Some 200-300 fans even sat on the tarmac at Athens Airport singing 'we shall not be moved' in an attempt to stay on until the replay. From the 5,000 fans that travelled to Athens, only 10% stayed behind for the replay, many of whom were only there thanks to the Chelsea players having a collection for the fans.

'The thing I remember most about Athens were the supporters,' recalls John Hollins. 'We had drawn on the Wednesday and we all went to see them off at the airport and half the planes seemed to go back to England half-empty. We kept saying to them 'get on the plane' and they would go 'we will be back tomorrow'. We could not get them all on the plane and on the Friday there must have still been 20,000 there. If there weren't that many there it certainly felt like there were.'

John Hollins' memory must have played tricks as only a few hundred had managed to stay behind. Long before the days of cut-price travel, Easy Jet and Go it wasn't cheap to travel to Athens in 1971. With most gone home before the replay, the 500 who stayed behind would be remembered, as 20,000 must have made a hell of a noise!

In the 48 hours since the first match, Chelsea had overcome the initial disappointment of being ten seconds from victory and Ron Harris promised all the Chelsea fans watching the replay on the BBC that Chelsea would win the cup.

'I promise all the fans who had to fly back to England that we will bring home the Cup. We know we didn't play well on Wednesday and were down in the dumps at the end of the night, but a day's break has worked wonders. We've come out of our depression, we've learned our lesson and we're ready to go. I don't think Real can get better, but we *know* we can, and we mean to do so.'

In the replay, Harris and Chelsea kept their promise. The first goal came in the 32nd minute and how appropriate that John Dempsey, with a rare goal, scored it. Having made the mistake that gifted Madrid the equaliser, Dempsey blasted Chelsea into the lead from a Charlie Cooke corner. Within a minute it was 2-0. Baldwin, in the side in place of the injured Hollins, slipped a ball through to Osgood and from the edge of the penalty area the great man scored his fourth and most crucial goal of the competition.

Although the Spaniards pulled a goal back with 15 minutes to go through Fleitas, there was no way lightning was going to strike twice and the Chelsea defence held on for a great victory.

The following year, Chelsea began the defence of the trophy in the tiny principality of Luxembourg against Jeunesse Hautcharage. Hautcharage were a small team from a village of only 704 inhabitants but they had put themselves on the European soccer map by surprisingly beating Luxembourg's top side Jeunesse Esch 4-1 in their domestic cup final. At the time, they were in the Third Division in Luxembourg so it was a giant killing act of the highest order. The reward for winning the cup was a place in Europe and the Grand Duchy's inhabitants were delighted when they drew the famous Chelsea in the first round with the first leg at home. The game caught the imagination of the nation and instead of the match being played in their usual 1500 capacity stadium, Jeunesse moved the game to the national stadium in Luxembourg and a crowd of 13,000 turned out to watch the village part-timers take on the professionals from London. The Jeunesse team was made up of steelworkers, a stationmaster, hairdresser, butcher, blacksmith and they even had four brothers in the squad, the Welschers, three of whom appeared against Chelsea. There was also the most memorable player of all, Guy Thill, a young student who only had one arm but who proved to be one of the best players in the Jeunesse side.

The game was the massacre most of the 13,000 spectators expected. After Peter Osgood had opened the scoring from a John Hollins pass after only two minutes, it was a question of how many goals Chelsea would score on the night. By half time Chelsea were already 6-0 up, and they eased up in the second half to eventually run out 8-0 winners with goals from Osgood (3), Houseman (2), Baldwin, Webb and Hollins. Chelsea had been professional in their performance but Ron Harris best summed up everyone's feelings after the game when he said, 'It was easier than training.'

After the game, Harris thought he was worth a few quid to get a goal in the second leg and Osgood confidently predicted that he would score six goals in the second leg. Peter Bonetti, who had a reputation amongst his teammates as being a bit of a tightwad, was first in the queue with a £5 bet to suggest otherwise. For two weeks all the talk was how seriously Chelsea would take the game in the second leg and whether or not they would try to beat the highest ever European aggregate held jointly by Benfica and Sporting Lisbon.

On the night, with the game over as a contest, a disappointing crowd of 27,621 saw Chelsea write a page in the European records books and produce the biggest win in our history.

After Osgood opened the scoring, the goals rained in and by the time Maltese referee Richard Navarra blew for half time, the score was 6-0, 14-0 to Chelsea on aggregate.

The second half was a repeat of the first with the home crowd willing Chelsea to the record score. By the time the record thirteenth goal went in, much to the delight of the crowd, the names of seven players were on the scoresheet – and Peter Osgood had scored five of the goals.

With time ticking away, Ossie had a chance to make it six on the night and 14-0 on aggregate to Chelsea but fluffed it as Bonetti nervously looked on at the other end. So 'The Cat' won the bet and Chelsea got in the record books with a score that will probably never be beaten – 21-0 on aggregate.

Sadly Chelsea went out in the next round to Swedish part timers Atvidaberg when the worst penalty ever taken at Stamford Bridge saw John Hollins miss and the cup holders go out on the away goals rule. When John Hollins missed that penalty, few people realised that it would be another 23 years before Chelsea played in Europe again.

During that period, the only time the Blues got close to qualifying for Europe was in the 1984/85 season when the combination of a home defeat by relegation bound Norwich City and the Heysel Stadium disaster stopped fans from digging out their passports again. However, having lost to double winners Manchester United in a rain sodden 1994 FA Cup final, the disconsolate Chelsea fans consoled themselves that at least they would be taking United's place in the Cup Winners' Cup and would be able to sample the delights of European football once again at Stamford Bridge.

When the draw was made and Chelsea came out of the hat first against Viktoria Zizkov, most fans were wondering who they were, although a few swore that they had been out with a girl of that name many years before! In 1993 Zizkov had won the Czech Second Division, and the Czech Cup the following season beating Sparta Prague on penalties in the final.

The first leg took place at the Bridge and after only four minutes, with thousands of supporters still trying to get in, Furlong and Frank Sinclair had put the Blues two goals up. Marjoros pulled both goals back for the Czechs, including a twenty-five yarder past Kharine just before half time, and the teams went into the interval level after a stunning opening forty-five minutes. The two away goals already scored by the Czechs would no doubt have given Glenn Hoddle some cause for concern until Rocastle chipped in from twenty-five yards and then Dennis Wise rounded off the game with a similar length drive for a 4-2 finish.

The Zizkov area of Prague is situated in the north of the city and, not having played in Europe for twenty three years, it seemed as if everyone wanted to go to Prague to make up for lost time. The club claimed that UEFA had demanded supporters were taken in and out straight away and there was nothing they could do about it. The week before the game, they issued a statement saying that only 700 tickets were available to Chelsea fans and that it was pointless to travel to Jablonec without one. However, it would be fair to say that if you wanted a ticket for the match and hung around in the Sports Bar in the centre of Prague long enough, you would have got one.

To make matters more difficult, the game was switched to three o'clock in the afternoon, as Jablonec apparently did not have floodlights. Well they did and, although they were not on a par with a Premier League ground, they were no worse than those you would find in the lower echelons of the Nationwide League. A school of thought running round Prague the day before the game was that the moving of the venue and the change of kick-off time were designed to prevent unofficial fans from getting there, when in reality most of them were already in Prague 24 hours before the game. The final irony was that the only people who missed the kick-off were the ones who travelled with the official club party.

To make matters worse, those Chelsea fans who nipped over to Zizkov's ground to check out if there were tickets on sale at the ticket office were stunned to discover that tickets were on sale only in Jablonec. When match tickets also had printed on them that they were invalid if they were in the possession of a Chelsea supporter it became obvious that the club were doing what they could to stop Chelsea fans travelling on their own, almost blackmailing them into going on the official travel package. The only people who were inconvenienced by all of this were the Ziskov fans who did not have the disposal income of Chelsea fans to hire a taxi to make the 50 mile journey north and then ask the driver to wait until the game was over.

Of the 6,000 fans in the ground, at least one-third had made the journey from London to see Chelsea's first match in Europe since the Heysel ban. A 20-page match programme greeted the travelling Chelsea fans on sale for the measly sum of 10p. The entrepreneurs among us bought dozens each and three days later at Stamford Bridge copies were being knocked out for £3 apiece! As for tickets marked 'Invalid in possession of a Chelsea fan', no one checked mine or many other fan's tickets, as we walked through the unmanned turnstiles - many fans even got in for free.

As for the match itself, a poor pitch did not help matters but Chelsea could not get going in the first half. The European rules about foreign players did not help Chelsea, especially as Scots such as Clarke and Spencer were classed as foreigners. Glenn Hoddle had to give Graham Rix his full first team debut at the age of 37, and with Paul Hughes and Michael Duberry having only a few appearances between them, it was not the strongest side Hoddle could have put out given the chance. Zizkov had all the early pressure and managed to get the ball into the net after fifteen minutes but the referee disallowed the goal for handball.

On the half-hour Anthony Barness tripped up Karel Poborsky but Kharine saved Vrabec's penalty. Perhaps Vrabec was put off by Queen's *'We Will Rock You'* which the Czechs played every time they got into the penalty area. The first time you heard it, it was funny but over ninety minutes it began to get on your nerves especially when you heard Freddie Mercury 'kicking his can all over the place' for the tenth time! With Zizkov unable to breakdown a stubborn Chelsea defence in the second half, the game faded into the inevitable 0-0 draw and Chelsea had qualified for the second round of the competition.

While supporters who travelled with the club made do with a complimentary drink on the way home, the 500 or so fans who had made their own way to Prague through various means hit the town and celebrated into the early hours of the morning with beer at the ridiculously cheap price of 30p a pint. Many of the travelling Chelsea fans were just arriving back home in London when the draw in Zurich paired the Blues with Austria Vienna or Memphis, as they were now known following a large injection of cash from a tobacco firm.

The first leg at the Bridge was a stalemate. In front of 22,560 fans and probably a few more at home watching the match on BSkyB, Chelsea could not break down a resolute Austrian defence, despite being reduced to ten men when one of their defenders was dismissed for persistently fouling Dennis Wise.

Two weeks later, in the Austrian capital it seemed as if most Chelsea fans who had planned to do at least one European trip that year had got the cash together to be in the Ernst Happel Stadium, just in case Chelsea were knocked out. The Austrians were favourites to go through and with a Chelsea side decimated by injury and ineligibility, Nigel Spackman was forced to turn out as a centre half for the first time in his career, so the omens did not look good when the two sides came out. However, with the game delicately poised at 0-0, Chelsea knew that one goal would mean the Austrians needed to get at least two to go through. Little did anyone imagine that the goal Chelsea managed to score before half time will probably go down as one of the greatest in the club's history.

With the Austrians throwing every man forward for a corner, the Chelsea defence managed to clear the ball to John Spencer. Surprisingly he found himself all alone, with not an Austrian player in front of him other than Memphis goalkeeper Frank Wolfhart. Spencer ran the length of the pitch and scored a valuable away goal. Although the little man has moved on from Chelsea since those days, his name will be permanently etched in Chelsea's history for that goal.

Since leaving Stamford Bridge he has played for Queens Park Rangers, Everton and has now joined up with another favourite wee man, Pat Nevin, at Motherwell. While most Chelsea fans in the Ernst Happel Stadium will never forget that moment, the little man has fond memories of the goal himself. 'The Austrians had a corner and the ball somehow came out to me and I was thinking, where was the sweeper? I just started running and running and the further I got down the pitch, I could see their keeper in the distance coming towards me getting bigger and bigger. I started thinking to myself that I had better score after running all this way with the ball but I could not decide which way I would go. At the last minute I thought that I would go round him but I looked up briefly to see that Eddie Newton was on the far side of the goal having made this amazing run and I thought should I pass it to him? Then I remembered that it was Eddie Newton and he would have blasted it out of the ground, so I thought sod it I will have to take this one myself. So I nipped round the keeper and stuck the ball in. I can tell you I was knackered after running all that way.'

Spencer and Chelsea dug in deep in the second half and defended with great resolve and although Narbekovas equalised for the Austrians, the Blues held out for the remainder of the game to go through on the away goals rule.

Other than the amazing celebrations that took place in the city centre after the game, there was one story doing the rounds in the bars of Vienna long into the night of the well-known Chelsea official who had been caught red handed coming out of one of Vienna's well known sex shops. A Chelsea fan had gone shopping looking for something to take back to his wife and having decided on a pair of silk stockings and sexy red knickers, he paid for his goods and left the shop. On leaving, he bumped into the said Chelsea official, who had a carrier bag from one of Vienna's well-known sex shops. When stopped by the Chelsea fan, the official looked embarrassed and tried to hide the name of the shop, but it was too late. The identity of this senior Chelsea official is sealed away in a brown envelope in a bank vault in the West End of London. For the right amount of money, I am sure the contributor of this story will reveal the guilty culprit's identity.

And so to Bruges and a repeat of the 1971 Cup Winners' Cup quarter-final. On a poor playing surface, Hoddle opted for a square back four and Spackman in the holding role in front of the defence, a three man midfield of Newton, Wise and Peacock with Spenny tucked in behind Paul Furlong or "Fucking Hell" Furlong as he had become to be known in the West Stand.

The majority of the first half saw Chelsea sit back and let FC Bruges take the game to them. Most first half chances fell the way of Belgians and the ever-consistent Kevin Hitchcock made a number of crucial saves. The second half seemed to fly by with neither side creating any clear-cut chances and with time running out Chelsea began to look as if they were going to pull off a great result to take back to the Bridge in two weeks' time.

Suddenly, Minto was penalised for a foul and the kick is quickly taken. Verheyen gets between Johnsen and Furlong to head FC Bruges into the lead - or was that Furlong who got the last touch? It certainly looked like it to me. The Olympiastadium erupts and for the first time in the evening, the Bruges fans strain their vocal chords to a chorus of 'We love you Bruges we do, we love you Bruges we do'. A strange one that. Why do Belgian fans sing their football songs in English?

Off the field, with the riots at the England v Ireland game in Dublin fresh in people's minds, many Chelsea fans are arbitrarily picked off the streets of Bruges and put in warehouses and detained for eight hours, even though they had tickets for the game. They were subsequently taken to Ostend and put on ferries to England. Some supporters had passports, luggage and car keys left behind in hotels that they were unable to return and collect. If any supporters had caused trouble in Bruges then the Belgian police had every right to crack down on them, but it seems many innocent fans were detained unfairly by the Belgian authorities.

With Chelsea and Arsenal now the only two British sides left in European competition, goals from Paul Furlong and Mark Stein saw Chelsea through to their third semi-final in a European competition where they were drawn to play Real Zaragosa in Spain.

In the Spaniards' stadium, the home fans created an atmosphere that many Chelsea fans had never experienced before. You had to be there to know how it felt with 35,000 Zaragosa fans producing a wall of noise, twirling 35,000 scarves at the same time all around the ground, synchronised Mexican waves, huge flags, banners and a major card display to put anything at Wembley to shame. The Spanish always seem to do it bigger and better. Forget the Roker roar, the Kop or the Gallowgate End, this was not noise from just one end but the whole ground.

The game kicked off and Chelsea were outclassed. The Zaragoza players wanted to win more than our players did. After the third goal went in, it all went pear-shaped for a while. If some Chelsea fans thought the police in Belgium had been bad then the Spanish police gave them an even bigger run for their money. There were many innocent Chelsea fans attacked indiscriminately by the riot police, including Club members who had travelled with the official Chelsea party and had opted to sit in the lower tier with their non-member friends. This killed off the argument that those seats were solely occupied by people who did not travel with the club. What chance did any law abiding Chelsea fan sitting behind the goal have when the Guardia Civil had been fed a continuous media message that Chelsea fans were 'los hooligans'? The riot police had been brought in for the occasion from Madrid and Barcelona and even before the game they were overreacting - one female fan had her perfume confiscated and another male fan had the duty free perfume purchased for his wife also confiscated.

In the return leg, it was important to get an early goal and Paul Furlong had a chance to beat Juaanmi after five minutes only for the Spanish keeper to save from eight yards out. However Furlong's persistent running made amends shortly after with probably the luckiest strike seen at the Bridge since an Alan Hudson shot into the side netting against Ipswich was given as a goal in the 1970/71 season. Zaragoza 'keeper Juaanmi went to clear a back pass and Furlong ran at him, the goalkeeper's clearance rebounding off Furlong's hand into the net. Unfortunately, an early second half goal by Aragon gave the Spaniards a valuable away goal and despite late goals from Frank Sinclair and Mark Stein's knee three minutes from time to give the score some respectability, Chelsea were out of the competition.

Nevertheless, despite the disappointment of going out of the competition, it was a proud Glenn Hoddle who spoke to the *Match of the Day* cameras after the game, 'It was a proud night for us and we came out of the game with honour. We really could have been out there playing extra time. We nearly got the five goals in the last knockings. It was an unbelievable performance from our boys. Not just the ones who performed tonight but the whole European Cup run has been magnificent. When we started the season I never dreamt we would get this far and under the circumstances the club should be proud.'

Chelsea only had two seasons out of Europe before they were back in the Cup Winners' Cup after their historic cup win at Wembley in 1997 under Ruud Gullit's management.

Their first round opponents were Slovan Bratislava from Slovakia and the first leg was held at Stamford Bridge; so the strategy was to build up a sufficient lead to make the second leg a formality. It did not quite work out that way. Although Robbie Di Matteo had sent the Blues in 1-0 up at half time, the second half goal feast never materialised due to some resolute defending from the Slovakians. Eight minutes from time it took a defender, Danny Granville, to dance through the Bratislava defence to score the only goal he would get in Chelsea's colours and what a beauty it was. Granville's goal meant Chelsea only had a two-goal lead to take to the second leg when they had hoped for more but Gullit was not too despondent afterwards.

'I am very happy. I thought it was an excellent performance today, despite the changes we made. We scored good goals and I'm pleased about the way the team approached the game. I am surprised we did not score more but on some days you can have worse luck when no goals go in, but at the same time we have given away nothing and that pleased me also.

'I said during half time that even if the game ends 1-0, it's still a good result because we know that we will create chances away from home. We were fully in control so I was not anxious about our second goal coming but I was glad when it did.'

For the fans who made the effort to go to the second leg, Bratislava was beer heaven. At fifty pence a pint, the 1500 or so the influx of Chelsea fans must have boosted the Slovakian economy where the average weekly wage is only £40 per week. Most bars served either the Czech beer Budvar or local beer Pivo. Even the best and most expensive hotel in town, the Forum Hotel, were charging less than £2 a pint which was considered extremely expensive by the locals. As hard as supporters tried, you would have been hard pushed to spend £10 on beer in Bratislava, even if you started drinking at breakfast and did not stop until you reached the stadium, which, considering the condition of many Chelsea fans on the flight home to London, was probably the case.

On the pitch, despite a two-goal lead from the first leg, an early Bratislava goal would have made the game a contest but thanks to Vialli's backside gifting Chelsea an early opener, the match was no contest and the Blues became the first English team to win in Bratislava.

As Ruud Gullit said afterwards, 'it was not a good match because of the pitch and the wind, but it was a professional performance by us.'

On Vialli's goal, Gullit was quick to confirm that it was not something that had been planned in training but Vialli had deserved the goal. 'It was a very lucky goal but Luca deserved it because he did everything but score in the first leg. He was the first to agree that it doesn't matter how you get the goals as long as they go in. It was a very important one for Chelsea.'

Although Bratislava were never really in the game, the home fans tried to get behind their team early on with their attempt at a Mexican wave. When Vialli's goal killed the game as a contest, the home fans then seemed more interested in selling any possessions they had to the travelling Chelsea supporters. Bratislavan scarves, hats, caps, badges and shirts were up for the highest bidder with the locals seeing a huge money making opportunity. Although the match programmes were given away free, I had to negotiate with one of the locals to buy one. He wanted 200 Koruna (about £4 for his copy). With my assertive hat on, I managed to beat him down to 50p. I later saw him trying to sell his sister for quite a reasonable price after the match to some other fans.

When Chelsea drew Norwegian side Tromso in the second round most people wondered where it was. Tore Andre Flo knew, as it was one of his former clubs. Tromso is an island just over 200 miles inside the Arctic Circle and in view of the small size of the ground, Chelsea and Elizabeth Duff Travel who organised travel for fans for European ties only had 350 tickets for sale. So this appeared to be one occasion where, unless you travelled with the club, there was little chance of getting in. Or was it? The club repeatedly spewed out the myth that if you do not travel with EDT you would not get in, but the Tromso trip shot that myth down in flames. With a capacity of only 8,000 and Chelsea only getting 350 tickets this was always going to be the hardest game to get into or so it seemed.

One group of 40 Chelsea fans had made their own way to Oslo having been promised match tickets by some dodgy Mancunian company, but they were then told that Ken Bates had threatened to shred the 150 returned tickets to Tromso rather than let independent fans travel. In the end the only people to get into trouble in Norway were two of Bates' £895 executive tour members, arrested for 'lining up' in a club.

As it turned out, finding a ticket was not a problem. Two hours before kick-off, the Tromso ticket office was selling to anyone who turned up, the locals had spares, and some were even offering tickets in return for a Chelsea scarf. Like nearly every other ground Chelsea have played at in Europe, there was a chance to pay at the turnstile! What a surprise!

On arrival in Tromso, the Chelsea fans were greeted with Christmas card scenery, snow was everywhere. Even the local sports shops had Manchester United shirts on sale and inside the ground there were plenty of youngsters in Man United colours. The global domination by the Man United brand name had even reached the Arctic Circle. Very scary. The Norwegian police were very hospitable, giving the Chelsea fans a chocolate bar each and when the travelling fans stopped singing in the ground the police went round trying to encourage them to get behind their team when most seemed content to try and keep warm.

The game itself saw Chelsea off to a slow start and they fell 2-0 behind. The bad weather in Tromso had left the pitch in very poor condition and even a Sunday league referee would have contemplated calling off the game. It was not until the arrival of a severe snowstorm that Chelsea got back into the game. Vialli had made it 2-1 before a comedy of errors, with Chelsea trying to make a substitution that the linesman failed to acknowledge, saw the Norwegians go 3-1 up and Gullit go mental. Just as Chelsea were in danger of leaving themselves with a difficult task in the second leg, up popped Vialli to score his second goal in injury time and leave Gullit's men on the wrong end of a 3-2 defeat.

Although most fans who travelled to Tromso had a good time, they were glad to get out of the country before being snowed in at the airport. One traveller who had been to Tromso a week earlier didn't even leave the airport on arrival in the country. A ticket tout had gone over to buy what tickets he could to sell to Chelsea fans but found none on sale. He had changed £2,000 to buy tickets but the bank clerk had put the nought in the wrong place. The lucky tout forgot about the tickets and got the first plane home out of Oslo - £18,000 richer.

The second leg was a personal triumph for Vialli as Chelsea made short work of the Scandinavians, winning 7-1 as the Italian grabbed his first hat trick in European football while Petrescu (2), Zola and Leboeuf were the other scorers.

However, having lost Ruud Gullit as manager since their second round, a trip to Seville to face Real Betis was always going to be a severe test of new manager Vialli's credentials in only his fourth match in charge. In the event, he passed with flying colours. An excellent all round team display saw two quick, carbon copy goals from Tore Andre Flo give the Blues the perfect foundation on which to build in the second half. The game made you proud to be a Chelsea fan. The support in the Benito Villamarin Stadium from the home support was tremendous but the 4,000 travelling Chelsea fans, most of whom had made their own way to Spain, were in fine voice. Their voices were no doubt well lubricated by an afternoon in the bars of Seville and until their escapades in the Champions League this was probably Chelsea's best performance in Europe since the 1970s.

In the next round, following a 1-0 defeat in the semi-final first leg in Vicenza, Chelsea's European Cup Winners' Cup dreams appeared to have gone up in smoke when Pasquale Luiso put the Italians 2-0 ahead on aggregate in the 33rd minute. Within three minutes, Chelsea were back in the match when Gus Poyet, playing his first game in six months following a cruciate knee injury, scored the equaliser.

Just after half time, player-manager Vialli sped down the right wing and sent a glorious cross over to the far post where the smallest player on the pitch, Franco Zola, was there to put the Blues ahead on the night.

It still meant that Chelsea had to score a third goal to win the tie and as the clock ticked down, it was beginning to look as if it was not going to be. On 70 minutes, Mark Hughes came off the bench to become the hero. Six minutes after his entrance, an Ed de Goey goal-kick bounced once and Hughes took the ball round defender Dicara and hammered a half-volley into the net. 3-1 to Chelsea and the Blues were going to Stockholm.

Hughes finished the game unconscious when a loose elbow caught him in the face. He was helped back to the dressing room where he was sick. Hughes had endured worse in his career and was just happy that Chelsea were in the final. Vialli was quick to praise the old warhorse. 'Mark Hughes does not mind getting punched or kicked to the ground. He is a warrior and never lets me down. I have to thank him.'

For three weeks leading up to the final, Gianfranco Zola had had extensive treatment in the hope of being fit. But on the night but Vialli did not want to risk him so he picked himself and Flo in the forward line and kept Zola on the bench.

With Chelsea making all the running Stuttgart, their opponents in the final, did their best to keep the Blues at bay and the magical moment didn't come until the 70th minute. Tore Andre Flo came off and the little Italian came on and within 17 seconds he had scored the winning goal. With his first touch of the ball, Zola lost possession to Berthold but luckily the ball rebounded to Dennis Wise. The Chelsea captain pushed the ball into Zola's path and as Stuttgart keeper Frank Wolfhart could not decide whether to come out or stay on his line, the Italian maestro made up his mind for him and blasted the ball into the top right hand corner. The 20,000 or so Chelsea fans in the Rasunda Stadium went wild and the celebrations went on long into the night in the streets of Stockholm. Twelve months earlier, Chelsea had not won any silverware for 25 years. After Zola's goal they were suddenly the holders of three different trophies.

The 1998/99 Cup Winners' Cup campaign kicked off at Stamford Bridge with the visit of Swedish side Helsingborg. A poor crowd of 17,714 on a cold night endured a below par performance from Chelsea and a sturdy defensive performance from the Swedes. Frank Leboeuf's free kick through the wall on the stroke of half time proved to be the only goal on the night and if left Chelsea with an uncomfortable journey to Sweden for the second leg. Vialli and Chelsea need not have worried. With the weather even colder in Sweden and Michael Duberry solid as a rock in defence, they kept their opponents at bay for the full ninety minutes, not even allowing them a single shot on target. It had been a poor game to watch but a professional away performance by Chelsea.

Chelsea were then drawn at home in the second round to FC Copenhagen. It was important that improvements were made on the Helsingborg performance with a healthy lead needed for the return leg in Denmark. It did not quite work out that way. A frustrating night saw Copenhagen's Bjarne Goldbaek score from the edge of the box with ten minutes to go to give the Danes the lead and put Chelsea's forty-year unbeaten run at home in Europe in severe jeopardy. With time running out Marcel Desailly pushed forward in the hope of grabbing an equaliser. With two minutes of injury time already gone and only seconds remaining it looked as if Chelsea had not only lost their unbeaten run but were in danger of going out of the competition. Then 'The Rock' curled in a beautiful goal from the edge of the penalty area to save Chelsea's blushes but as the Danes had the advantage of an away goal. Chelsea had to win in Denmark to make sure of going through. However, a week before the second leg, at a press conference held at Stamford Bridge, Chelsea announced that summer signing Brian Laudrup would be leaving the club. Laudrup had not settled in London and Chelsea had agreed to his request to return home to Denmark, ironically to FC Copenhagen. This meant that the second leg was to be Laudrup's swan song in a

Chelsea shirt and, as if the story line had already been scripted, the Dane duly scored the only goal of the game against his new team mates to help his old teammates qualify for the quarter-final where Chelsea were paired with Valerenga of Norway.

Valerenga manager Egil Olsen, former manager of the Norwegian national side, had done well to get his side to the quarter-finals. While Chelsea had struggled to beat Helsingborg and Copenhagen, they dealt comfortably with Valerenga, winning 6-2 on aggregate. At Stamford Bridge, goals from Celestine Babayaro (11 minutes), Gianfranco Zola (29 minutes) and Dennis Wise (85 minutes) had seen the Blues build a comfortable 3-0 advantage to take to Scandinavia. The second leg saw two early goals from Gianluca Vialli (11 minutes) and Bernard Lambourde (15 minutes) put Chelsea a comfortable 5-0 up on aggregate but a madcap eleven minutes before half time saw Valerenga grab two goals either side of a Tore Andre Flo header.

For the third time the Blues had made the semi-finals of a European competition and had avoided favourites Lazio and drawn Real Mallorca instead. For the third year it ended in disappointment. Having been held 1-1 at Stamford Bridge, when Dani's away goal proved crucial, it was always going to be difficult for Vialli's men to get a result in Spain. When Dani scored again in the second leg to put the Spaniards ahead both in the tie and on aggregate, Chelsea needed two goals to make the final at Villa Park. Chelsea had desperately wanted to win, as they would have gone down as the last winners of the Cup Winner's Cup and also become the only club in history to win the trophy two years in a row. Sadly it was not to be, but third place in the Premier League gave them the compensation of playing in the Champions League the following season.

Having waited forty-four years to get into the Champions Cup, now the Champions League, Chelsea were drawn against Skonto Riga of Latvia in the final qualifying round of the tournament. Victory would see them through to the first group stage.

With the first leg at home and the ITV cameras in situ, the 22,043 loyal Chelsea fans and the millions watching at home looked forward to a goal feast. It was a long time coming. The Latvian champions defended superbly for most of the game until an inspired double substitution in the 66th minute swung it in Chelsea's favour. Deschamps and Zola came off and were replaced by Flo and Babayaro. After another nightmare evening in front of goal, many were surprised that Chris Sutton had not been taken off but Vialli's substitutions immediately paid off and Sutton played his part in the build up to the first goal. A Wise cross was chested down by Sutton into the path of Babayaro and he blasted in from the edge of the penalty area. Within sixty seconds a Gus Poyet special made it 2-0 and then with six minutes remaining those fortunate enough to be there witnessed something they would not see many more times that season, a Chris Sutton goal at Stamford Bridge. Another Vialli substitute, Barney Goldbaek, broke free on the right and his low cross into the area was touched in by Sutton.

After the game, Sutton was in great demand and had a smile wider than the distance by which he had missed a sitter the previous Saturday. He told reporters he was pleased to get off the mark for his new club. 'Of course I am pleased to get off the mark, especially after the chances I missed on Saturday against Sunderland. However, I have always been confident in my own ability and I knew I would get a goal eventually'

Vialli was a much happier man knowing that three late goals had as good as killed the tie and the second leg in Riga appeared to be a formality. He saved all his praise for his new signing. 'He does not have to prove anything to me. He played very well tonight, he led the line well and he scored the goal which he deserved for his all-round play. He had a lot of criticism after Sunderland but he is big enough to handle the situation at a club like Chelsea.' Two weeks later, on a ground that would have been more at home in the Rymans League than the Champions League, Chelsea played out a tedious 0-0 draw to secure entry to the Champions League group stages.

Chelsea were drawn with the mighty AC Milan, Galatasary and Hertha Berlin with Chelsea's first Champions League game a mouth watering encounter with the Milanese. If this was not the greatest 0-0 draw you had ever seen, you would be hard pushed to pick a better one. With Gianfranco Zola in inspirational form in front of a full house at Stamford Bridge and millions watching at home, Chelsea played some of their best football under Vialli. Had it not been for three marvellous saves from Milan keeper Abbiati, the Italians would have returned to the San Siro empty handed

After making a promising start against the pre-group favourites, Vialli and his squad travelled to Berlin for their first away game in the vast Olympic Stadium arena. Michael Caine, many years earlier, in his role as secret agent Harry Palmer, had starred in *'Funeral in Berlin'*. On a cold, wet September night Chelsea experienced their own Berlin funeral with a below-par performance that started badly and got worse. After only two minutes Berlin number nine Ali Daei managed to get between Frank Leboeuf and Marcel Desailly to score the opening goal. The second crucial goal came after seventy minutes, when another Leboeuf and Desailly misunderstanding allowed Daei to race clear thirty yards from goal and slip the ball past Ed de Goey. Leboeuf made partial amends with a late penalty, but on a night when Chelsea were optimistic about taking a point but hoping for all three, they suddenly found themselves bottom of Group H after two games. Vialli was honest in his assessment of the game but too harsh on himself in the process.

'Tonight we were poor physically, mentally and tactically. I have to accept some of the responsibility for that as I am the one who trains the team, picks the team and when the team does not perform than I must be doing something wrong.' Other than the absence of Poyet through injury this was arguably Vialli's strongest side on paper and for them to perform so badly for their manager in such a crucial game, having just been humiliated at Watford a few days earlier, said more about them than the manager.

On the eve of the next game, Galatasary coach Fatih Terim made sure that whatever happened at Stamford Bridge, Chelsea would be guaranteed a hostile reception in the return game in Turkey. Terim suggested that Chelsea had deliberately failed to send someone to meet the Turkish party on their arrival at Heathrow airport, not provided security guards for his players and had not laid on training facilities for his players. The Galatasary players and management were held up at Heathrow Airport for ninety minutes at passport control and the Turks hired QPR's training ground in Ealing because they believed that Chelsea had arranged nothing for them.

'We have had to get a training pitch a long way from the ground and we had to pay for it. I have never seen anything like it. We will be complaining to UEFA.' said Terim to anyone who could be bothered to listen to his rants. 'We were also told at Heathrow by passport control that we were held up because they had not been told by Chelsea that we were coming. They will get it back with interest. I'm asking that of my chairman, directors and supporters. I feel so strongly about this. All my players are upset about this and I have never been treated like this before.'

Coming from the manager of a team whose fans regularly greeted opposing teams and fans with 'Welcome to Hell' banners at Istanbul airport, it certainly smacked of double standards. In the end all Terim's hot air succeeded in doing was to wind Vialli and his players up and make sure they got the points.

Having lost in Berlin, this was a game Chelsea had to win. A draw would not be good enough. They got the three points they badly wanted and had to thank a combination of Sutton and Petrescu for the spoils. With Galatasary reduced to ten men when Brazilian international Taffarel was sent off in the first for handball outside the area, the Turks seemed content to hold on for a point. However in the 56th minute Sutton created a clear chance for Petrescu who saw substitute keeper Mehmet save before he shot home the rebound.

With the group evenly poised, the next game in Istanbul was a stern test for Chelsea and a game in which they had to take at least a point. Vialli once again rotated his squad, leaving Dennis Wise, Chris Sutton and goalscorer Dan Petrescu on the bench.

Galatasary, their fans armed with drums and flares, had built up a fortress in the Ali Sami Yen stadium, with their intimidation of opposing players and fans and 'Welcome to Hell' banners designed to intimidate the opposition. They provided a reception committee when Chelsea arrived at Istanbul airport and on a hot October night the home fans were in the ground nearly four hours before kick off making a noise that would scare many opposing teams into submission. However, Chelsea produced one of their best-ever performances in Europe and discovered that, just as Australian heavy metallers AC/DC used to sing, *'Hell Ain't a Bad Place to be'* running out 5-0 winners. Dennis Wise even took a video camera on to the pitch before the game to film the crowd. It was Chelsea's second biggest away win in Europe, behind the 8-0 thrashing of Jeunesse Hautcharage in 1971. The goals on the night were scored by Tore Andre Flo (2), Gianfranco Zola and substitutes Ambrosetti and Wise got a piece of the action late on with a goal apiece.

Vialli happily told journalists after the game, 'I have never doubted my team's character. My players do not have to prove anything to me. We knew we would be intimidated but we were superb at the back and I can not believe that we won 5-0.'

The even more surprising news filtered through that surprise team Hertha Berlin had beaten AC Milan 1-0 in Berlin, a result which put them top of Group H after four games. Vialli knew that it would be between Milan and his side for second place, 'it looks as if it will be between Milan and us for second place now. We will have to go to Milan next week and get a result. It will be a massive game as there is so much at stake but we have proved here tonight that we can achieve anything we want to.'

Less than a week later and the Champions League roadshow relocated to Milan. This was clearly looking like a winner takes all game. If Milan won, Chelsea would have to beat Berlin in their final game to be sure of qualification. If Chelsea won, then Milan were as good as out of the competition. The odds on a Chelsea victory were 10-3 with Milan 4-5 on favourites. The 2-1 odds for a draw looked the safest bet, which would still leave Chelsea in a very strong position. With history against Chelsea, as no English club had ever won in the San Siro, Vialli was confident before the game that his side would be able to cope with the intimidating atmosphere of a full San Siro. If they could cope with Hell than Milan would be Heaven in comparison, 'I believe that we will be able to cope with the atmosphere in the San Siro. There might be 78,000 supporters in the ground, but my players will be fired up for this game. It is a great place to play football and we have players in our team who are good footballers.'

Having gone behind to an Oliver Bierhoff goal, Chelsea looked in danger of missing out on qualification when Roberto Di Matteo came on as substitute for Petrescu. With thirteen minutes to go, and time running out, Di Matteo's first touch slipped the ball through to Dennis Wise and the Chelsea captain skipped through to score a memorable goal in the San Siro. Not only did it salvage a point for the Blues but it also put Chelsea in a good position to qualify for the next group stage.

With a dramatic sense of timing, the press had a field day before the Berlin game, putting even more pressure on Vialli. A draw would have been enough for Chelsea but if Berlin did the unthinkable and actually won at the Bridge and Milan won in Istanbul, Chelsea would be out.

Vialli need not have worried. Many bookmakers, realising that a draw would see both teams through, were even suggesting that gamblers might want to stake a few quid on that outcome. They would have been wasting their money as from the kick off this game was only going to have one outcome - a Chelsea victory. Chelsea were professionalism personified and won 2-0 when perhaps they could have even won by a greater margin. The only surprise of the night were the goalscorers. Having played what seemed an eternity in the Champions League, but was in fact forty-eight matches, Didier Deschamps scored his first-ever Champions League goal. His twenty-five yard effort after eleven minutes gave keeper Gabor Kirally no chance and Chelsea the perfect start. The game itself was over before half time when Dennis Wise sent Albert Ferrer through and the vastly underrated Spaniard scored from close range.

The win put Chelsea top of the group but even more surprisingly and particularly pleasing for the Berlin fans who thought they were out of the competition with fifteen minutes left, was the stunning news from Istanbul. Having been leading 2-1 with time running out, AC Milan had been hauled back to 2-2 by Turkish international Hakan Sukur and then sensationally dumped out of the competition with a last minute penalty by Davala Umit. The only cloud on a glorious night was the foolish sending off of Chris Sutton. Until then, despite his indifferent start to the season, most Chelsea fans had been supportive of the £10 million striker. Having already been booked and with the game won, Sutton inexplicably body checked Eyjolfur Sverrisson and had to go. The sending off meant that Sutton automatically missed the next Champions League tie but after that moment of stupidity it did not matter. Sutton had clearly struggled in the Champions League and despite Chelsea's successful run through to the quarter finals, Sutton would only play a combined total of twelve more minutes in the rest of the competition in the shape of two late substitute appearances.

In a week when he had been exposed to unnecessary pressure, Vialli had a grin larger than Ken Bates' bank account when he met the press and TV cameras afterwards. 'It was a great night for the players, the supporters and the club. It will be tough competing against the best in Europe and it will not matter who we get – Lazio, Barcelona or Real Madrid, it will be a great honour to play against such strong opposition.'

While Vialli was relaxing downstairs in the dressing room with a much-needed cigarette or two, Bates was upstairs, a glass of pink champagne in hand, defending his under-fire manager to *Evening Standard* journalist Steve Stammers. 'Those suggestions about him being under pressure were nonsense, total nonsense. All I did was stress on the Chelsea Clubcall line that, despite what some fans might think, we want to win the league very much. In fact, I want us to win everything. We are not like Manchester

United and some other clubs who put out weak teams in some competitions. When we played against Huddersfield in the Worthington Cup we had six full internationals in the side. Yet they lost and I was livid about that. I still am. The players who played that night did not earn their wages. Maybe it is true that we have lost our way a bit. Maybe the wholesale changes in the line up were mistakes. Vialli has said that himself. But you just can't blame the manager. Managers are always blamed. It was the players who went on the pitch and didn't fight. Vialli is the best of them all and all those suggestions earlier in the week were nothing more than troublemaking. Look at his record and what he has won – the League Cup and the Cup Winners' Cup and the European Super Cup. He helped us to third in the Premiership, our highest-ever position. We also reached the semi-final of the Cup Winners' Cup last season. This season we are in the second stage of the UEFA Champions League. That is an achievement.

'I have no doubts about Luca Vialli. None at all is the truth. I had no hesitation when it came to appointing him and I wouldn't swap him for any other manager in the Premiership. Talk of him being under pressure is absolute nonsense – he has never been under pressure here, only the pressure he likes to put himself under because he wants to be a success.'

Having achieved the remarkable by winning their group, Vialli could sit down, relax and listen to the draw for the second stage on Friday 5 November. On Bonfire night the draw produced its own fireworks when Chelsea were drawn with pre-tournament favourites Lazio, Dutch champions Feyenoord and Marseille who had defeated Manchester United in the first group stages.

Chelsea's first opponents were Feyenoord at home. The Dutch champions were unbeaten in the Champions League but despite a disappointing crowd of only 29,704, Chelsea romped home with their best performance of the season to date in the Champions League.

They had 37 shots on goal, but the Blues did not take the lead until the 45th minute when Babayaro got on the end of a Petrescu cross. The biggest culprit was Flo, who could easily have had a hat-trick before the interval. He made amends in the second half with a brace, before Feyenoord substitute Julio Cruz scored a consolation to make the score a respectable 3-1, when the Dutch could not have complained had they conceded six or seven.

Chelsea's next opponents were group and potential tournament favourites Lazio in the Olympic Stadium in Rome. This was going to be the severest test so far, even tougher than the trip to the San Siro. On a cold December night, Chelsea once again surprised their critics by not only holding the Serie A league leaders to a goalless draw but coming within inches of a winner when Celestine Babayaro nearly got on the end of a Zola cross.

Four points from their opening two games was a good start and after a three month winter break, Vialli and Chelsea resumed their Champions League activity at the end of February with a visit to the Velodrome in Marseille.

With Celestine Babayaro just back from African Nations' Cup duty, Vialli stuck with in-form John Harley and gave him his first full Champions League start following his eight minutes in Riga earlier in the competition. Unfortunately, the decision backfired early on as Robert Pires, not for the first time, got in behind Harley and from a seemingly impossible angle, somehow squeezed the ball between Ed de Goey and his near post. Harley redeemed himself moments later when he made a last ditch tackle to prevent future Arsenal signing Pires scoring a second goal but on the night, Chelsea could not get into first gear and lost 1-0. A late rally, with Chris Sutton and Jody Morris on for Ferrer and Flo, nearly brought an equaliser. Four minutes from time Marseille goalkeeper Stephane Trevisan produced the save of the match from a close range Gus Poyet shot to deny Chelsea a point and keep Marseille's remote Champions League dream alive.

The Marseille coach lit the blue touch paper for the return game seven days later when he had a dig at the attitude of the Chelsea players after the match. 'Maybe the Chelsea players were surprised by some of the problems my players caused them tonight. Maybe they came here thinking that this would be an easy game and an easy three points for them. They will respect us a lot more next week when we come to Stamford Bridge.'

No one was sure about the respect side of things but the following week a tight game was decided by a solitary Dennis Wise goal. On 27 minutes the unlikely combination of a Flo cross and a Zola header put the ball into the path of Wise who ran into the six yard box to calmly slip his shot past Trevisan. It could have been so different though, had it not been for the exploits of Ed de Goey in the Chelsea goal. Instead of being top of the group with two matches to play, Chelsea could have been in third place and in danger of going out of the competition. Having taken the lead the Blues failed to add to it and in true Chelsea 'hanging on by their fingertips' style it was only de Goey's own fingers that prevented ex-Everton striker Ibrahima Bakoyoko from scoring a late equaliser. Bakoyoko inexplicably put a last minute shot wide when it seemed easier to score.

The Feyenoord game now had great importance. Chelsea had to get a result. A draw would have been good but the manner of the win was beyond everyone's wildest dreams.

The Blues took the lead on the 39th minute when Zola scored with a half volley from the edge of the penalty area that broke his goal drought and sent the 3,000 travelling Chelsea fans into ecstasy. They could even afford a rare penalty miss by Frank Leboeuf as early as the 8th minute when Jerry Dudek in the Feyenoord goal easily saved his tame spot kick. After Feyenoord substitute Kalou had equalised on the hour, Chelsea stepped up a gear and within minutes they had killed off the game as first Wise headed a rare goal and then, in the 69th minute, Flo cut in from the right and hit a low drive into the far corner. The goal from Wise had an irony about it as Vialli had already signalled for Jody Morris to replace the Chelsea captain when his goal ensured he would stay on the pitch until the final whistle.

Sitting in the stadium in Rotterdam the greatest Dutch player of all, Johann Cruyff, came away impressed with what he had seen, 'I was very impressed with Chelsea. They have only one English player in their line up but they still play a very English game. It was pressure, pressure, pressure - very bold and very English for a team playing away from home in Europe. You would not see a Spanish side or an Italian side play that way.'

Although Vialli suggested that to reach the final Chelsea would have to rely on the hand of God, his players may have wanted to say a few prayers of thanks for the bumper pay day their good night's work brought them. Having already earned £25,000 for qualifying from the first stage, the win over Feyenoord ensured a guaranteed £5 million payday for the club. In return the players were handsomely rewarded with a further £25,000 each for reaching the last eight. For players like Zola, however, it was not the money that motivated him but the fact that they were now amongst the cream of European football and had as good a chance as any of winning the Champions Cup.

'There will be eight teams left now and they are the best teams in Europe,' he explained at the time, 'we have proved that man-to-man we are as good as anybody but also as a team we have shown we can compete with any team in Europe. Our display against Feyenoord was the best we have played since I came here. There is no reason why we cannot go all the way and win the trophy.'

Although his players had won through to the quarter-finals, Vialli still had the small matter of a final home game against Lazio to contend with. If Vialli and his men could avoid defeat at home they would win the group and avoid the seeded teams: Manchester United, Bayern Munich and Barcelona in the quarter-finals. With a forty-two year unbeaten record in Europe to defend there was nothing to suggest that anything untoward would happen when Gus Poyet took a Didier Deschamps pass a minute from half time and rifled the ball into the top corner. In the absence of the rested Dennis Wise, Poyet had been made captain and his unusual goal celebration saw him take off his captain's armband and pull it around his head.

The second half was a different story however. Lazio, needing a victory to qualify, thoroughly outclassed Chelsea with a quick passing game that saw defence turn swiftly into attack. It was only a matter of time before Pavel Nedved crossed from the right hand side for Inzaghi to beat Desailly to the ball and slip it past De Goey. While a draw would have been enough to ensure Lazio's qualification, Sven Goran Ericksson's men were not content to settle for a point. They wanted to win the group and on 67 minutes, Celestine Babayaro needlessly gave away a free kick for handball. Mihajlovic needed no invitation and his direct free kick sailed past De Goey into the top corner of the net and the Italians were in front and on top of the group. The goal should have been the catalyst for Chelsea to fight back to defend their proud record of being unbeaten for 33 ties in Europe spread over 42 years, but the fight back never materialised. Even when Couto was booked with seven minutes left for a vicious tackle on Tore Andre Flo, the equaliser never came and Chelsea had placed their Champions League dreams in severe jeopardy.

After the match Vialli acknowledged that his players had panicked after Lazio's equaliser but he did not see Dennis Wise's absence as the reason why his side had lost.

'We missed Dennis' leadership on the pitch tonight, but he needed to have a rest as he has played so many matches lately. It is important that players rest every now and again so I do not regret my decision to leave Dennis out. The problem was we panicked after they scored and things started to go wrong for us out there. Lazio took advantage as we did not show more caution when they scored and they exploited the gaps we left.'

When the draw was made for the quarter-finals it had an element of high comedy about it. Chelsea, having finished second in Group D, knew they had to play their first leg at home. The Blues were out of the hat first and were drawn against Bayern Munich. Immediately, there was activity on the Internet as Chelsea fans started logging on to low cost airline web sites to find the cheapest flights to Bavaria. Minutes later, with some about to complete their bookings, they had to pull the plug when UEFA embarrassingly realised they had cocked up the draw. They had somehow managed to draw two group winners together so it all had to be done again.

This time it was Barcelona and a cheap flight with Easy Jet and a two-night stay left just the small matter of sorting out a match ticket. But first there was the matter of the first leg and a return visit from the side that had knocked out Docherty's diamonds in the semi-final of the Fairs Cup in 1966.

Considering that Chelsea beat Manchester United 5-0 at Stamford Bridge and won the FA Cup in 1999/2000, I have to say I don't think it will ever get any better than that night at home to Barcelona in April. Yes, we might win the Premier League this season and unless it comes down to the last minute of the last game and we score against Manchester United to pip them to the title, then nothing for me will get near to how I felt at half time, 3-0 up against Barcelona. When Zola stepped up to take the free kick leading to the first goal, it seemed as if the whole ground was wishing that ball into the net. The diminutive Italian stepped up and floated the ball over the Barca wall and beat Hesp into the top corner. 1-0 up against Barcelona would have done for most people but moments later it was 2-0 when Zola and Ferrer combined down the right and Flo was on the end of a perfect cross to send the whole ground into dreamland. By now, Stamford Bridge was rocking and if someone had said to me before the game that Chelsea would be 3-0 up at half time against Barcelona I would have been checking under which part of the Mental Health Act I would need to section them.

Out on the concourse of the Matthew Harding Upper Tier the place was alive and I had not seen such buoyant half time celebrations since a Micky Fillery goal on the stroke of half time against Tottenham in 1982 had us all believing that we were going to Wembley. In all that blue sea of joy it was funny to see that the true spirit of supporting Chelsea shining through. Amid the usual pandemonium and scrum for the toilets everyone was deliriously happy, while the Chelsea psychology was still evident amongst many fans who had been around long enough to remember when getting into Europe was a pipe-dream, never mind being 3-0 up against the Champions League favourites and supposed best team in Europe. It was a case of 'we may be 3-0 up but remember this is Chelsea, so we better score a couple more goals in the second half to make sure we get through to the semi-finals!'

There was only one dissenting voice shouting at the top of his voice 'Yes, yes, we're in the semi-finals already.' As everyone looked up from their urinals, all had a look that said 'must be one of these new Chelsea fans.'

Clearly, 3-0 down away from home, Barcelona were going to make a game of it in the second half and with Figo pulling the strings it was only a matter of time before they grabbed a valuable away goal. Figo had given away the free kick that led to Zola's opener so his second half performance demonstrated why Real Madrid recently paid £40 million for him. For twenty minutes in the second half Figo made things happen and it was he who started and finished the move that led to Barcelona's valuable away goal.

It certainly made for an interesting second leg and no matter what happened in the Nou Camp two weeks later, nothing could possibly take away that feeling at half time on April 5 2000. Moments like that do not come around very often and anyone following the Blues through the gloomy years of the eighties would say they come along even less at Chelsea. If my children or grandchildren grow up to be Chelsea fans (they better had!) I will happily tell them about that night and yes 'I was there!'

Afterwards, Vialli summed up the thoughts of most Chelsea fans, 'My team were magnificent. They were great and it was a great night for us.' Amen to that. Let's hope we get to see some more nights like that in years to come.

With Manchester United having wrapped up the title and with Chelsea's league form in kamikaze mode, qualification for the Champions League via the Premiership top three was beginning to look distinctly unlikely. Vialli knew that if his side were to be in the Champions League again they might have to win it to be in it! 'It is vitally important to win in Barcelona because we need to be in the Champions League again next season,' he said, 'it will be difficult, if not impossible, for us to qualify for the Champions League with a place in the top three of the Premiership.'

Two weeks later, having lost away to Sheffield Wednesday, Chelsea headed to Barcelona for their most important match of the season. Vialli's players knew that it would be a different game in the second leg and most knew that the Catalans would put up a far better performance in their own back yard than they had done at Stamford Bridge. Marcel Desailly certainly thought so as he told journalists at Heathrow airport, 'I was a bit surprised the way they reacted when we put them under pressure. When they arrived in London the weather was cold. Perhaps they just wanted to play the match quickly and go home to their nice stadium and hot weather.'

Gianfranco Zola had taken advantage of the school holidays to bring his children on a trip of a lifetime but he was quick to emphasise how he and his teammates' minds were focussed on the tough task ahead. 'We know how important it is to get to the semi-finals, but we still have a chance of third place in the League as well. We are not doing so badly and we can still try to make up ground in our last results, though it will be a hard finish. Barcelona have been having a bad time since we played them but they can turn things around with the players they have. We have to force them to make mistakes but we can't expect them to play as badly as they did at Stamford Bridge.' Since playing Chelsea, Barcelona had lost to 3-0 at home to Real Mallorca, 3-1 away to Atletico Madrid in the Spanish Cup and then 3-0 away to Oviedo the previous Saturday. Rumours were rife that all was not well in the Barcelona camp. The players had fallen out with Van Gaal and having lost four games in a row the pressure was not only on Chelsea but on the Catalans as well.

With Chelsea only receiving 1,700 tickets for the game, the EDT finally got a result. For the first time since Tromso the club trip completely sold out and no tickets went on general sale to season ticket holders or club members.

With the weekend leading up to April 22 a bank holiday weekend, it was difficult for Chelsea fans making their own way to Barcelona to get a cheap direct flight. Most fans had to take a detour of some kind to a non-Spanish city and then get a connecting flight to Barcelona. Brussels, Munich and Frankfurt were popular and some fans even flew as far as Rome before getting a flight back across Europe to Catalonia. However, for the fans who made it to Barcelona, the hard work had just begun. Tickets were thin on the ground and the starting price was £100. If any fans had hoped to see history being made and Chelsea reaching the semi-finals of the Champions League they would have to pay top dollar prices.

Although the history books will show in later years that Chelsea got a right spanking, they were, in fact, a mere seven minutes from knocking the Champions League favourites out of the competition. Those lucky enough to get in to the Nou Camp saw a classic which had several twists and turns to it before Chelsea were reduced to ten men by the dismissal of Celestine Babayaro. We finally conceded two extra-time goals that saw the Catalans win by the somewhat flattering score of 5-1. Barcelona produced arguably the greatest performance of the season from any club in Europe and few teams could have kept up with them on that hot night in the Nou Camp. Chelsea performed wonders in reaching the quarter-finals at the first attempt and as Vialli said afterwards 'My players are very down in the dressing room at the moment but we have to remember that we have done something very special in the Champions League this season. We are disappointed because we were so close and could have done better in some situations. But we can be proud of ourselves because we reached the quarter-finals of the Champions League and gave Barcelona a really hard game. But in extra time they had the upper hand and with so many quality players we just could not handle it.'

It was not just Chelsea fans who were disappointed by the Barcelona defeat. Eurostar felt the pinch as well as the Blues missed out on a trip to Paris on May 24. Why you may ask? Well, in February, *the Times* ran a promotional offer that allowed up to four people to travel together on Eurostar for a negligent sum and the most optimistic fans in football rushed to snap up the offer to the extent that most Eurostar trains to Paris on that day sold out quickly. The trains to Paris on the day of the Champions League final were half empty due to the number of cancellations made by Chelsea fans who had had high hopes of their team making the final. The final itself was won by Real Madrid who Chelsea had defeated only a season earlier in the European Super Cup Final in Monaco.

There were many Chelsea fans that night thinking that it could so easily have been the Blues in the final. Probably a few senior players such as Wise, Zola, Poyet and Leboeuf must also have sat at home thinking that their best and last chance of reaching the Champions League had passed them by. Sadly with Vialli now gone his ambition to win the Premier League and then the Champions League has also disappeared for the time being.

Chelsea's 2000/1 European campaign was the briefest in the club's history. In the First Round of the UEFA Cup Chelsea were drawn against Swiss national champions St Gallen. With the home leg coming first only two days after Chelsea had sacked Vialli, it was never going to be an easy game especially with the Swiss defending in large numbers. A solitary Christian Panucci goal was the difference between the two sides at Stamford Bridge but with Claudio Ranieri installed as manager the following day, the second leg two weeks later looked certain to produce a better result.

Sadly, Chelsea were sensationally dumped out of the competition by the gallant Swiss who comfortably won 2-0. It was a bad night all round for Chelsea and Ranieri (a further down side was the loss of Roberto Di Matteo for the rest of the season with a broken leg). Although not as financially lucrative as the Champions League, there was still a financial incentive for a lengthy run in the UEFA Cup. It remains to be seen how significant the early exit in the UEFA Cup will have on the rest of Chelsea's season. One thing is for certain – Chelsea must be in the Champions League next season – anything less would be a financial disaster for Chelsea Football Club.

Foreign Policy v Youth Policy

If the press and some of the more respected names in professional football are to be believed, the blame for the demise of the national game and the failure of the English national side to make an impact on the world stage can be placed squarely at the door of Chelsea Football Club. The 'policy' of clubs like Chelsea, where the purchase of foreign players is supposedly stifling the opportunity of young English players to get in a Premiership first team and eventually, the national side, has been blamed for recent English failures in major international championships.

Howard Wilkinson's viewpoint is that if he were a young player today he would not join Chelsea, as he believes that he would have few opportunities to play in the first team. An alternative view might hold that anyone old enough to remember Wilkinson play would be that Chelsea would never have signed him as, frankly, he was not good enough! Instead, it is time we took a closer and more mature look at Chelsea's youth policy and concentrate on what really is going on at the club. There is optimism for the future. Contrary to the belief that the Chelsea team is little more than a resting-place for foreigners past their sell-by who prevent talented youngsters making the first team, the club is committed to nurturing English talent at all levels.

Since the introduction of the Bosman ruling, over 30 foreign players have signed and played for Chelsea. Dan Petrescu played 208 games before he left for Bradford City in the close season. That was equal to the number of games Chelsea legend Alan Hudson played and far more than Ray Wilkins' number of appearances in a blue shirt. Frank Leboeuf, Roberto Di Matteo and Gianfranco Zola have all made more than 170 appearances for Chelsea and they should all pass the 200 game landmark this season as well, which would mean they would overtake the likes of Jimmy Greaves, Barry Bridges, Andy Townsend, Nigel Spackman, and Gordon Durie to name but a few. Of the 30 foreign players who have played for Chelsea during that time, 24 players were still with the club at the start of the 2000/01 season.

Although the signing of foreign players has worked very well for Chelsea, with nearly every signing made by Hoddle, Gullit and the recently-departed Vialli playing regularly in the first team, it has not all been plain sailing as the Brian Laudrup saga bears out. Granted, this crisis never quite reached the same scale as the headaches suffered by Harry Redknapp in his initial ventures into the foreign transfer market (where the likes of Marco Boogers and Florin Radiciou failed to live up to expectations and threatened the club with relegation) but the Laudrup saga was a soap opera in itself.

Soon after joining Chelsea, Laudrup, while out of the country, spoke to a Danish journalist and told him that he was unhappy at the Bridge. He had come to Chelsea in the belief that he was guaranteed a starting place in the team and Vialli's 'rotation policy' frustrated him. Five weeks later, the story hit the British media in the run-up to the Cup Winners' Cup tie with FC Copenhagen at Stamford Bridge. By then Laudrup had made eight appearances for the club, three of them as a substitute and had only played for the full 90 minutes on one occasion.

As a result, the press conference before the Copenhagen

game focused on whether Laudrup would leave Chelsea rather than the match itself.

As far as the manager was concerned, Vialli was unhappy with the way the story had found its way into the press but accepted the explanation Laudrup gave at the time. 'He told me it was a very old interview from when he was still unsure about his position in the squad. Now he knows I consider him to be a decisive player and it is my intention to play him as much as possible because he can do a great job for Chelsea.'

A week passed and most Chelsea fans thought that was the end of the saga. However, as supporters made their way to Stamford Bridge for a Coca-Cola Cup-tie against Aston Villa, they were greeted with an *Evening Standard* story that suggested that Laudrup was leaving to join Chelsea's Cup Winners' Cup opponents FC Copenhagen. The following afternoon Chelsea held a hurried press conference with managing director Colin Hutchinson and Laudrup present. The story that had emerged from Denmark, that Laudrup had signed a ten-year deal with the Danes, was reinforced by news that Laudrup's father was set to join Copenhagen as merchandising manager. The press conference, although well marshalled by Hutchinson, confirmed that although Laudrup had not yet left Chelsea, it was only going to be a matter of time before he did.

Hutchinson advised that no deal had taken place between Copenhagen and Chelsea, although the Danes had asked to take Laudrup on loan until the end of the season, a deal turned down by Hutchinson. He went on to elaborate that although no deal had been done, Chelsea could not rule out a deal taking place in the future. The press got the story they wanted. It did not matter when Laudrup would go, just that he would go eventually.

When Hutchinson gave way and allowed Laudrup to speak to the press, his body language indicated that he wanted to leave. When he opened his mouth he confirmed everyone's suspicions. 'You get to a certain stage in your career when you feel you would like to return to your home country and go back to your roots. I feel like this now and that is why I have to do what is in my heart rather than my head. The money is not important to me if I am not happy.'

Hutchinson had tried as hard he could to persuade Laudrup to stay, even suggesting he should spend more time in Denmark, train over there and commute to England to train occasionally with the first team and then play in matches. But with the Dane's mind made up, Hutchinson struck a deal with FC Copenhagen to ensure that if Laudrup were to play for another club other than Chelsea or Copenhagen, then Chelsea would be 'suitably compensated.'

Laudrup's swan song for Chelsea was due to be the Premier League game at home to Aston Villa the following Saturday. However, with the match postponed, Vialli was left with a difficult decision – should he play Laudrup against his new club in the return leg in Copenhagen? And if he played him would he run the risk of putting his new club out of the competition and upset their supporters? Or would he have a 'mare' and add to the anger already felt among Chelsea supporters?

In the end, Vialli opted to take Laudrup at his word when he promised that he would continue to give 100% until he left the club. But I don't think Vialli could quite have imagined the events of the 32nd minute of the match. With some sections of the travelling Chelsea support jeering Laudrup's every touch and the old Tommy Langley chant resurrected into 'We're going to shoot Brian Laudrup', Vialli could easily have seen his gamble backfire. However up popped Laudrup at the far post to head a Le Saux cross into the net. On 67 minutes, the number 7 went up on the substitute board and Brian Laudrup left the pitch for the last time as a Chelsea player. His job done, Chelsea won the tie 1-0 and went through 2-1 on aggregate.

It had been a difficult couple of weeks for Laudrup, Chelsea and Vialli but the manager was quick to compliment Laudrup for his role in Chelsea's victory. 'I always had faith in Brian and I knew before the game that he was having a difficult time because of everything going on. But in training and in previous matches he has always been outstanding so I didn't have any problems picking him this evening. He responded very well. Sometimes you think that football is such a funny thing because Brian has played ten matches without scoring and then he comes to Denmark in front of his own supporters and scores. That is the prize for what he is doing at the moment - working really hard and being professional.' Within a couple of days, Colin Hutchinson had finalised the deal with his opposite number Flemming Ostergaard and as canny as ever the Chelsea managing director managed to purchase Copenhagen's best player over the two legs - Bjarne Goldbaek - for a modest £300,000.

However, despite his return to Copenhagen, the Laudrup saga had not yet run its course. On his return to Denmark most FC Copenhagen fans began to think that Chelsea had got the better of the deal, getting rid of Laudrup and replacing him with their crowd favourite Bjarne Goldbaek. Laudrup did not excel in Denmark and stunned Danish football when he announced that he had an opt-out clause in his contract that gave him the option of leaving Copenhagen after only six months.

Immediately, when faced with criticism from the Danish press, Laudrup denied the existence of such a clause in his contract. Clearly however, Laudrup had forgotten to prompt his agent who, when questioned by the press, confirmed that the clause did exist. This created a huge dilemma. If Laudrup was unhappy in Copenhagen it meant he had to return to Chelsea. Whether Colin Hutchinson smelt a rat with Laudrup when he claimed to be home sick or not, he had thought of every eventuality. The agreement that allowed the homesick Dane to leave Chelsea was watertight.

'We hammered out a complex agreement to try to meet every eventuality. I am not suggesting there was ever any intention, but if he left Chelsea for a short stay in Denmark to join a big European club, the protection was such that they had to guarantee a fee of over £5 million if he left Copenhagen,' Hutchinson confirmed afterwards. As a result, when Laudrup left Copenhagen for Ajax, Chelsea pocketed around £2.5 million on the two deals. 'An excellent bit of business,' as Ken Bates said at the time, 'we acted honourably. It was a nice piece of business because Brian is no longer on the wage bill, we don't have a malcontent in the dressing room and we're one of the few clubs that does not have trouble in the dressing room. In addition we recouped our financial outlay.'

Of the few foreign players who have left Chelsea, several were on-loan signings, George Weah and Laurent Charvet being prime examples. The only other players who have left for a transfer fee in addition to Petrescu were Bjarne Goldbaek and Didier Deschamps. The sale of Goldbaek disappointed many Chelsea fans who had taken to the Danish midfielder in the short time he had been with the club. His standing among the fans had been done no harm by the 35-yarder he scored at Three Point Lane at the end of the 1998/99 season. Deschamps, on the other hand, was said to have had some very good games for Chelsea but he was truly effective in less than half the 47 appearances he made. Many fans were disappointed to see Petrescu and Goldbaek leave, but there were few tears shed when the World Cup winning water carrier moved to Valencia in the close season.

Meanwhile the foreign players who have stayed the distance have been part of the most successful Chelsea era of all time. Two FA Cups, a European Cup Winners' Cup, a Coca Cola Cup, European Super Cup and Charity Shield have all been added to the Stamford Bridge trophy cabinet in that time.

However the critics have suggested that this success has come at a steep price. The predominant view seems to be that Chelsea have spent a lot of money to lure the players concerned with the result that the club has one of the highest wage bills in the country. This has, according to many in the game, been to the detriment of youth development and has led many young players to leave the club for regular first team football elsewhere.

Yet this criticism is unfair. The successful Liverpool teams of the seventies and early eighties had few players who had graduated through the ranks. Dalglish, Hansen, Souness, McDermott, Rush and Whelan came courtesy of the chequebook rather than the youth team. Even Manchester United, who have clearly been extremely successful over the last ten years in producing young players, have not been slow to buy big on the continent. Although they have been held up as an example of how to develop quality English players for the long-term, a closer look at their current first team reveals otherwise. Most people would have the following in Alex Ferguson's first choice team: Barthez, Stam, Johnsen, Irwin, Silvestre, Keane, Yorke, and Cole. Cole may be English but cost United £6 million – of Ferguson's first choice only Beckham, Giggs, Gary Neville and Scholes have graduated from their youth team. Since that initial rush of players that also included Nicky Butt and Phil Neville, how many United youngsters have broken into the first team? It was only yesterday that a so-called future Manchester United star such as John Curtis was going to play for England. Where is he now? He has joined Barnsley. Danny Higginbotham has gone to Derby and Ben Thornley has gone to Huddersfield, leaving Wes Brown as the only United youngster to have broken through in the past two seasons.

As Vialli himself said last season, it seems that nobody gets criticised as much as Chelsea for not signing English players. 'look at the flak we keep getting about not signing English players. But just look at what other clubs have done. Everybody is going in the same direction. We made enquires for a few English players but nothing came off for us.'

If you look at Chelsea's rivals in the top half of the Premier League, most of them did not get their chequebooks out until they passed the white cliffs of Dover. Arsenal purchased Pires, Lauren and Wiltord. Leeds United signed Viduka and Dacourt and although Liverpool broke the mould by signing England international Nick Barmby they also signed Ziege, Traore, Babbel and Gary McAllister. Even Tottenham chairman Alan 'Carlos Kickaball' Sugar broke the club's transfer record by spending £11 million on Sergei Rebrov.

For all the criticism Chelsea receive, people forget that Chelsea were one of the first clubs in the football league to launch a youth team. In 1947/48 then manager Billy Birrell realised the savings in transfer fees and wages that could be made by discovering and developing your own players. The most successful Chelsea youth era on the pitch was between 1956 and 1963 when the Blues reached the FA Youth Cup final three times and won the South East Counties League seven years in a row. In 1958 Chelsea reached the final of the FA Youth Cup, which had been set up in 1952 and when they won the first leg against Wolves 5-1 it looked as if the youngsters had done the double. Unfortunately, in a style reminiscent of the senior Chelsea side, they rescued defeat from the jaws of victory, losing the second leg at Molineux 6-1 and 6-7 on aggregate.

Fortunately in 1960 and 1961 they made amends by winning back-to-back trophies - beating Preston North End 5-2 on aggregate in 1960 and Everton 5-3 on aggregate the following year. However, since the heady days of the early sixties Chelsea have only won the South East Counties League twice and their performances in the FA Youth Cup have produced very few cup runs over the past few generations. The Chelsea Youth team in that era also produced a number of players who not only excelled at home but also represented their country at international level. During the 1960s, Barry Bridges, John Hollins, Ken Shellito, Bobby Tambling and Terry Venables came through the ranks and later played for England. In the 1970s, Peter Osgood carried the tradition forward but sadly Ray Wilkins' 24th cap against Austria in 1979 was the last time a former Chelsea youth player represented his country.

So before anyone gets too excited about the lorry load of foreign players arriving at Stamford Bridge to stifle the ambitions of young players, it is useful to remember that Chelsea have not won the FA Youth Cup since 1961 and we have not produced a full England international through the ranks since Ray Wilkins made his England debut in 1976. So while it is fair to say that the Chelsea youth scheme has produced countless first team players in that time, few of them have made a significant mark on the national game. And although the youth team has produced some good servants for the club and even provided inspirational moments from a few players (usually on their debuts), they have failed to emulate Manchester United's youngsters. Indeed the furthest any Chelsea player has got in that time is appearing for the England Under-21 side, selection for which seems to have become a graveyard for Chelsea youngsters down the years. No sooner do they play for Young England and are touted as the next best thing than they embark on a downward spiral to lower division football and obscurity.

Michael Duberry is a classic case in point. Having left Chelsea for Leeds United his career has apparently gone into reverse. Leeds paid £5 million for Duberry and yet his replacement, Marcel Desailly, cost Chelsea just £4.6 million. Duberry left Chelsea to play more regular first team football but in the 1999/2000 season he played fewer first team games for Leeds than he had done for Chelsea the previous season. Had he remained at Chelsea, Duberry would have been in Vialli's squad and played regularly last season. Bernard Lambourde made 21 appearances last season while Jes Hogh appeared 17 times. Duberry would have been ahead of both players in the pecking order when deputies were required for Chelsea's first choice central defenders Leboeuf and Desailly. Unless Duberry can oust the Leeds first choice of Radebe and Woodgate, expect a transfer before the end of the season and if he is not careful, Nationwide football may be beckoning sooner than he thinks and that would be a shame.

When Duberry first broke into the team in 1995 he made a sensational start when put up against the likes of Tony Yeboah and Ian Wright in his first couple of games. However, he was prone to injury, lapses of concentration and the odd faux pas - none more so then the infamous game at home to Leicester City in 1999. Chelsea were pushing Manchester United and Arsenal for the Premier League title when Leicester came to Stamford Bridge on April 18. With seven minutes to go, Chelsea were coasting to a 2-0 win which would put them a point behind United with five games to go. What happened next, not only destroyed Chelsea's championship challenge but signalled the end of Michael Duberry's Chelsea career. Duberry replaced Ferrer in the 74th minute for what appeared to be little more than a brief run out.

Within minutes of his arrival, confusion reigned in the Chelsea area when a Neil Lennon cross saw the ball ping around the area until Duberry clumsily put it into his own net.

A minute from time, with the Chelsea defence still at sixes and sevens, Leicester wide man Steve Guppy cut inside Dan Petrescu. Usually there would have been a covering Chelsea defender but Duberry was nowhere to be seen and the room between Petrescu and him was wide enough for Guppy to look up and curl the ball past Ed de Goey into the bottom corner. Chelsea's title ambitions evaporated in those mad seven minutes and Duberry (widely blamed for both goals) saw his career go the same way.

All might have been forgiven among supporters had it not been for Duberry's reaction after the match. Vialli, like the 35,000 people in the ground, was extremely upset to see Chelsea's Premiership prospects go down the pan in the last ten minutes. He could not believe how uncaring Duberry was in the dressing room afterwards and from that game it seemed only a matter of time before the young defender left the club. He missed most of the rest of the season and was only recalled on the final day of the season for the home game with Derby, his last appearance in Chelsea colours. To make matters worse, once he left the club Duberry took the opportunity to slag off both Vialli and Hoddle in the tabloids, which hardly endured him to supporters and seemed to confirm that the club was better off without him.

Another former Chelsea youth, Graham Stuart, is back in the Premier League following Charlton's promotion last season but here was another player who never quite made the grade. He scored some important goals, especially one against Sheffield United in the FA Cup in 1992, but he was a typically underachieving and inconsistent Chelsea player. Stuart joins a long list of graduates from the youth team who were shipped out after a couple of seasons in the first team and ended up in the Nationwide League. Eddie Newton is another classic example. He was fortunate at one stage to train with the national side and was being tipped as a future international, he'd established himself in the first team and scored the winner in the 1997 FA Cup final. Since then Eddie has been blighted by injury but that aside it remains a mystery why his career has plummeted so quickly and so soon since leaving Chelsea only a season ago. He went to Birmingham City, failed to gain a regular place in their first team and Trevor Francis sold him on to Oxford United. Amazingly, Newton's contract was cancelled by the Bulls at the end of last season and he is now playing at Third Division Barnet.

Newton, like Duberry, blamed the club's 'foreign policy' for his departure, 'I knew it was time to leave - even after eleven years at the club. I have had great times here, especially when I scored the second goal in the FA Cup final. But Chelsea are a team in a hurry. There will be a few more home-grown products like me, but not many. The club are after big trophies and they are prepared to pay big money for foreign players to get them.'

A look back at the Chelsea youth graduates of the past decade begs the question where are they now? Darren Barnard and Neil Shipperley are at Barnsley, Jason Cundy (Portsmouth), Steve Hampshire (Dunfermline), Nick Colgan (Hibernian), Gareth Hall (contract cancelled at the end of last season), Joe Sheerin (Bournemouth), Damien Matthew (Northampton, last time I heard) and if anyone wants to explain how David Lee failed to get a regular place in a Crystal Palace side desperately short of players, then send me a letter via the publisher. This is a sad indictment of how too many players have flattered to deceive.

Andy Myers was also quick to jump on the bandwagon, criticising Vialli's foreign policy despite never really fulfilling his early potential soon after he had been sold to Bradford City. Despite making his first time debut in 1991 Myers failed to establish himself as a first team regular in eight years in the first team squad and was unsympathetically dubbed 'sicknote' by a section of the Chelsea crowd. He seemed to spend half his time at Chelsea on the treatment table, although he was some distance behind Darren Anderton's leave of absence at Spurs.

Myers was particularly critical of Vialli in a conversation with *Daily Mirror* journalist Ian Edwards, 'Luca has got to do what he feels is right for the club and if he feels it is right to bring in international players that is his choice. There were loads of us who came through the youth system and the club has a good youth policy, but Vialli let us go. A few years ago there were English players breaking through and it was a great base to take Chelsea through the next five years. But that all stopped under Vialli and no player wants to be around two or three years. I was sad to leave Chelsea. I grew up there and it was part of my life. I loved the club but I had to be realistic. When I saw who they were bringing in I knew that it was not going to happen for me.'

So why are English players such as Eddie Newton, Michael Duberry and Andy Myers being left behind at clubs like Chelsea? Chelsea chairman Ken Bates, who has overseen the opening of the club's chequebook on more than one occasion, has his own views on the failures of English footballers

'It is the beer belly culture which has led to English football lagging behind the rest of the world for so long. Look at the foreign players like the guys we have here at Chelsea. Not only would they never consider acting like that, it is beyond their comprehension that any professional could. It's no contest. And it's a viewpoint they totally buy into and carry onto the training ground. We can see this professionalism catching on amongst our young up and coming players too. Who are going to be the brightest hopes for England's future? Young lads brought up alongside the Gascoignes of the game? Or those who train with people like Zola and Bergkamp?'

Players' Union chief executive Gordon Taylor has pointed the finger at Ken Bates as the villain in the piece on more than one occasion, citing Chelsea's 'buying foreign' policy as harmful to the English game and to the future development of young players in this country.

'Ken Bates has done a great job for Chelsea and made them the club they are today. But what about when he puts on his other hat as a leading member of the FA Council? It is his club that has played a leading role in creating a situation that could cause problems for the England team in the future. How many

English youngsters get a chance in the Chelsea first team to learn and gain experience?'

Taylor has gone on record as saying that if he had a son, he would not allow him to join Chelsea. Clearly Bates has no intention of sending Taylor a card next Christmas and, never one to duck any form of criticism he has hit back at the Players Union chief.

'People always say that parents should not send their children to Chelsea as they will not get into the first team. Gordon Taylor has said that if he had a son he would not let him come to Chelsea. Well, if he had a son we wouldn't have signed him anyway because within three weeks Gordon Taylor would be organising a players' union picking the team and changing the tactics. So it is a load of rubbish what he has said.'

Paradoxically, Chelsea are now forced to turn away kids because of the numbers who want to play for the club. They would rather play for Chelsea as Bates says 'than some other club who are stuck in the beer-belly and fish-and-chips syndrome. And if the lads don't make it to the first team at Chelsea, they can go on to a better career elsewhere than if they had been at a more mundane club.'

As an example of their dedication, at a Chelsea club function early in the season every one of the players was present and everyone one of them left at 9.45pm to go home to bed. In years gone by the 'Player of the Year' dinners and Christmas get-togethers had been a good opportunity for the players and fans to mix and have more than a few drinks together. It was not uncommon for the boozing to go on until after midnight and for the odd one or two in the first team to overdo it. The early departure of the players angered one supporter who sought Bates out and asked him why they had gone so early. Bates' answer summed up how dramatically things have changed amongst playing personnel and exemplified the new professionalism running through the club. He turned to the fan and dismissed his question with one of his own, 'Do you want them boozing all night or in perfect nick to win three points for you on Saturday?' he asked him.

Bates also went on record in the summer on the day Chelsea sold £10 million misfit Chris Sutton to Celtic. 'Why haven't we bought any English players?' asks Bates rhetorically. 'Because they are not good enough.' Although Bates may have ruffled a few feathers with his usual abrupt style, in particular with relation to his old adversary Gordon Taylor, the club's experiences with their one English signing last season has convinced him that Chelsea are doing the right thing. Chelsea not only broke their transfer record when they signed Chris Sutton they as good as doubled it for a player many hoped would be the man to score the goals and lead Chelsea to Championship glory. But from his first day disaster against Sunderland things never got much better for Sutton and, although supporters remained tolerant, his record at the end of the season of just three goals in thirty nine appearances in the first team (twelve of them from the substitute's bench) spoke volumes. Following his departure to Celtic, he beat that record in his first four games for the Scottish club.

Sutton is typical of the English footballer Ken Bates mentioned earlier. Chelsea are probably one of the best in the business in doing their homework on a player, on not just their professional life but also their private life. Looking into Sutton's previous off-field track record before he came to the club would have suggested he was precisely the wrong type of player to bring to the club as a potential role model for younger players. Perhaps whoever did the research on Sutton decided that as a married man, he would be a good example to some of the younger players at Chelsea and that if he had a skeleton or two in his closet, that had been some time ago. Sutton though, did not just have the odd skeleton in his cupboard, he had half a bloody cemetery.

Although Sutton was a married man when he joined Chelsea, his wife, Page 3 model Sam Williamson, had to issue a few ultimatums to him before they walked down the aisle. Sutton, while still at Norwich City, was well known in the city for holding 'trawler' parties. This involved Sutton and his teammates 'trawling' the pubs of the town with invites back to his house for 'nocturnal activities'. Samantha put a stop to Sutton's wanderlust but that it did not stop him behaving like a prat when he had too much to drink.

His goal-scoring success at Norwich City made Sutton a transfer target and when Kenny Dalglish raided the late Jack Walker's piggy bank he broke the Blackburn transfer record to pay £5 million for Sutton. However, the night before his move Sutton went out on the town in Norwich to celebrate and ended the night in the police cells. Sutton and his friends had apparently vandalised a local restaurateur's car who, rather than asking for Sutton's autograph, quickly rang the local constabulary. When the police arrived Sutton, by now hiding in the restaurant toilet, tried to do a runner by jumping into a taxi. Unluckily for him the police gave chase and he was caught and arrested. Although Sutton got off with a caution, the hard man act disappeared when he was locked in the cells - his tears would have given Paul Gascoigne's 1990 World Cup effort a run for its money. Indeed on the very day Sutton joined Celtic he was fined £750 for common assault having been found guilty of spitting in the face of some Manchester United fans months earlier on a night out in the West End with family and friends including the easily-distracted Jody Morris.

Another figure who could never be described as a Chris Sutton fan is former Chelsea boss Glenn Hoddle who, as England manager, resisted the huge media campaign to make Sutton a permanent fixture in the England side. When Hoddle selected Sutton for the 'B' squad the striker refused to join the team and ensured that he probably never appeared for his country again. Sutton, like so many English footballers, exemplifies a football culture at odds with the dedication of Zola, Desailly and the rest.

When Hoddle first took over at Chelsea he appointed Graham Rix. Both believed from the start that winning the South East Counties League was not the best way of producing players for the first team. They believed that individual progress was far more important than team progress. So they set about a huge restructuring programme at youth level, with the same playing set-up instilled throughout the club from first team to youth team – at this stage the idea of a completely non-English Chelsea first eleven seemed an anathema.

In Rix's first season in charge Chelsea finished an encouraging fourth in the table but the most staggering statistic was that during that first year Mark Nicholls, who finished top scorer with 22 goals, is the only player still at the club. Whatever happened to Junior Mendes, Ben Papa, Clinton Ellis, Lee Carroll, Chris McCann and Russell Kelly?

The goalposts have even moved since Glenn Hoddle's day. Back then Chelsea were picking players to play at Premier League level. Now, with one successful season and ambitions to return to the Champions League, Chelsea have to produce youngsters capable of performing in the Champions League against Barcelona, Real Madrid and AC Milan.

It will be interesting to see what develops at Chelsea now Vialli has left the club. Will Claudio Ranieri turn to some of the younger players in the squad that have been produced through the Chelsea youth team? Will Chelsea put a greater emphasis on the academy and will we see more young players breaking through at Chelsea?

The man in charge at the Chelsea academy, responsible for coaching the young Chelsea players of tomorrow is Jim Duffy who came to the club at the recommendation of Graham Rix having worked together with him in Scotland at Dundee.

'The expectations at this club are so high now.' says Duffy. 'Before, a young player would get a dozen or so games in the first team, the fans would say "Great here's a good young kid" then he'd be put back in the reserves and brought on a bit. But now you can't have a dozen games, you might get two and if you are not top quality in those, they'll want somebody else in and go and buy another £4 million star. That's the level of expectation.'

The thing about the foreign players at Chelsea is that too much emphasis is placed on the passport they carry. Chelsea does not have a policy of signing foreign players. They now have a policy of only signing quality players. Sadly for English football most of them are foreign but that probably says more about the state of English football rather than anything that can be particularly attributed to Chelsea Football Club

The whole set-up has changed at Chelsea now. In the old days, when Chelsea returned to London after an away game, it would not be uncommon for there to be a couple of crates of beer on the coach or a stop at a pub on the way back. There would also be the occasional stop at a chippy where one of the Chelsea entourage would rush in and order twenty fish suppers and make the chip shop owner's evening. That was just the way British footballers did things, a concept alien to foreign players. Training at Chelsea used to start at 10.30 and be over by 12.30 with the likes of Andy Townsend, Kerry Dixon and Gordon Durie heading off to the nearest bookmakers, golf club or pub to while away the rest of the day. Now it is not uncommon for the first team squad to follow a morning's training with lunch at Harlington and adjourn to a nearby hotel for some rest before another afternoon training session.

So how has the Chelsea policy of buying predominantly foreign players benefited the club in terms of future youth development? The foreign players bring with them their own way of doing business, particularly in attitude to diet, training, alcohol and their responsibilities as a professional footballer. The benefit to Chelsea Football Club is that this attitude and professionalism rubs off on all Chelsea's younger players as they can see the standards and professionalism needed to succeed as a footballer.

Chelsea hope that their young players will learn from foreign players. It has been universally accepted that European players are better disciplined than British players. They train more, eat better and take better care of their body. Bringing in this quality of player can only improve the quality of our home grown players. This should not only benefit Chelsea but, in the long term, it should also benefit the England side.

As Graham Rix said many times as youth coach, it is no so much a case of foreign players keeping young English players out of the side but more a case of 'if you are good enough you will play for Chelsea' and Jody Morris, John Harley and John Terry have proved that in recent seasons. Far from being a hideous threat to the future of Chelsea, the success of Chelsea's foreign imports should be seen as a massive bonus. It is no coincidence that Chelsea's youth side are playing outstanding football and Chelsea's schoolboys are also playing well with kids encouraged to go forward - using the likes of Zola, Vialli, Poyet, Desailly and Flo as positive role models. The young players at all levels of the club see that they are part of a fantastic, multi-cultural collection of players and want to remain part of it for years to come.

Basically, what the media have failed to appreciate is that youth development is not a quick-fix scenario. Chelsea will not see the benefits of it for some years, but there is no doubt that if the club have eleven English kids good enough and available for selection, then Chelsea will play an all-English team. As an illustration, the last time Chelsea played an all-English team was at the start of the 1982/83 season, a staggering eighteen seasons ago. It also coincided with the season Chelsea were nearly relegated to the Third Division. So much for playing only English players!

There have actually been only two occasions in Chelsea's history when the side was made up mainly of graduates from the Chelsea youth team. Chelsea, despite some of their financial problems over the years, have never been slow to dabble in the transfer market. However, the Tommy Docherty side of the mid-sixties was possibly the greatest group of young players that Chelsea ever produced, although the Eddie McCreadie graduates who formed the nucleus of the 1976/77 Second Division promotion team would give them a run for their money. One man who played with both sets of players was Chelsea stalwart Peter Bonetti. (Ironically Bonetti was the only signing a cash-strapped McCreadie could afford following a free transfer in 1976 having spent nineteen years at the Bridge.) He served under both Docherty and McCreadie and was probably in the best position to make comparisons between the two young sides back in 1976:

'It's impossible to compare the two sides. I do know that Eddie, like Tommy, has a team capable of doing great things. I'm a great admirer of the Doc. But he was impetuous in those days.

He pushed players out and that left others wondering where they stood. What has changed is the mental attitude of the players this season against the lads who were in Tommy's team. Eddie has got these lads thinking about nothing else but Chelsea. Like Tommy he is a great motivator, but he also makes sure the players keep their feet on the ground.'

Any move towards a younger and predominantly non-continental side is still a number of years off though and the change will be transitional with one or two players breaking through each season rather than a wholesale avalanche of youngsters, as happened during Eddie McCreadie's reign.

However, from a look at the numbers at Chelsea, it has been some time since eighteen young professionals were graduates from the Chelsea youth team. What people fail to realise is that since Chelsea turned to foreigners, the schoolboy recruitment drive also turned around and they now have to turn people away. Previously, despite having one of the best youth setups in the country, along with Arsenal and West Ham United, Chelsea really struggled to get good players. Six or seven years ago a promising youngster would not think of Chelsea but Arsenal, Manchester United, Leeds or West Ham. Joe Cole is a classic case in point. If the rumours are true the young West Ham starlet supported Chelsea like his father but opted to join West Ham United many years back as a schoolboy.

To entice the better prospects, Chelsea launched their Academy three years ago and invested a substantial sum in development for the future. Despite their interest, Ken Bates and Colin Hutchinson have got the small matter of running a successful football club and ideally the Academy should be separately funded but it has, to date, proved very difficult to get sponsorship. The youth team used to have sponsors before the academy was created but corporate sponsors have yet to emerge which has left the club to foot a growing bill alone.

Clearly companies such as McDonald's or Coca-Cola are reluctant to sponsor just one club when there are nineteen other Premier League teams developing their own youth teams and academies. But it is surprising, with all the criticism surrounding the national side and the concerns for the future of the game, that the powers that be have not been able to secure a deal with a large company to raise the profile of youth football. Another area where the development of Chelsea's youth scheme could rise to prominence is through various media. BSkyB showed England youth and FA Youth Cup games last season and when Chelsea entered the Premier Youth League there was talk of some games being shown on television. To date, this has not materialised although Chelsea do have the benefit of Channel Chelsea, the club's own in-house TV channel, which is one area where Chelsea could push their youth team more by showing their games on TV before first team home games.

Any kids who were taken on as twelve year-olds when the academy started are now only fifteen or sixteen, so we may have to wait a little while longer to see the full benefits of the Chelsea Academy. However the twelve-year-olds taken on after Glenn Hoddle dramatically changed the youth set-up at Chelsea are now eighteen and nineteen and the early signs are good.

In the 1999/2000 season, John Harley, John Terry, Rob Wolleaston, Sam Dalla Bonna and Luca Percassi (all of whom were youth team players just two years ago), have played in the first team with Harley (26 first team appearances) and Terry (nine) making most appearances. Aside from these youngsters and Jody Morris there remains a gap between the younger players and the older players, many of who will never see thirty again. Both Dalla Bonna and Luca Percassi, who has now left the club, have had to adjust to a different language, a different culture and a different style of football. Percassi settled in quicker both on and off the pitch and swiftly mastered the English language. Dalla Bonna admitted that he found it difficult to adapt to the English game at first, but his continued good form in the reserves and his two substitute appearances last season will have helped him enormously. The appointment of an experienced Italian manager should also help him.

'At first it was difficult. I did not understand English football. In Italy, football is about tactics and technique, over here it is more about strength and the game is much quicker as well. You have to learn to get rid of the ball quickly because you do not get as much time as you do in Italy. In the beginning that was a huge problem for me but I find it much easier now.'

Dalla Bonna has suffered probably more than Terry with the lengthy queue of midfielders ahead of him in the pecking order. He is now in his third year of a five-year contract and will need to push himself up the pecking order and be knocking on the door of the first team during the season. The early signs this season are encouraging and since Ranieri's arrival he has featured in the first team. But competing with Dennis Wise, Jody Morris, Roberto Di Matteo and Gus Poyet will not be easy despite two promising seasons at the club. After his first season, when he scored eighteen goals from an attacking midfield role, he was played in a defensive holding role last season in an effort to improve that area of his game and to make him more able to adapt to the demands of the English game.

Rob Wolleaston was a player I saw on many occasions in the same youth side as Harley and Terry, and although both have made the breakthrough into the first team, Wolleaston has had to content himself with two substitute appearances, against Huddersfield and Sunderland. A player of immense talent, Wolleaston reminded me of the generations of young players before him who, despite the ability, remained dreadfully inconsistent. He is probably one of the most skilful members of the first team squad, which is a huge compliment to him in view of the esteemed company he is keeping, but he needs to perform more consistently at a higher level for his chance in the first team to come. Last season though, with the aid of the coaching staff and with the benefit of taking Dalla Bonna's attacking midfield role, he was probably the most improved young player at the club.

Other youngsters who may make the breakthrough soon are Warren Cummings, Sam Parkin, Courtney Pitt, Danny Slatter, Leon Knight and ex-National School graduates Joe Keenan, Paul Thornton and young goalkeeper Rhys Evans. For Keenan, Thornton and Knight to receive contracts was exceptional, as all three players were only first-year trainees and to get a professional contract before their second year as trainees shows how highly they are regarded at the club.

Indeed, if Albert Ferrer's injury problems persist and Mario Melchiot is also injured, Cardiff-born Slatter could get his chance this year. Welsh manager Mark Hughes, remembering the youngster from his time at the club, has already called him into the Welsh squad without him appearing in the Chelsea first team. Danny Slatter is not the type of player who would immediately catch the eye but he's a hard working full back in the Albert Ferrer mould who will chase everything and not stop running for ninety minutes. He has a good future ahead of him.

Leon Knight is another potential first-teamer. His progress from the youth team continued last season when he played for the reserves fourteen times, five them as a substitute. Knight exemplifies why young players prefer Chelsea over other clubs - in his last two games last season his striking partners were Zola and Vialli. Playing alongside this quality of player can only benefit Knight and the back-room staff have high hopes for the young striker during the coming season - for one so young he has already had his share of media coverage.

The *Sunday Express* dubbed Knight the 'English Zola'. He is only slightly built (like the gifted Italian) but he has the pace and ability to score spectacular goals and if he is half as good as his Italian mentor he should have a long future in the game. Moreover, media pressure is nothing new to Knight, Chelsea fans with longer memories may recall a 1997 *News of the World* article describing the then fourteen year old as the new Pele! At the end of last season the Chelsea youth team flew to Hong Kong to take part in a seven-a-side competition. Against very strong local opposition they played superbly and made the final only to lose to a 'golden goal' in extra time. The player of the tournament award went to Leon Knight.

Jim Duffy is a quiet admirer of Knight's talent but is adept at keeping the young man's feet on the ground and is always there to remind him that it is a team game.

'Although he is quite small he is strong on the ball,' says Duffy. 'But what he wants is midfield players to give him the right passes, the possession and the chances. If they do that then he will score.' It is Duffy who has the hard task of sorting out the wheat from the chaff and he does his best to get to know his young protégés and understand what makes them tick. It is not enough just to be a good footballer to make the grade at Chelsea; the players have to be professional on and off the pitch. Duffy makes sure his players observe the behaviour of the first team professionals and learn from them, 'You say to the boys 'Look at these players, look at their diets, look at their weight programmes'. It's not about having six pints at the weekend with a curry to finish'. These lads are like any sixteen year-olds. They want to go to nightclubs, they read the papers, see the glamour side of the game and how much you can earn. But there is a multitude of things that can go wrong for a young player. Be it problems with girlfriends or their home life. They can get homesick because they live in digs. Any one of these things can contribute to them struggling. You have got to get to know them, try to get under their skin a little bit, so they learn to trust you so they can speak to you about any problems they might have.'

Another of Duffy's charges is young goalkeeper Rhys Evans. Since he joined the club, former Chelsea keeper Eddie Niedzwicki has been inspirational in his development of Evans to the extent that many felt Chelsea were right not to enter a bidding war for the young Ipswich Town goalkeeper Richard Wright, although he is tipped as a future England keeper.

As a sixteen-year-old, Evans played for England against Germany in front of 69,000 in Berlin in the same stadium where Chelsea froze in the Champions League last season. He also played in the traditional pre-season friendly against Kingstonian before the 1998/99 season. 'Playing at Kingstonian was a great experience,' says Evans, 'I was told beforehand that I might get a chance. But as I ran out, people were asking who I was. It was great just to see people were interested.' Evans played for England Under-15s and, like John Harley and Leon Knight, trained at the FA

School of Excellence at Lilleshall. For a young man, Evans is already a six-footer but trains hard and is ambitious, with aspirations to one day replace one of the goalkeepers he trains with on a regular basis:

'I watch what they do although I have never tried to model myself on anyone. I will try to pick up on things but my ambition is that one day I will take their place. But working with these keepers is great experience for me. It gives me a standard by which I can judge myself.'

Last season he went on loan to promotion-chasing Bristol Rovers and played four games for them, keeping two clean sheets in the process. Bristol Rovers manager Ian Holloway had seen Evans playing in Chelsea's reserves and when their first choice keeper got injured, he took a gamble, and put the inexperienced eighteen year-old straight into the first team. The England Under-18 goalkeeper did not let Holloway down and returned to Chelsea better for the experience. 'I'm highly delighted with his progress,' says Eddie Niedzwicki in the club programme, 'we have high hopes for him, as long as he continues in the same vein. He has had a very good season.' In Evans, some of the back-room staff at Chelsea believe they have a future Chelsea goalkeeper in the making and a huge transfer fee saved into the bargain.

Other players looking for professional contracts and names to look out for in years to come could include Pat Baldwin, Scott Cousins and Andrew Ross who were all first-year trainees last season. In addition, among the new breed of trainees for the coming year include James Pidgeley, who is currently the England Under16 goalkeeper, and Joel Kitamirike, who plays for England Under 17s.

The most encouraging thing looking at the list of professional players assembled at Stamford Bridge for the 2000/01 season is that there are eighteen players (and that does not include Jody Morris) who have played for the Chelsea youth team in recent years. Clearly not all of them will end up having a career at the club but many are likely to establish themselves in the first team in the next few seasons.

BLUE TOMORROW?

While a lot of positive things have taken place at youth level in recent years, that is not to say that there have not been unfortunate casualties along the way. A couple of years ago, Neil Clement and Jody Morris appeared to be joined at the hip, both signing professional forms at the same time having come up through the youth team and reserves. But while Morris is now an established member of the first team, with over 100 first team appearances to his name, and has had the honour of captaining Chelsea, Clement only managed one appearance last season as a substitute for the last 17 minutes of the 5-0 thrashing of Gillingham. Injury has restricted him to just four first team appearances, three of which were made from the substitutes bench. After making his debut under Ruud Gullit's reign, Clement saw John Terry overtake him in the pecking order and in the summer he joined First Division West Bromwich Albion for £100,000.

Another close season exit was 21 year old Nick Crittenden, who failed to break into the first team after making his debut three years ago in a Coca-Cola Cup tie against Southampton when Gullit was manager. With no squad number being allocated to Crittenden at the start of last season, the writing was already on the wall for the young wingback. Despite being the second highest appearance maker in the reserves, Crittenden is now a free agent looking to make a living outside the game.

Perhaps the main danger to Chelsea's young stars could be the huge salaries and temptations that come their way. The *News of the World* had a field day in the summer at the expense of Kieron Dyer, Rio Ferdinand and Frank Lampard following their exploits with a few young ladies and a video camera. The Sunday tabloids are regularly filled with sex scandals, players getting in fights or being arrested. Unsurprisingly all of the players involved have been English and there do not appear to be any Italians, French or Dutch among them. A classic case is Jody Morris. There is no question that Jody is the heir apparent to Dennis Wise as a future Chelsea captain and likely England international. The only barrier to achieving all this is probably Jody himself. Although he was in Ayia Napia with Dyer and co, he did not step out of line (or was not caught in the act), but his behaviour at times seems more at home with the Chelsea of the seventies rather than the current generation. The Monday afternoon of February 21 2000 was a classic example. Having played his part in Chelsea's 5-0 victory over Gillingham in the Fifth Round of the FA Cup, Morris spent the next day celebrating in the Fox and Hounds pub in Wimbledon.

After being thrown out of the pub, the Chelsea midfielder and his friends were picked up by the police and were only released after they sobered up. Morris also had his collar felt after getting into a fight in a pub in Epsom just before Christmas and on June 27 2000 he pleaded guilty to causing actual bodily harm. Ironically, his fellow defendant was an ex-Chelsea youth team colleague Paul Quinn who failed to make the grade at the Bridge and who has since drifted out of the game altogether. Quinn got a two-month jail sentence and Morris was fortunate to get community service.

It was not the first time that Morris has gone off the rails while he has been on professional terms at Chelsea and sooner or later, if this talented young man does not grasp the need to stay on the straight and narrow, his Chelsea days could be numbered.

Back in the 1997/98 season, Morris was the first to admit that he had been 'a complete waste of space' and had not been doing the right things off the pitch. He had started the season in the side against Manchester United at Wembley in the Charity Shield but when he got injured and did not recover his place in the side, he sought solace in the bottle rather than in his mentor Graham Rix. As he said at the time, 'if I am honest I wasn't 100 per cent professional while I was injured: in the way I looked after myself and the things I did. I wasn't doing things right off the pitch because I wasn't keeping myself fit and I wasn't looking after myself. I suppose you could say it was complacency and that's bad – especially from a lad who has been a Chelsea fan all his life and has always wanted to play for them.' In the end it took some intimidation from Chelsea fan Dennis Wise who pinned

Morris against the wall and read him the riot act. The added intervention of Graham Rix made Morris realise how close he was to no longer playing for the club he loved. 'In the end, a few people at the club, including Graham Rix, told me to pull my socks up and I realised what was happening. Graham has known me since I came to the club, and when someone like that tells you to buck up, you do.'

Another reason for Jody Morris making the headlines last season followed Ken Bates' infamous programme notes which related his fondness for burgers rather than the pasta and salad favoured by his continental team-mates. 'Jody could become a great Chelsea captain. But he must learn from his current peers. Don't let me see you eating hamburgers at Gatwick Airport, forget your flash cars and the nightclubs. If you really dedicate yourself, you could become one of the Chelsea greats. It's up to you - how much do you want it?'

For someone who can be outspoken on a majority of topics, Ken Bates has always been supportive of the young players at Chelsea. Morris confided to close friends that Bates' programme notes did not offend him and that it had all been meant in a jovial manner. 'It wasn't as bad as the press made out but it was disappointing. He phoned me the next morning at the training ground and said it was half in jest and that it's only because I was doing so well that he was having a pop at me.'

Clearly, Morris did not take offence, although taking offence at your club chairman would probably not be a good idea. The problem though, is that Ken Bates' programme notes are the most read item these days in the club magazine (sic) and you can usually guarantee that at least one lazy journalist will pillage something from them and make it into a story for the Monday papers. The Jody Morris story was a Ken Bates article hijacked by the press and it swiftly spiralled out of control.

Jody Morris is probably the best Chelsea youth product of recent times. He played two Champions League games against the mighty Barcelona last season and on that disastrous night in the Camp Nou it was Morris who emerged with most distinction for an outstanding midfield performance. With the likes of Frank Lampard, Joe Cole, Stephen Gerrard and Lee Bowyer ahead of Morris in the England pecking order, he will need to play more games of this calibre and perhaps, with the departure of the water carrier to Valencia, he will get the opportunity to stake his claim to a regular midfield berth this term. Another blessing for the young midfielder was the departure of Chris Sutton to Celtic. From the moment he joined the club, Sutton was quick to make friends with Morris and the two were regularly seen out on the town together. The trouble with Chris Sutton was that as well as not being the greatest footballer going, he was the worst possible influence for a young player such as Morris.

The two success stories of last year, with whom high hopes rest this season, are John Harley and John Terry, both of whom broke into the first team squad last season. Although Harley made a far greater number of appearances, both made a substantial enough mark for many to believe that the two Johns will form the backbone of the Chelsea defence in future.

Harley could hardly have imagined the impact he would have on Chelsea last season. Despite being ever present in the reserves during 1998/99, the only first team football he had to show for it was a one-minute substitute appearance in the Coca-Cola cup against Aston Villa. Prior to that he had made only three league appearances at the tail end of the 1997/8 season. As a third year professional, time appeared to be running out, however when opportunity knocked, Harley grabbed it and never looked back.

For Harley, breaking into the Chelsea side was particularly special having supported the club as a boy. He went to his first game at the Bridge in 1989 when his father took the nine-year-old to see the Blues beat Bournemouth 2-0 with goals from Graham Roberts and Gordon Durie. The promising young footballer was initially scouted by Millwall and it was at their Centre of Excellence that he first came to Chelsea's attention.

The first time Harley cught my eye was when I saw him play at Fratton Park in February 1998 in the FA Youth Cup. The Chelsea team that night featured current professionals Stephen Broad,

John Terry, Rob Wolleaston and Jay Richardson but it was Harley who stole the show. Within fifteen seconds of the kick-off a Chelsea attack was cleared by the Pompey defence, the ball fell to Harley and from 35 yards he hammered the ball into the top left-hand corner. Within a matter of weeks Harley had made his first team debut.

John was forced to wait another two seasons before a further run in the first team. But following a long-term injury to Graham Le Saux, Harley took his chance. He played for the first team 26 times, 7 of them as a substitute and managed to get on the score sheet on two occasions, both of them winning goals: the first at home to Watford followed by an excellent strike in the 1-0 victory against Leeds at Elland Road. The greatest compliment that could be paid to John is that if a straw poll was held tomorrow among Chelsea fans concerning our first choice left back/left wing back, Harley would probably beat Babayaro and Le Saux. Most importantly, the young man from Kent has helped dispel the myth that only foreign players prevent young players breaking through.

Harley's 1999/00 season was made complete when he was selected to play for England Under-21s at the end of the season. Harley clearly feels that his career has been boosted by training with Desailly, Leboeuf and Zola, 'If anything it is helping me by being at Chelsea. I am learning a lot from the foreigners. When you get your chance you learn as much as you can from them and you try to be as good as you can. You cannot help but learn from these players and I feel that they have made me a better player. They have certainly influenced me and I have learnt from them. They have made me feel welcome and they're always willing to give advice to the younger players.'

When the national team found themselves bereft of left sided players in the run up to the Euro 2000 championships, Harley's name suddenly leapt to the top of the pile. Whilst complimenting his player when being questioned about whether or not he should go to the Championships, Vialli made sure he kept the young man's feet firmly on the ground, 'he is a very nice lad and he wants to get better. He has enthusiasm, self-belief but you have to give him time. But he has a chance to be a great player.' Perhaps the most encouraging thing of all is that Harley still lives in the same digs as when he was in the youth team and, unlike the wayward Jody Morris, he drives a modest car and is more likely to be found in his native Maidstone at a weekend taking his girlfriend to see Toy Story 2, than painting the town red with a complete waste of space such as Chris Sutton.

The 2000/01 season looks to be crucial for John Harley, but you will not find him running to the press bemoaning his lack of first team opportunities like some of his former team mates. 'I am proof you can get through at Chelsea. The players we produce have to be of a high standard. We get the best education here. I know that if someone is playing well and they are good enough, they are going to get a game at this club. It is not a question of who you are.'

Even after he was put out on loan in October to Wimbledon and certain sections of the media were already predicting the end of his Chelsea career, Harley was quick to confirm where he believed his future lies. 'It is a chance for me to play first team football and that's good. I don't see it as a backward step. My future is still at Chelsea.' Chelsea have successfully farmed out their younger professionals to Nationwide League clubs recently. It regarded as part of their long term development with young striker Sam Parkin recently benefitting from a loan spell at Millwall. Nevertheless it was a strange transfer even by Chelsea standards. Harley has in effect gone to Wimbledon for a third of the season and with the injury prone Le Saux and Babayaro's wonderlust to travel the globe but not return, few fans could see the benefit of releasing such a talented young player to a lower league team. Many fans were asking themselves what Harley could possibly learn at Wimbledon that he could not learn better at Stamford Bridge.

Also, with the club bereft of left-footed players and their continuing, yet fruitless search for a talented left sided midfielder player – most questioned Ranieri's motives. The only benefit I could see was that is if there is a weakness to his game then it is his often fragile nature - perhaps three months roughing it in the Nationwide League would toughen him up to Chelsea's long term benefit. Personally, I do not think John Harley will be leaving Chelsea and I look forward to welcoming him back in the blue shirt before the current season is over. After all, with Peter Taylor taking temporary charge of the national side with a promise to give younger players a chance at senior level who is to say that the Leicester manager will not select John Harley for the national squad before the year is out. After all English football, like Chelsea, is not over run with left sided players at present.

The other successful John at Chelsea last season was John Terry, a young man from Barking who did not sign a professional contract until March 1998 but made his debut seven months later. For John Terry, every season is a stepping-stone and having made seven appearances in the 1998/99 season, he made eight further starts in 1999/00 and even managed to get on the bench for the FA Cup final against Aston Villa. Although he did not get on he picked up a winners' medal and no doubt in years to come he will add to that.

He also had the opportunity of a loan spell at Nottingham Forest towards the end of last year, as a favour to David Platt from his old team-mate Vialli. Terry went to a Forest side in danger of relegation but helped them pull away from the drop zone and remain unbeaten during his loan period. It was good experience for Terry and he has probably helped his long-term development. If there was, though, one moment last season that John Terry will remember for many years to come perhaps, a moment even better than collecting his FA Cup winners' medal, it was his first goal for the club against Gillingham in the fifth round of the FA Cup at Stamford Bridge. When Terry scored Chelsea's second goal and threw himself into the front row of the lower tier of the Matthew Harding stand, there was only one man happier than the young 19 year-old from Essex.

Sitting up in the Gods of the Upper Tier of the East Stand was his father Ted, a forklift truck driver from Essex. Ted Terry cried tears of joy at his son's first goal for Chelsea. However despite that goal, Terry couldn't make the bench for the next two games but this did not get to him, 'I am just happy with the situation at the moment training with the first team every day. We have so many good youngsters at the club who hopefully will get their chance in the first team. You cannot help but learn from the likes of Frank Leboeuf and Marcel Desailly and Luca has said that if you are good enough, you are old enough. I also tell myself that although the team is full of household names they are not going to be here forever and I hope to be a first team regular in a couple of years' time.'

So what will the future hold for the young players at Chelsea Football Club? Now Gianluca Vialli has gone, will Claudio Ranieri look to foreign shores, or will more youngsters be blooded in the coming seasons? John Harley and John Terry have set the benchmark for other youngsters to follow. Chelsea now have a professional squad of 44 players, which is the largest it has been for several years, but Vialli used 31 players last season, so although the squad could do with some trimming there should still be an opportunity for some of those young professionals to make their mark this season. If some do not get a chance this year, they have plenty of time on their hands. Within the next couple of seasons Dennis Wise, Gianfranco Zola, Gus Poyet, Marcel Desailly, Ed de Goey and Frank Leboeuf will all have finished their careers at Chelsea and it should come as no surprise if the Chelsea side of 2003 lines up as follows:

Cudicini

Slatter **Terry** **Broad** **Cummings**

Dalla Bonna **Morris** **Harley** **Wooleaston**

Knight **Gudjohnsen**

Team Manager: Dennis Wise
Coaching staff: Steve Clarke/Dan Petrescu

A Season to Remember

Chelsea's 1999/2000 season was memorable. Although there are many who feel that having just the FA Cup to show at the end of the season of such promise was an underachievement, these people clearly have short memories. A few years earlier and most fans, having waited since 1971 for a trophy, would have been delighted with an FA Cup appearance let alone a win. It is, though, a demonstration of how far Chelsea have come in recent years that expectations are now so much higher than *just* the FA Cup and the club are regarded as genuine Championship contenders.

Although for most supporters, the season began in earnest on August 7 with the first home game, for Colin Hutchinson, the previous season probably never ended and just merged in with the new, particularly in view of the unusually high amount of transfer activity during the close season. Hutchinson had been busy attempting to bolster Vialli's squad. France's World Cup winning captain and renowned 'water carrier' Didier Deschamps was signed for £3million from Juventus. Danish international Jes Hogh arrived from Fenerbache and Hutchinson also acquired Mario Melchiot from Ajax.

Most of Hutchinson's time and effort, though, was spent trying to lure Italian striker Marco Delvecchio from Roma. The deal at one stage seemed done with the player keen to come to Chelsea – he made all the right noises and Roma seemed prepared to sell. Suddenly, Fabio Cappello took over as Roma manager and the Italian was staying after Roma significantly increased his salary. It had been clear the previous season that Vialli needed to strengthen his forward line so the loss of Delvecchio was a major disappointment for Hutchinson and Vialli.

However, with the new season approaching and the clock ticking down, Hutchinson still had a rather large cheque burning a hole in his pocket and he wanted to spend it on a new striker. All summer Chelsea had been linked with Chris Sutton who had made no secret of his wish to leave Blackburn following their relegation to the Nationwide League. However Chelsea had shown no interest so far and with George Graham showing an interest in the tall striker, Sutton seemed destined for a move elsewhere. Then, with the season about to start, Chelsea stunned football, Frank Leboeuf and a large section of their own supporters by signing Sutton for a club record fee of £10 million to make the tall striker the third most expensive player in English football after Dwight Yorke and Alan Shearer.

The signing produced a mixed reaction among supporters and media alike but Vialli was quick to defend his new acquisition and his reasons for purchasing the Blackburn striker. 'We were in contact with Roma and made an offer for Marco Delvecchio but he chose to stay with them,' he said, 'so we looked at Chris Sutton because he was on the transfer list and he was available. I chose to sign Sutton and I want to say that I am happy that he is here. It takes any player joining a new club time to settle down but I think Sutton has fitted in well. He has the right attitude and he will do well.'

It did not take long for the press to put the knife in with Des Kelly in *The Mirror* offering an unusual description of Vialli's new signing. 'Sutton is the Waterworld of strikers – an over-hyped, budget-busting Kevin Costner style catastrophe playing at a Premiership ground near you. He is like watching a car crash in slow motion.'

The first opportunity many Chelsea fans got to see the £10 million signing was at Kingstonian where Chelsea had played each pre-season since the early nineties. The match is always a sell-out and the 5,000 crowd, mainly made up of young Chelsea fans who cannot get to Stamford Bridge very often, use the game to get as many autographs as they can for their collections. The laid-back Family Day atmosphere at Kingsmeadow Stadium and the lax security makes the players more accessible to the public than they are at Stamford Bridge on match days when security men provide a barrier between fans and players at the tunnel after each game.

As the players got out of their expensive cars, they were mobbed by hundreds of young fans and the Poyets and Zolas were extremely accommodating, signing as many autographs as they could and delighting a lot of young Chelsea fans into the bargain.

When Sutton arrived and got out to be greeted by hundreds of autograph hunters, he could not have provided a more contrasting image as he signed two autographs, refused to sign any more and barged his way through the young crowd and fled to the dressing room. It was clear from the number of new home shirts with the number nine on the back that many fans had taken to Sutton. At that moment, however, he managed to alienate a number of angry dads with what was perceived as an arrogant attitude and this was before he had even kicked a ball for his new club.

After an ordinary pre-season slipped by, the great day finally arrived. August 7 1999. The opening day of the season and the most optimistic football fans in the country turned up at Stamford Bridge thinking this could be Chelsea's year.

The first opponents of the season were newly-promoted Sunderland who had run away with the First Division the previous season thanks to the goal scoring exploits of Kevin Phillips. It was not going to be an easy start to the season but little did anyone expect the eventual outcome with Vialli's men cruising to a 4-0 victory which could easily have been double figures. Goals from Gianfranco Zola, Tore Andre Flo and two from Gustavo Poyet did the damage leaving Sunderland manager Peter Reid shell-shocked, 'they gave us a right hiding,' said Reid. 'I now know what Davey Crockett fell like at the Alamo.'

The only disappointment following such a buoyant start was the form of Sutton. With the weight of his transfer fee weighing heavily on many Chelsea fans' minds, he had two perfect first half opportunities to start his debut with a goal. Ten minutes before half time Sutton beat the Sunderland offside trap and raced towards the Wearsiders goal with only keeper Thomas Sorensen to beat. With the fans in the Shed End willing their new number nine to score, Sutton inexplicably put the ball wide. If that wasn't bad enough, just on half time Sutton again beat the offside trap and bore down on goal. With Chelsea already 2-0 up it would have given the Blues an unassailable lead. However it was not to be. With only the keeper to beat, Sutton once again failed, somehow managing to trip over the ball just as he was about to shoot. To crown a disappointing debut, Vialli rescued Sutton from more misery and replaced him with crowd favourite Tore Andre Flo who scored Chelsea's third within 4 minutes of coming on.

After the match Vialli was quick to console his record signing. 'Obviously Chris can do better and we are going to help him. However from my own experience I know that sometimes the more time you have on the ball the more difficult it is to score.'

For a man with a huge mistrust and dislike of the press, Sutton had to take credit for coming out after the game to face his detractors who probably already had their articles written for the Sunday and Monday papers. 'I probably won't get two better chances to score than I did today but I am not worried,' was Sutton's opening gambit. 'I have missed hundreds of chances before so I am not worrying now.' For a man who had just missed two of the easiest chances he would get all season they were brave words indeed. He may not have been worried but there were thousands of Chelsea fans who were pondering whether

Chelsea had bought the new Robert Fleck rather than the new Kerry Dixon.

'I had so much time for the first chance I was expecting a defender to tackle me. When I missed I just wanted the ground to open up and swallow me. On the second one I just slipped but it was still a good chance. The lads have given me terrible stick in the dressing room.' Somehow a bit of Dennis Wise banter about fat cows, arses and banjos should not be filed under terrible stick. Fortunately for Sutton, the jury was still out on his signing and having endured the likes of Robert Fleck, Tony Cascarino, Paul Furlong and Pierluigi Casiraghi in recent years in the coveted number nine shirt, every Chelsea fan desperately wanted him to succeed.

The following week Chelsea gained a creditable draw at Filbert Street thanks to the head of Chelsea old boy 'Mad' Frank Sinclair who for the second week in succession scored an own goal in the last minute of the game. A minute earlier, the match seemed lost when Emile Heskey fell on his arse in a manner that he would repeat on countless occasions throughout the season but on this occasion he got a penalty. Another Chelsea old boy, Muzzy Izzet, made it 2-1 but then up popped Sinclair to give his old teammates a share of the points in a 2-2 draw.

Aston Villa were next at the Bridge and in a manner that would be repeated nine months later at Wembley, made little attempt to make a game of it. An own goal from Ugo Ehiogu, deflecting an unlikely goal-bound attempt from Dan Petrescu past Calamity James, gave Chelsea the only goal of the game. While most Chelsea fans were none too impressed by Villa's negative tactics, Vialli saw it differently. 'I take it as a compliment that a team of Villa's undoubted calibre came to stop us playing. We must be patient,' continued Vialli, 'and expect teams to play like that when they come to Stamford Bridge. They will do the same at Old Trafford and Highbury so we have to expect teams to do it here. This was a very big test at such an early stage in the season. It was hot out there today so my players found it difficult to breathe at times. I am happy though that once we got into the lead my players had the character to hold on to it.'

A week later, a short trip across London to Selhurst Park saw a late Dan Petrescu goal grab the points for Chelsea. But against a poor Wimbledon side already looking like relegation candidates Chelsea made hard work of their victory. So four games into the season and Chelsea were third in the table. Things got even better following a third 1-0 victory on the trot at home to Newcastle, and all the pre-season hype seemed justified. The Newcastle game turned on two penalty appeals. Chelsea got theirs but the Geordie's appeals were turned down by referee Graham Poll. On 38 minutes Gary Speed clumsily hauled Celestine Babayaro down in the penalty area and Leboeuf scored from the spot. In the second half, Newcastle had what seemed a decent shout for a penalty dismissed by Poll and after only five games Chelsea were second in the table.

After the plaudits given for the midweek nil-nil draw with mighty AC Milan, the next game at Vicarage Road should have been a formality. Watford appeared to be prime candidates for relegation and before the game, Graham Taylor even suggested that Chelsea's cosmopolitan side would be a match for England, never mind Watford. Whether it was a bit of shrewd psychology by the ex-England manager, who knows, but his Watford players were clearly psyched up for Chelsea's visit. If what happened over the next 90 minutes was a warning for Vialli's players not to be too complacent in the Premier League it was not heeded. Watford won 1-0 with a goal from Alan Smart and deserved the three points. Chelsea were a disgrace and no player could take any credit from their performance. While much criticism over the season was levelled at the foreigners in Vialli's side, at Watford it was the English players who let him down. None more so than Chris Sutton who, despite being made captain, did little to inspire his team-mates and his only contribution to a poor afternoon's performance was a booking. Vialli had made Sutton captain as a way of demonstrating that he valued him highly and perhaps it was also a way of boosting the failing striker's confidence. It sadly backfired this time. 'Bring on the Arsenal...' sang the jubilant Watford fans, who could not believe their good fortune at turning over one of the favourites for the Premier League title. 'Bring off the English...' sang their Chelsea counterparts already realising the weak links in Vialli's side tended to have the same passports as the supporters.

Vialli didn't pull his punches after the game and for once was refreshingly honest in his appraisal of his team's performance. The Chelsea fans who had been forced to endure humiliation at Vicarage Road would have been livid if Vialli had trotted out the well-worn phrase about his players doing their best but the better team on the day won. 'We were poor today. It is our duty at Chelsea to take three points from places like Watford. We have to be able to play as well against Watford as we do against the likes of Milan. This result could work one of two ways for us. It might cause problems for the players because morale may be low but we have another game on Tuesday so we have a chance to put this performance behind us.'

The long trip up to Middlesbrough's Cellnet stadium proved worthwhile when Bernard Lambourde was first to react to a first half Gianfranco Zola free kick that hit the bar - the Frenchman scrambling in the only goal of the game. It was Chelsea's first victory on Teeside for 68 years and kept the Blues fifth in the table. The Man United game was the biggest of the Premier League season so far. United came to Stamford Bridge unbeaten in 29 games and unbeaten on their last seven visits to the Bridge. It was going to be Chelsea and Vialli's sternest test of the season to date.

At the training ground at Harlington on the Friday Dennis Wise revealed that Chelsea would be changing their style of play to try to accommodate Chris Sutton more than they had done so to date. 'We know that we can get the ball into the box quicker and sometimes we should be prepared to do that, especially with Chris in there. Luca has asked us to be more direct in our play and hit the ball into the box whenever we have a chance of crossing for Chris in the area.' The players had clearly listened to Vialli as no one could have predicted the immediate impact his Friday team talk had had. After twenty-eight seconds, Dan Petrescu crossed for Gus Poyet, whose header beat the hapless Massimo Taibi in United's goal to give Chelsea a dream start. Poyet's goal was the fourth-fastest ever in the Premiership. Fifteen minutes later, it got even better when a similar ball from Albert Ferrer saw an unmarked Chris Sutton make it 2-0 with a perfect header. For Sutton it was a particularly pleasing moment scoring his first league goal for Chelsea. The game was as good as over before half time when the temperamental Nicky Butt lashed out at Dennis Wise after he'd pulled a couple of hairs out of Butt's leg when they clashed on the ground.

Taibi's nightmare continued in the second half when he palmed a Frank Leboeuf shot straight into Gus Poyet's path to make it 3-0. Minutes later, Henning Berg, reluctant to trust his keeper to collect a Zola cross, only succeeded in turning the ball into his own net. To complete a match that effectively terminated his United career, Taibi left his legs open wide enough for a late Jody Morris shot to go straight through them for 'one, two, one, two, three, one, two, three, four, five nil!'

October though was Chelsea's annus horriblis rolled into 31 days. It had all started so promising with the win over United and victory by the same score in Galatasary. There was also a draw in Milan to celebrate but sandwiched in between were woeful performances in the Premier League and Worthington Cup. Their Cup defeat by First Division Huddersfield Town was particularly painful to watch. Liverpool at Anfield has never been a particularly happy hunting ground and the Vinnie Jones-inspired 2-1 win in 1992 seems a dim and distant memory now. Chelsea travelled to Anfield as favourites to win the game with Liverpool having already lost three times in front of their own supporters. Even Liverpool manager Gerard Houllier took a cautious approach, electing to play Michael Owen as a lone striker and pack his midfield with five players. On the day though, despite Vialli playing his strongest eleven, it was Liverpool who once again collected the points while Desailly and Wise collected a red card apiece. Referee Mike Read had endured the wrath of the nation when he gave Chelsea a hotly disputed penalty in an FA Cup replay against Leicester in 1997 and since then he seems determined to put that matter right. In 1998/99 at Elland Road he dismissed Frank Leboeuf and booked eight Chelsea players so it was perhaps not surprising that Wise and Desailly walked at Anfield. Wise clearly caught Vladimir Smicer with what looked like a stray arm but Desailly's red card even mystified the fans at the Kop End who sportingly applauded him off the pitch.

But if there was a defining moment for Chelsea's whole season then it was the home game against Arsenal. For me this was the turning point of the season and the moment we blew any slim chance of winning the Premier League. Having seen off Manchester United in the previous home game, we held a two-goal lead against Arsenal and looked likely to increase it. If we had held on to our lead we would have had the huge psychological advantage of beating our main rivals in successive home games which would have done wonders for morale. But in a mad last fifteen minutes our defence somehow disintegrated.

It had all started so promisingly, with goals either side of half time by Tore Andre Flo and Dan Petrescu and two weeks after the historic home win, the home fans could not have predicted what would happen next. With time ticking down, the gangly Nigerian striker Kanu scored what appeared to be a consolation with fifteen minutes left. Minutes later Kanu scored again and the heavens opened soaking the already dejected Chelsea fans in the uncovered West Stand. With a minute of normal time left, Ed De Goey made a disastrous charge towards the corner flag, Kanu beat him to the ball and from the tightest of angles chipped the ball into the top corner.

The last day of the month saw another dreadful away performance when, just days after drawing in the San Siro, Chelsea rolled up at Pride Park to face a Derby side who had lost five of their first six home games. If there was an arrogance about the side that day, naturally assuming they only had to turn up to collect the points, they soon got a shock when diminutive striker Deon Burton gave Derby the lead after eight minutes. Although Frank Leboeuf scored a quick equaliser, two late goals from Irish international Rory Delap stunned Chelsea and Vialli, who was already showing signs of losing patience with some of his players. 'We have a psychological problem somewhere,' he told the press after the game. 'I will spend the next few days trying to work out what is going on in the players' minds. We have not played well in our last two away games and that is a problem. The game seemed more important to Derby than it did my players, which is a state of affairs I do not regard as acceptable. It is no good beating Manchester United and Galatasary 5-0 and drawing against Milan in the San Siro if we cannot do the same at places like Derby and Watford. We did not play as well as we did in Milan and I don't know how we can do so well away from home in Europe but not in the Premier League.'

Days later, on the eve of the Hertha Berlin Champions League tie, Bates gave his viewpoint on the Chelsea Clubcall phone line. It may cost 60p a minute but that day it seemed it did its best business in years when word spread of what had been said by Captain Birdseye. 'I think possibly errors of judgement have been made in certain games with the rotation system and to be fair, Vialli has acknowledged that in a number of circumstances. After several years with nothing, we are now on a roll and want to keep it going, but we want to do well in the Premiership because that is the home competition. In a way it hurts us more to lose to Arsenal than to Hertha Berlin because Arsenal are just down the road. They were three points thrown away and we have to ask ourselves why. They were left for dead and we surrendered.

'We want to win the championship and the Champions League and the FA Cup. I was concerned that we went out of the Worthington Cup to Huddersfield because the team we fielded should have won. We should have beaten Watford and Derby but we didn't and that's not necessarily down to team selection, it's down to the players' attitude on the pitch. We are still not firing on all cylinders but the idea that we are concentrating on the Champions League to the detriment of the Premiership is nonsense.'

The reality of the clubcall speech by Bates was he was only

saying what a lot of Chelsea fans had been thinking. Bates had only repeated what Vialli himself had said, namely that the defeats the team had suffered were not down to team selection but down to the players and their attitude. Those fans who travelled to Pride Park and Vicarage Road would happily name the players they thought were not up for two crucial Premiership games that, had Chelsea won, would have qualified them for the Champions League at the end of the season and possibly saved Gianluca from the chop twelve months later.

A few days later, the euphoria of qualifying for the next stage of the Champions League was forgotten when West Ham, a team with a reputation of playing the beautiful game the right way, came to Stamford Bridge intent on frustrating Chelsea. Harry Redknapp's tactics worked and the subdued 34,935 Sunday afternoon crowd saw their one and only 0-0 of the season.

Chelsea were already ten points behind Manchester United and although they had two games in hand, signs were that this was not going to be a championship challenging season. Vialli, as ever, remained optimistic, 'we have two games in hand on Manchester United and could close the gap to four points if we win both of them. With half the season left to play there is still a long way to go but we have to do better and get results away from home as well as at home.'

It did not get any better the following week when a mid-table Everton side were only seconds away from beating ten-man Chelsea when Tore Andre Flo popped up in injury time to score a much needed equaliser. The fact that Chelsea had to play most of the second half with ten men was down to the stupidity of Frank Leboeuf who was sent off for fouling Nick Barmby just after half time right in front of the referee. Surprisingly the hero of the day aside from Flo was Chris Sutton who moved back to centre-half after the Frenchman's dismissal and had a sound game. More embarrassingly for Chelsea, as the ten men tried to chase the game in the last ten minutes, it was centre half Desailly who was pushed forward and not striker Sutton. Ten million pounds seemed a lot of money to pay for a centre half.

Fortunately, Chelsea once again redeemed themselves with a magnificent performance in the Champions League beating Dutch champions Feyenoord 3-1 and got back to winning ways in the Premier League when a Tore Andre Flo goal was enough to beat struggling Bradford. More surprising was the fact that it had been almost two months since Chelsea had won in the league – the defeat of Manchester United had been their last league victory.

The next game was at the magnificent Stadium of Light and despite the fact that a midweek trip to Lazio in the Champions League would make a large dent in many fans' pockets, many Blues fans were keen to add a new ground to a growing list, so Chelsea took a large following to Wearside. They may as well have stayed at home and suffered the Capital Radio commentary as Chelsea capitulated from the 46th second when Niall Quinn opened the scoring. The next 36 minutes saw Sunderland avenge their 4-0 thrashing on the opening day of the season as they tore into Chelsea. By the 38th minute they were 4-0 up with leading scorer Kevin Phillips bagging a brace and Quinn adding his second to send Chelsea in at half time humiliated. Young John Harley, drafted into the side for his first appearance, was replaced by Barney Goldbaek at the break while an out of sorts Marcel Desailly was replaced by John Terry for his first league appearance of the season.

The re-jigged side either did the job or Sunderland ran out of steam but the only consolation those Chelsea fans singing 'Are you watching Lazio?' had was a late header by Gus Poyet eight minutes from time. By then, many Chelsea fans were already on the long journey back to London. 'I can't explain a defeat like that,' said Vialli. 'We started badly and it did not get any better.' With another defeat sandwiched by two Champions League ties questions were being raised about Chelsea's real aims this season. To most it seemed the Blues were concentrating too hard on the Champions League at the expense of the Premier League.

When asked if Chelsea's early success in the Champions League was affecting their league form having lost to Derby and

Watford, Vialli was honest, 'it is much easier to play in the Champions League than in the Premier League at the moment. My players have not let me down in Europe and I am sure they will not let me down in Rome. But that is not my priority. I want to have a successful team at Chelsea that is good enough to win the Premier League.'

Having drawn magnificently in the Olympic Stadium in Rome the third round FA Cup tie at Hull City's Boothferry Park represented a potential embarassment. The history of Chelsea is littered with cup reverses against lower league opposition and many pundits on the morning of the game were whispering that Hull might pull off the shock of the round. I suspect some might have been disappointed as Chelsea ran riot at Boothferry Park, Gus Poyet helped himself to a hat-trick and even Chris Sutton managed to get on the scoresheet in a 6-1 win. Sadly, Sutton then made a fool of himself by gesturing to the home fans who had taunted him prior to his goal. One Chelsea player who acted in a more dignified manner was John Harley. Having made only one appearance all season, and that in the fiasco at the Stadium of Light, Harley played an inspired game on the left-hand side, creating two of Chelsea's goals with inch-perfect crosses. He also impressed throughout the game, supplying the kind of crosses that even Chris Sutton would have appreciated.

Despite Sky's presence at Chelsea's next home game, against David O'Leary's promising Leeds team, the Blues' biggest crowd of the season (35,106) braved the December chill hoping to see the Blues gain three valuable points over their long-standing Yorkshire rivals. For sixty minutes Chelsea dominated the game but once again, despite good approach play, their forwards once again failed to shine. The turning point came with the loss of Marcel Desailly at half time who was replaced by Jes Hogh and then Hogh himself had to limp off after 65 minutes. Three minutes later, a gaping hole in the centre of Chelsea's defence got wider after Frank Leboeuf went searching for Harry Kewell. Leeds midfielder Stephen McPhail nipped in to score and all hell broke loose soon after.

Kewell and Leboeuf clashed in the centre of the pitch and while the Australian lay on the ground after Leboeuf had tripped him, Leboeuf then stamped on him in full view of the referee who already had a red card in his hand. With both sets of players pushing and shoving, Leboeuf did not disappear down the tunnel immediately. His former rival for the Chelsea centre half shirt, Michael Duberry, was sitting on the Leeds bench and as the Frenchman walked off the pitch Duberry made a passing remark to his ex-teammate that seemed to wind him up even more.

While all this was going on a football match was struggling for attention, McPhail scored his second of the game to seal the points for Leeds and kill off what little chance Chelsea had of remaining in the title race. With nearly half the season gone Chelsea were now tenth, already seventeen points behind Leeds at the top of the table. 'We lost our heads a bit. After creating so many chances, my players got frustrated as the game began to slip away,' said Vialli, 'I might be biased but I think we were the better team today. We did not take the chances we had today and Leeds did. It might be difficult for us to win the league now but we will keep going.'

Goals from Gus Poyet and Tore Andre Flo secured the points at the Dell despite a late panic caused by Kevin Davies scoring for the Saints with ten minutes left. However all the talk after the game was about Vialli's decision to pick the first-ever all foreign Premiership side. With Dennis Wise, Graham Le Saux and Chris Sutton unavailable through either injury or illness, Vialli picked his side more out of necessity rather than to create history. Sadly, the jingoistic journalists preferred the 'Johnny Foreigner' side of the story and neglected to look at the Chelsea bench which included four players who had graduated from the Chelsea youth team – Jody Morris, John Harley, John Terry and Mark Nicholls.

Two days later, in the last match of the millennium, Vialli once again stuck to his all-foreign line-up as Bernard Lambourde replaced the unavailable Albert Ferrer. However, as if it had been scripted just to please the press, two Englishmen came off the bench to grab the headlines. In front of the BSkyB cameras a rather sterile first half was going nowhere when Didier Deschamps was forced from the field after a clash of heads. With Vialli's squad decimated by injuries, Dennis Wise, still suffering from flu, had been put on the bench and was called into action to replace the Frenchman. His impact on the game was emphatic. He scored one goal and had a hand in two others Chelsea scored on the night, when Chelsea's other substitute, Jody Morris, shot in from close range late on and wrote his name into the history books as the last footballer to score a goal in the twentieth century. Although Morris' name will go into the record books it was Dennis Wise who won all the praise afterwards. 'Dennis plays well for us but more importantly he makes the team play well.' said Vialli. 'He has shown great loyalty to Chelsea over the last ten years. He has the right mentality and on top of that he is a very good player. He is more mature now, more experienced. The older you get, the more you realise that you do not have many chances left in the game to win something.'

After the millennial festivities the serious business of football returned with a visit to Highfield Road. Coventry had beaten Chelsea on their last four visits, so the omens were not good when the Sky Blues took the lead. However within sixty seconds Chelsea equalised through Tore Andre Flo. Coventry once again regained the lead through wonderboy Robbie Keane but amazingly Flo equalised within sixty seconds once again to earn a point.

Tore-Andre was in a rich vein of form and after a slow start he was now leading scorer with13 goals. So not surprisingly he kept his place for the visit to Bradford four days after his brace at Highfield Road. Unfortunately Bradford turned out to be one of those days. You had to be there to believe it. In ninety minutes Chelsea made 35 attempts on goal (almost a chance every three minutes) and yet somehow only scored one goal and came away with a solitary point when clearly they should have won all three long before half time. Like Sunderland at the Stadium of Light before Christmas, Bradford struck in the first minute when Mills headed home from archenemy Saunders' cross. The goal shocked

Chelsea out of their slumber and with Didier Deschamps for once in inspirational form, chance after chance was created but all went begging. The main culprits were Poyet and Flo, who would both have scored a hat-trick on any other day. Credit has to be given to Bradford goalkeeper Matthew Clarke who had an inspirational game. Only in the 57th minute did Dan Petrescu finally get the equaliser and Chelsea went in search of a winner that sadly never came. Sad to reflect that it was in games such as this that Chelsea's title challenge faded – they need to find the winning habit if they are to sustain a title challenge year in, year out in future as the manager commented, 'they tell me we had 30 attempts at goal. At times it was like shooting practice but if you do not score you do not win.'

Perhaps Vialli had been patient long enough with his strikers and within forty-eight hours of the Bradford debacle he managed to stun most Chelsea fans with news of his latest signing. A rumour had been doing the rounds for weeks that George Weah was joining Chelsea. Now the story was true. George Weah, former World Footballer of the Year, was coming to Chelsea. Vialli had certainly learnt from his mistakes the previous year when the goals dried up following Tore Andre Flo's absence through injury.

After the record-breaking number of chances spurned at Valley Parade, the forward line clearly needed an injection of life and they did not come any larger than the Liberian international. No individual though could have written the script for his debut 24 hours after signing in Milan following a meeting with Colin Hutchinson. On Wednesday 12 January 2000, the giant Liberian flew into London, briefly met his new team-mates and then lay down in his hotel room for a couple of hours sleep before the London derby with Tottenham. Vialli decided not to risk Weah from the start and left him on the bench and left Zola out of the side completely, preferring instead to play a five-man midfield.

A rather sterile game, dominated by Spurs, was heading nowhere other than perhaps George Graham's side sneaking a point when, in the 56th minute, the number 19 sign flashed up indicating that Tore Andre Flo should come off as Weah's new squad number 31 flashed up on the board.

A morgue-like Stamford Bridge came to life. There was a buzz around the ground every time the giant Liberian got the ball and you just knew that this game was only going to have one winner. After ten years of trying and failing, Spurs seemed resigned to handing over the three points but somehow Chelsea and Weah could not score. Then it happened. Other than the eight amazing minutes against Barcelona and the 1,2,123, 1234 5-0 against Man United, this was probably the most memorable moment at the Bridge all season. With three minutes left on the clock, Bernard Lambourde split the Tottenham defence with an inch-perfect pass for Dennis Wise who had broken free on the right. The little man looked up, crossed and, with what seemed like half the Tottenham defence challenging him in the air along with Chris Sutton for good measure, Weah rose above them all and blasted the ball past Walker into the net. There have been many players down the years who have scored on their debut but few have managed it in more dramatic circumstances than Weah did on that cold January night. As Vialli commented, 'George's arrival has given everyone at the club a huge lift just at the right time. He is one of the best strikers in the world and I am delighted he has come to Chelsea. He is keen to show that Milan should not have let him go and he has made the best possible start for himself and for the team.'

The only cloud on such a memorable night was the walk out of Gianfranco Zola, an hour before kick off. Had he been in the side the little Italian would have reached a landmark 150 appearances for Chelsea but Vialli left him out of the side and did not even include him among the five substitutes.

Vialli made no apologies for leaving the little Italian out. He told reporters that, as manager, there would be occasions he would have to leave out players and make decisions that made him unpopular. This night had been repeated on many occasions throughout the season and Zola would not be the first and certainly not the last who would be unhappy with Vialli for not playing them. Days later, an unhappy Zola was recalled to the side and paired with Weah for the visit of Leicester City. I suspect the Italian would rather have been left on the bench. With a Leicester side decimated by injuries Martin O'Neill filled his side with defenders content to camp in their own half and settle for a point. There was nothing more frustrating than watching the Chelsea defence hump the ball into the Leicester box time and again with Zola valiantly attempting to win the ball against defenders who were nearly a foot taller than him.

It came as little surprise that Leicester scored from a rare attack and despite Poyet coming on for the increasingly ineffective French water carrier, even Gus seemed out of sorts. Just as the home fans were resigned to an unexpected home defeat, a Zola free kick near the corner flag was headed home by Dennis Wise for an undeserved equaliser. Chelsea had been very poor and there were many in the disappointingly low 30,000 crowd who booed the players off the pitch.

Goals from Leboeuf and Wise saw the blues ease into the fourth round of the FA Cup against David Platt's struggling Forest and the week was rounded with a rather dull 0-0 draw against a decidedly dull Aston Villa side. The only moments to remember were a sensational John Harley effort that shaved the crossbar and the form of George Weah who on any other day could have grabbed the hat-trick he had forecast when he signed for Chelsea.

The opportunity to make amends for the poor home performance two weeks earlier against Leicester was provided when Martin O'Neill's men returned to the Bridge for a fifth round FA Cup tie. Vialli opted for a Weah-Sutton strike force and the double act seemed to work wonders. Weah laid on Poyet's goal just before half time, then, early in the second half, a moment that will now be remembered as perhaps the highlight of Chris Sutton's season with the Blues. Sutton went for a 50/50 ball with Leicester defender Steve Walsh and used all his power to barge past Walsh and leave him on his arse. Sutton looked up and crossed for Weah to volley first time into the Leicester net.

When the number nine was held up with fifteen minutes to go for the eighth time that season, Sutton left the pitch to a standing ovation from the Chelsea crowd. The form of Sutton had impressed Vialli and for the game at White Hart Lane, Weah and Sutton were partners again up front. Lambourde's second goal of the season stretched Chelsea's run against Tottenham to 22 games in ten years but after the match it was the strikers who received Vialli's praise. 'They did well. They create and set up chances. But they know there is competition for places and the pressure is on them. With Gianfranco Zola and Tore Andre Flo on the bench they can take nothing for granted.'

If a Chelsea season ticket holder is ever going to miss a home game during the season you can bet a great deal of money on Wimbledon being the one. The home fixture against the Dons has never been attractive and although in recent years, Chelsea have rid themselves of the jinx the Crazy Gang had on them at Stamford Bridge, you know what sort of game it is going to be, even before a ball is kicked. This game was no different with the Dons employing their usual spoiling tactics, sending most of the crowd racing for the bar at half time five minutes earlier than usual. When Norwegian debutante Andreas Lund put the Crazy Gang in front 15 minutes from the end some disloyal Chelsea fans even headed for the exits.

However, the goal woke Chelsea from their slumber and in a frantic last 10 minutes they ran in three first-class goals to comfortably win a game they appeared to be sleepwalking through for eighty minutes. The first goal was a Gus Poyet special, volleying in from the edge of box. You get no two-yard tap-ins from the Uruguayan. Within a minute, substitute Jody Morris slipped round the back of the Dons defence to cross and George Weah's head did the rest. In the final minute, Morris scored his third goal of the season (all from the subs bench) from twenty yards. However, the headlines the next day were not about Chelsea's comeback, but the fracas in the tunnel when players apparently swapped punches and Vialli got a smack in the face from an unknown assailant.

Despite an unbeaten run in the league, Chelsea's best chance of a trophy still lay in the FA Cup and the draw for the sixth round once again gave Chelsea home advantage, presenting delighted season ticket holders with their fourth 'free' home game of the season. Gillingham had captured football fans' hearts with their giant-killing exploits already, against Premier League Bradford and Sheffield Wednesday, but they found Chelsea a completely different proposition altogether. The Chelsea sides of yesteryear might have regarded this game as a potential banana skin but for the modern-day Chelsea, the tie presented few problems. The travelling 'pikeys' from Kent sold out the West Stand and had their FA Cup final that day. However, Chelsea remained professional and for the third time in the season ran out 5-0 winners. Tore Andre Flo began the rout after 16 minutes, and after the interval, the goals rained in. Four minutes into the second half John Terry scored his first senior goal, from a Zola corner and George Weah made it 3-0 a minute later. Goals from Morris and Zola completed the rout.

The following week, it was back to the bread and butter of Premier League football again with the visit of relegation bound Watford and a chance for Chelsea to avenge one of their worst performances of the season, at Vicarage Road. Another home game was descending into tedium when it was temporarily rescued by Marcel Desailly's first goal of the season - 'The Rock' heading home a Zola free kick. Watford scored just before half time when that man Allan Smart netted again and at half time some of the more pessimistic Chelsea fans sitting in the Matthew Harding were predicting a Watford double. Those foolish thoughts were buried in the 65th minute when a young man, who still has pictures of Kerry Dixon on his wall, emulated his hero by scoring for Chelsea. John Harley ran the length of the pitch to get on the end of an inch-perfect Dan Petrescu cross before being mobbed by the fans in the lower tier of the Matthew Harding. Not surprisingly the youngster, who was yet to make 20 appearances for Chelsea, was the hero of the hour and even found himself being touted as a possible solution to

England manager Kevin Keegan's lack of left-sided players. 'John Harley is already one of the best left-sided players in the country,' said Vialli. 'He still needs to work hard on the defensive side of his game but to be fair to him, he has not been playing there for long. He needs to keep learning and improving but who knows, he might then get a chance to play for England.'

With the games coming thick and fast, Harley kept his place for the 1-0 Champions League defeat in Marseille. However, a few days later a tough trip to St James' Park saw Harley rested and bad boy Babayaro (forgiven after going AWOL) was restored to the side. For two men in particular, Chelsea's 1-0 victory was particularly pleasing. Firstly, goalkeeper Ed de Goey's clean sheet saw him break Peter Bonetti's club record of 21 clean sheets in one season. Secondly, Emerson Thome turned in another outstanding performance as he managed to lay a few ghosts from his last visit to St James' Park earlier in the season when he was part of the Sheffield Wednesday side beaten 8-0 by Alan Shearer and co. No one would deny the Brazilian his moment of joy at helping secure a Chelsea victory, 'It was such a wonderful feeling coming here today,' said the man nicknamed the Wall, 'especially after what happened the last time I was here. That 8-0 defeat left me feeling ashamed and it was my worst ever day in football. I had never lost a game more than 4-0 before that day. I knew it was going to be a hard game today because you are playing against Alan Shearer and Duncan Ferguson. I asked for Alan Shearer's shirt at the end of the game but he had promised it to someone else. Newcastle were also on a great run so we responded well. This was an important result for us and hopefully it will be an important step towards qualifying for the Champions League next season.'

Chelsea were unbeaten in eleven games and had not lost since 19 December. The win at St James' Park was crucial, especially as Manchester United had lost there 3-0 three weeks before and the Blues were due to face the Geordies in the FA Cup semi-final a month later. Vialli was happy with the three points and in his after-match appraisal of his team's performance he was quick to praise his under-fire centre half Frank Leboeuf. 'We are having a good run at the moment but need to keep it going. It was good to come here today and get three points and we should be proud of that. We defended well but we knew it was going to be a physical battle. Alan Shearer and Duncan Ferguson are two powerful forwards and Frank dealt with them really well.'

When Everton visited the Bridge, Vialli made one of his stranger tactical moves of the season as Wise was asked to play on the right hand side of midfield, while Jody Morris and Roberto Di Matteo were played centre midfield. With Wise in the best form of his career it was an unusual experiment to say the least. Vialli probably thought his decision was vindicated when Wise put Chelsea into the lead on the half hour. Sadly, out on the right, Wise was not his usual, effective self and Chelsea laboured painfully all afternoon and surprised few fans when Danny Cadamarteri nicked an equaliser with 20 minutes to go.

At Upton Park the following week, the 0-0 bore that took place earlier in the season at the Bridge was repeated. Vialli banned his players from talking to the press after the game. Was it because of how badly his side had played against a rather ordinary West Ham? Or rather that Steve Lomas accused Gus Poyet of smacking him in the face with his elbow? Vialli may have described the game as enjoyable but he was in a minority on that count, 'It is a difficult place to come to, to get three points but I still think we should have won today.'

Having failed to beat West Ham and then lost to Lazio, a disappointing week came to a conclusion when Southampton took a well-earned point from a 1-1 draw at the Bridge. However, it could have been a great deal worse had Southampton defender Dean Richards not managed to head home an aimless punt into the Saints' area to gift Chelsea an undeserved equaliser.

For the trip to Elland Road, the pressure was on Frank Leboeuf. Since his arrival from Sheffield Wednesday, Emerson Thome had missed only one league game, turning in a series of solid performances. But there was added pressure as, during his two previous appearances against Leeds, Leboeuf had received two red cards on each occasion and, having stamped all over Harry Kewell in December, he was guaranteed some stick from the fanatical Leeds supporters.

The Chelsea-Leeds match is traditionally explosive, but on this occasion referee Jeff Winter only reached for his yellow card twice for each side - Jody Morris and Chris Sutton being the Chelsea miscreants. The only flare-up followed straight after Smith elbowed Leboeuf in the face as players from both sides joined in a sixteen-man free-for-all. Stephen McPhail appeared to head-butt Jody Morris and Chris Sutton showed a rare turn of pace by sprinting forty yards to extract retribution on the young Leeds midfielder. The game was settled in the 63rd minute with John Harley starting and finishing the move that saw his second goal of the season grab all three points for Chelsea.

As it turned out, Leboeuf rose to the challenge and the occasion. Turning a deaf ear to the jeers, he turned in an inspirational performance in keeping his old adversary Harry Kewell quiet making sure Alan Smith caused little danger either.

The only mark Smith made on the game was a deliberate elbow in Leboeuf's face. Smith got booked and Leboeuf took the plaudits after the match from Gianluca Vialli. 'Frank was the best player on the pitch today. I am pleased for him. He got a lot of abuse out there today but it was marvellous how he responded putting in a performance like that.'

Chelsea's next game was one they had to win. The Champions League dream was still alive but with league form still inconsistent, the FA Cup was still the best chance of glory. The knives would be out for Vialli's foreign imports if they lost in the semi-final at Wembley. Many in the press thought they would come unstuck against a Newcastle side who surely could not lose at Wembley for the third year in succession. Vialli rotated his side once again, making a staggering six changes from the side that had beaten Barcelona. Out went Thome, Babayaro, Petrescu, Morris, Flo and Zola while in came Leboeuf, Harley, Di Matteo, Poyet, Weah and Sutton. This was no easy league game after the exertions of a midweek Champions League game, this was an FA Cup semi-final. Some said Vialli took a gamble. Perhaps, but it was more a reflection of his confidence in his playing personnel. Despite his recent departure, one of Vialli's strengths was that he seemed to know which eleven to put out to win important games such as this.

Newcastle dominated the early stages but it was Gus Poyet who broke the deadlock in the sixteenth minute. The Uruguayan started the move, receiving a quickly-taken free kick from Dennis Wise found Sutton who flicked the ball on to George Weah and Poyet was there when the Liberian pushed the ball through to him – he beat Shay Given with an exquisite lob. On 67 minutes Robert Lee pulled Newcastle back into the game and just when it seemed that Newcastle would go on to win the game Poyet scored a timely second goal five minutes later. John Harley had a below-par afternoon with Norbert Solano giving him the runaround in the first half. But with his first decent run down the left, he sent a perfect cross into the crowded Newcastle penalty area. There, waiting at the far post, was Poyet to head the winning goal and break Newcastle hearts at Wembley for the third successive season.

One Newcastle fan, though broken hearted after losing again at Wembley, at least had the consolation of going home with a rather valuable souvenir of the day from Gianfranco Zola. 'I was clapping the Chelsea lads as they came off,' Newcastle fan Tony Spooner later told the Newcastle programme. 'I was with most of the United fans behind the goal at the tunnel end and Zola caught my eye and indicated he wanted my shirt. I threw it down to him and he took his own off and insisted it was passed to me.' Despite being offered a king's ransom from Chelsea fans, the Geordie kept the prized shirt and gave it to his three-year-old daughter Amy as the medium-sized shirt of Zola would not fit Tony's extra large waist!

A few days later, Coventry were the visitors to Stamford Bridge. This was a potential banana skin as Coventry were the only team in the Premiership without an away win all season and their run had to come to an end some time. Vialli rotated his line up once more, making five changes from the victorious semi-final team. One significant inclusion was the return of Jody Morris to the centre of midfield. Following the disappointment of missing out on the semi-final, Morris was rewarded with the captaincy for the Coventry game.

For a young lad who had grown up on the West Kensington Estate in North End Road and had supported Chelsea as a boy, this was the highlight of his season. 'When I was told I was captain, I was really buzzing. I mean this was the team I supported as a boy. You can imagine how it felt to wear the armband. I didn't do anything different or anything like that. It was just a great, great honour. Keep the armband? No, I didn't take it home.'

Despite his critics, it demonstrated once again Vialli's skills as a man-manager. He had suffered more than most under the reign of Ruud Gullit, especially when he was left out of the 1997 FA Cup final, so he could empathise with Morris at missing out on such a big game. However, on one of the wettest nights of the year, Chelsea were slow to get going and fell behind to an eighteenth minute Gary McAllister effort. Gordon Strachan's men held out until half time but a couple of early second half substitutions turned the game Chelsea's way. Much to the crowd's displeasure Gus Poyet gave way to the normally ineffective Gabrielle Ambrosetti and Tore Andre Flo made way for George Weah. Surprisingly it was the Italian Ryan Giggs who proved to be the unlikely hero on the night. Within a matter of minutes, Ambrosetti sent a hard low cross into the Coventry penalty area that was intended for George Weah but the huge Liberian slid in and missed. Fortunately the pace of Ambrosetti's cross meant that Coventry defender Colin Hendry could do nothing but deflect the ball into his own net. Minutes later the other substitute George Weah crossed for Zola to score only his second of the season. For Chelsea fans with good memories, the last league goal the little Italian had scored was way back in August on the first day of the season. Chelsea won the game and as the fans queued at

Fulham Broadway and got a soaking for their troubles, most were talking of how inspirational Ambrosetti had been with his willingness to take his man on, his endless running and his crossing. He could even have got a couple of goals for himself. Having frustrated Chelsea fans for most of the season, the quiet Italian must have been pleased with his performance. I suppose, as the saying goes, everything comes to those who wait.

After the game, Vialli was a happy man. His clenched fist salute to the fans in the middle tier showed how badly he wanted to win the game. For a man who rarely displays emotion it showed how much he cared about Chelsea.

Despite the number of games Chelsea had played, team spirit had pulled them through, a fact he was quick to recognise: 'All round, our performance tonight was excellent. We wanted to win this game, you saw that. Our spirit was fantastic. We were superb tonight. This was always going to be a difficult game for us because of the conditions and because we have played so many games recently. Also, Coventry had not had a game for ten days and were much fresher than us. But we won the game and we played some very good football.'

The win and the valuable three points had once again put Chelsea back in contention for a Champions League place as they leapfrogged Arsenal and moved to within two points of Leeds who were in the third Champions League spot. One man who had other things on his mind after the game was Dennis Wise who was up before the FA on a misconduct charge the following day. Wise was convinced he would be found innocent, 'A lot has been said about the case that is just not true. I am sure I will be found innocent.'

The following day the Football Association fined Wise £7,500 for using insulting behaviour against Kenny Cunnningham but they clearly accepted that he was not responsible for the brawl that took place in the tunnel against Wimbledon on February 12. Referee Peter Jones' report into the fracas confirmed that no punches had been thrown by Wise. Wise had been accused of being the instigator by spraying Lucozade over Cunningham in the tunnel after the game. Another version of events was that Cunningham had suggested that Wise's team mate Chris Sutton had fathered his recently born baby Henry. Clearly, no fan believed that story with the £10 million striker's continual failure to hit the target all season!

Chelsea were fined £50,000 and found guilty of failing to control their players. The club had turned up at the hearing armed with evidence but reluctantly accepted the three-man commission's verdict. They had no points deducted, they still had their captain free of suspension and now they could concentrate on their trophy ambitions for the rest of the season. 'We feel aggrieved at the £50,000 fine. We believe we took all steps necessary,' said Colin Hutchinson. 'Our attitude is we acted reasonably with our stewards in trying to break up certain incidents.'

Anyone who has been in the Chelsea tunnel before a game will know there are more stewards in there than you can shake a stick at and Hutchinson confirmed that on the match in question Chelsea had at least six stewards on tunnel duty. 'Dennis pleaded not guilty to misconduct and violent conduct. We subsequently changed that to lesser charge of insulting behaviour. We came here to vigorously defend ourselves and we have done that.'

On the eleventh anniversary of the Hillsborough disaster Chelsea travelled to north to play Sheffield Wednesday. Before the game Ken Bates joined a small group of the bereaved families outside the stone memorial by the main stand for a minute's silence for Hillsborough victims. Bill Pemberton, whose son Roy was one of the 96 killed that day, laid a basket of red roses in his son's honour but as the moment became too much for him, Bates leant forward and hugged him. For the few people there it was a touching gesture and it showed a human side to the Chelsea chairman rarely seen in public.

With Wise and Ferrer missing and Zola rested, Chelsea still fielded a strong side on paper but it seemed as if everybody's mind was on the Barcelona game. De Goey brought down De Bilde and as he was the last man, most Chelsea fans expected the

Dutchman to walk, but Paul Durkin only issued a yellow card along with the penalty, which Wim Jonk scored. Things were not looking up as far as any Champions League ambitions were concerned. A win would have taken Chelsea above eventual qualifiers Leeds while defeat brought an end to Chelsea's sixteen match unbeaten run. Few Chelsea fans were fooled about the run as seven matches had been drawn and three of the draws had been at home in games Chelsea should have won, against Leicester, Everton and Southampton. In hindsight, if we had won those games we would have qualified for the Champions League next season.

Vialli confirmed everyone's suspicions afterwards, 'Nobody expected us to lose this game. But we were playing three days before probably the most important match in the club's history so mentally they had something more to give. We did not come here to lose the game, but subconsciously, the match against Barcelona was in the back of the players' minds and Sheffield Wednesday probably wanted to win more than we did. I want to play offensive and aggressive football. I want to press the opposition. But looking at the age of some of our players I know that this is almost impossible especially when you play 55 games in less than eight months.'

After the titanic disappointment of the Nou Camp it was back to domestic action and a last-gasp attempt to put the bitter memory of Barcelona behind them with qualification for the Champions League. A promising twenty-minute start, when a Gus Poyet goal gave the Blues the lead, soon diminished and the remainder of the match saw Chelsea's performance deteriorate rapidly. The greatest travesty of all for the 35,000 spectators present was to endure the substitution on 62 minutes of Chris Sutton for Gianfranco Zola, the one player likely to win the game for Chelsea. Not surprisingly the home crowd was in an unforgiving mood and the ground resounded to a chorus of booing. After the match Vialli was in an unrepentant mood:

'I make my decisions without taking note of what supporters think. I know not everyone agrees with me but it does not really matter. I have got to do whatever I think is right. We still have a chance to make the Champions League. It is difficult and we know that. The matches are coming thick and fast now. It will be interesting to see how we can play at United. They are the best team in England. We should have been more clinical, though, this season, especially against sides we expect to beat. But this is part of the learning process. We will learn the lessons and try to improve. Everyone wants to improve and sign new players to bridge the gap with United. At the moment they are a top class side and out of everybody's league. We have got to look at them and try to get there.'

Two days later Chelsea had the chance to take on the best when, having just won the Premier League title for the sixth time in eight years, travelling supporters hoped to gatecrash the Championship party by winning once again at Old Trafford. It did not bode well when Lambourde passed the ball back to Ed de Goey and in a similar fashion to a goal scored by Southampton's Kevin Davies three years previously, the Dutchman took too much time and saw his casual clearance hit Yorke on the shins and rebound into the net.

Although Petrescu and Zola then scored two quick goals to put the Blues in front, a Solskjaer strike just before half time and another from Yorke on 69 minutes gave United the points on a day when they did not get out of second gear. Sadly they did not have to, as second gear was still too much for a poor Chelsea to contend with.

Having watched Chelsea wave a white flag in surrender against a Manchester United only half-interested in playing football, Luca Vialli was doing his best to contain his anger in the post-match press conference. 'In the final month of this season I have to see who wants to stay at this club, who wants to make the club successful, who wants to die on the pitch for the club and who doesn't. The last four matches are important. There are nine points available. We have the FA Cup final and I am sure all the players want to play. I am not threatening anybody. We have done well in Europe this season but we are still not good enough in the League. We want to be there at the last match of the season with Manchester United, to be in the final of the Champions League and to do that we have to improve things.'

When questioned about whether or not he would still be at Chelsea for the following season Vialli was equally forthright, 'I am going to try and stay here. I am going to try to make Chelsea as good as I can. I am not worried about my own position. I might one day be fired, who knows? As part of the job I just to want to get on with it. I will be there doing my best for the club. If my best is not good enough then okay, they will obviously find someone else instead. I have twenty-three players. I signed most of them. I train them and I pick the team. If they are tired, which they looked against Manchester United, then it is down to me. They either train too much or not enough. I am the guy in charge. My future? I don't worry about that. I was given the opportunity to be the manager. One day I might be fired but all I can try to do is my best for the club. If my best enough is good enough, okay. Otherwise, they will find someone else. If my best is not good enough then that is someone else's decision.'

The warning fired by Vialli at his supposedly underachieving squad seemed to be heeded as, with a Champions League spot looking less and less likely, it was important that his side tried to finish in a UEFA Cup qualifying place rather than having to rely on winning the FA Cup to avoid the dreaded Inter Toto route into Europe.

Liverpool were the visitors for the penultimate home game at Stamford Bridge and they were still chasing a Champions League spot. But in one of Chelsea's most impressive home performances of the season, Gerard Houllier's side were beaten within the first fifteen minutes as the two new fathers in the Chelsea camp grabbed both goals for Chelsea.

After two minutes the recalled Di Matteo, in for the now out of favour Dan Petrescu, sent George Weah through on goal and the giant Liberian hammered the ball past Westerveld in the Liverpool goal. On thirteen minutes Weah returned the compliment by setting up Di Matteo for his first league goal of the season and the game was as good as over. Chelsea had chances to increase the lead but in front of their third largest crowd of the season, Vialli's side turned in a performance that restored their battered reputation, they had set themselves up nicely for the their final away game of the season against Arsenal and a chance to avenge that manic defeat back in October.

John Bumstead's winner ten years ago was the last time Chelsea recorded a league at Highbury, so revenge was long overdue. With eight of Vialli's eventual Wembley side in the starting line up and two more making appearances from the bench, it was clear that the players had something else on their minds two weeks hence. Vialli described his team's performance as sloppy and confirmed everyone's suspicions that his players' minds were on the FA Cup final. The fans had travelled to Highbury hoping that Chelsea would go for it as a UEFA Cup was still within their grasp, but left the ground desperately unhappy at such another below par Chelsea performance. The contrast between the two £10 million strikers was clearly evident. Both men had cost big money during the summer and while Sutton sat on the bench for the full ninety minutes, Thierry Henry continued a rich vein of goal scoring form, hitting both Arsenal's goals on a day when the minds of the Chelsea players seemed to be elsewhere.

And so to the final game of the season. Nine months after Chelsea had hammered Sunderland 4-0 on the opening day of the season at Stamford Bridge, there was a sense of déjà vu when Derby were routed on the final day of the season. The first half saw Derby keeper Mart Poom and the woodwork deny Tore Andre Flo at least a hat-trick that would have made him the first Chelsea striker to break the 20-goal barrier since Kerry Dixon. Two minutes into the second half, Zola broke the deadlock and then Poyet, Di Matteo and finally, and most deservedly, Flo himself scored in the last minute to round off an end-of-season showboating performance from Chelsea.

The following week the season reached a climax with the FA Cup final at Wembley. It was the last cup final to be played at the old stadium before demolition but those football fans expecting a classic final to give the old girl a good send off were very disappointed at the outcome.

Aston Villa seemed content to play a defensive game from the outset and it left to Chelsea to produce the goalmouth action the millions watching around the world had anticipated. Sadly, a stale first half produced little excitement but whatever Vialli and Rix said at half time spurred Chelsea into action and within ten minutes of the restart Dennis Wise had the ball in the net. Delighted though I was that Chelsea had scored, remembering that I had a fiver on Wise for first scorer and the beers would be on me tonight, it soon turned to disappointment. The cheers at the Chelsea end quickly evaporated as in the middle of the pitch I could see referee Graham Poll with his hand raised to signal the goal offside. The apparent culprit was George Weah and nearly £100 suddenly had evaporated from my back pocket. There are some bad referees in the Premier League no doubt, but why does Graham Poll continue to aggravate myself and other Chelsea fans? Earlier in the season Poll had even had the honour of being only the second referee after David Elleray to have his own song at Stamford Bridge. In my view though, 'Graham Poll is a fuckin' arsehole" does have a better ring to it then the plain old 'Elleray is a wanker.' Within seconds, the Graham Poll song had started and like a vocal Mexican wave it worked its way around the Chelsea end of the stadium.

The disallowed goal lifted the crowd and when Gerry Kelly from the Matthew Harding lower tier stood up and was counted down from ten to cry out 'Zigger Zagger' you could almost feel the hairs on the back your neck, as if the ghost of Micky Greenaway had been reincarnated in Gerry's body. The whole Chelsea end responded and with the crowd behind them in full voice, the game was only going to have one winner.

Poyet spurned a chance, Weah somehow missed one Chris Sutton would have put away and then Robbie Di Matteo, who only seems to score at Wembley these days, did it again. In 1997 it took him 43 seconds to get on the scoresheet. This time he had to wait 72 minutes longer but when the goal came it was worth waiting for.

Man of the Match 'Super Mario' Melchiot had made only five appearances all season through injury but Albert Ferrer's injury in Barcelona had opened the door for him to grab a cup final place. The Dutchman grasped the opportunity and having spent most of the afternoon keeping Benito Carbone quiet, he surged forward on a superb run that took him from one side of the pitch to the other, leaving four Villa players in his wake before Ian Taylor took his legs from him. Zola stepped up and took the free kick, Calamity James came out, flapped and missed, and there was Di Matteo for his third goal in a cup final for Chelsea. It was enough to win the game and put another trophy in the cabinet at Stamford Bridge. Having won the FA Cup only once in over 80 years, Chelsea had now won it twice in four seasons.

When Poll blew the final whistle at just before ten to five on Saturday, 20 May 2000 he brought the curtain down on the longest season in Chelsea's history. They had played 61 competitive games in all competitions with Ed de Goey missing only one of those games. Despite all the criticism of Vialli's side they had finished the season with a trophy, winning the last FA Cup before the most famous stadium was demolished.

So was it a bad season? Of course not. So we did not win the Premier League. So what. We do not have a divine right to win the Premier League and if, a few years ago, someone had said you would win the FA Cup, League Cup, Cup Winners' Cup and the European Super Cup most Chelsea fans were so desperate for success they would taken just one of them. The measure of how successful a football club has been is usually measured in what is in the trophy cabinet, so with an FA Cup won, season 1999/2000 must go down as a successful one.

From my own point of view, I always used to be a pessimist about Chelsea but now I tend to look for positives rather than negatives on the playing side. My memories of the 1999/2000 season are many from Gus' amazing goal on the opening day against the Mackems to Tore Andre Flo's amazing back heel on the last day of the season against Derby. When Kanu did the same up at Middlesbrough last season the press and *Match of the Day* went crazy over a wonder goal. Flo scores a carbon copy just over twelve months later and is lucky to get a few lines in most tabloid newspapers. Sandwiched in between were many joyous moments: our games with Feyenoord home and away, Wise's great goal in the San Siro, the 5-0 demolition of Galatasary and the eight minute, three-goal blitz against Barcelona. The only strange feeling I have is that although it was great to win the FA Cup again, it did not have the same feeling about it as when we won in 1997. For me the highlight of the 1999/2000 season were those eight minutes against Barcelona. Perhaps those eight minutes are the highlight of my Chelsea supporting career over the last thirty years. That is unless the 2000/01 football season can produce something even more special than that.

The 2000/01 season started perfectly for Chelsea with a convincing Charity Shield win over Manchester United with goals from new signing Jimmy Floyd Hasselbaink and the ever improving Mario Melchiot in the penultimate game played at the old Wembley stadium.

When, on the following Saturday, Chelsea beat their bogey side West Ham United 4-2 with goals from Hasselbaink, Zola and a double from new signing Mario Stanic, the pundits pre-season prediction of Chelsea being Manchester United's likeliest Premiership challengers seemed accurate.

Three days later however, an embarrassing 2-0 defeat at Bradford alerted outsiders that all was not well at Stamford Bridge and a boring 0-0 draw at Villa Park the following Sunday did little to dispel the doubters. The press were already readying their pens for the season's first managerial casualty.

When Arsenal skipper Tony Adams suggested, on the eve of the London 'derby' with Chelsea, that Vialli's days were numbered, Chelsea chairman Ken Bates blasted back in his programme column defending his under fire manager. Whereas Arsenal's comeback at Stamford Bridge last season as good as killed off Chelsea's Premier League intentions, their comeback this year as good as killed off Vialli's position as manager. Eagle-eyed observers the following Saturday at St James Park were quick to spot

Vialli's body language before, during and after the game and many felt the likeable Italian already had the look of a condemned man.

The pressure had been building on Vialli since the previous season and despite Bates dreaded vote of confidence, by 12 September he had finally pulled the plug on the most popular and successful manager in Chelsea's history.

With Chelsea only five games into the season, Bates could not claim the dismissal had been because of a disappointing start to the season. Vialli's agent, Athole Still, confirmed that the reason for his departure had been due to Vialli losing the confidence of key players. Still advised: 'Gianluca accepts that he has lost the confidence of some of the players and therefore accepts the club's prerogative in choosing to dismiss him. The spirit in the camp was not what he or Chelsea wanted to have.'

Having been present at the Civic Reception at Fulham Town Hall the day after last season's Cup Final, I witnessed some strange goings on among certain Chelsea players. Some were being very non-committal when asked if they would still be at Stamford Bridge in August. Rumour had it that some had already begun plotting the downfall of Vialli. During Euro 2000 gossip had risen from the French camp, where Chelsea had three players on duty, that Didier Deschamps was going to replace Vialli as Chelsea manager. Deschamps went to Valencia instead but that did not stop certain players undermining their manager at every opportunity from the moment pre season training began.

If the true reason had anything to do with the alleged training ground scuffle the day before his departure, which suggested to many that Vialli had lost the confidence of his players, that would be very sad. If there was any weakness on Vialli's part maybe it was his softness with his players. Had it been Alex Ferguson in charge the likes of Leboeuf and Zola, they would have been sold for undermining the manager's authority in the press. Managers must be allowed to manage and one of the main reasons for Chelsea's appointment of Claudio Ranieri was his reputation as a strict disciplinarian. It would also suggest that some of the current playing squad need taking down a peg or two.

However, one of the more worrying aspects of Ranieri's appointment was his later confirmation that he had been offered the job by Hutchinson 24 hours before Vialli got his P45. If this is true, it made a mockery of Hutchinson's claim that he had an in-tray full of applications from Europe's elite to succeed Vialli. It also debunked the official line that Chelsea had no one immediately in mind to replace Vialli.

Stranger still is Ken Bates role in this. For a man who wasted no time in disposing of Ruud Gullit he seems to have found the task of disposing of Vialli that much harder. In the Chelsea match programme against St Gallen he wrote, 'It was the most difficult and distressing action I have had to take. He goes with my affection, respect and tremendous best wishes.'

For once, I believe Bates meant every word of that statement. He thought the world of Vialli and having only a week earlier given him his vote of confidence, it seems strange that he was party to a decision to get rid of a man he had so much respect for.

Perhaps Bates would be the first to admit that, having devoted all his time to his beloved Chelsea Village, he might have taken his eye off the playing side for too long. He has already given control of the day-to-day running of the football club to Colin Hutchinson and perhaps on this occasion he has lent Hutchinson too much control, allowing himself to be persuaded that a change of manager was necessary.

Then again, perhaps Ranieri needs to be successful not just for his own sake but also for Colin Hutchinson's. Ken Bates might later come to rue being persuaded to get rid of a man he had previously said had a job for life at Stamford Bridge. Maybe the Chelsea fan who is rumoured to have already placed a bet on Vialli returning as manager of Chelsea knows more than he is letting on!

Stranger still is the role that agent Vicenzo Morabito seems to have in the whole affair. Vicenzo Morabito who he? I hear many Chelsea fans ask. His name was linked with the Brian Laudrup saga two seasons ago as a result Morabito was well known to managing director Colin Hutchinson.

More recently Morabito's name hit the headlines when Chelsea made a £7.5 million bid for Ajax star Jesper Gronkjaer as a result of which the player openly criticised his agent for negotiating with Chelsea without his authority. It was later revealed that Morabito also happens to represent Claudio Ranieri now manager of Chelsea. So was Chelsea's manager trying to buy a player with whom he shared an agent or was this a mere coincidence?

Rumour has it that Morabito also represents Jimmy Floyd Hasselbaink and Winston Bogarde, the player who, it was alleged, had been signed without Gianluca Vialli's knowledge. This suggestion was hotly refuted by Colin Hutchinson at the time, 'Like all the transfers during Luca's time here the signing of Winston Bogarde was carried out with his full knowledge and authority. To suggest anything else was the case is absolute nonsense.' Fair enough, but you do begin to wonder whether, unbeknown to Vialli, his days were numbered long before he finally got his marching orders on September 12.

Add to this the uncomfortable fact that the recent personnel changes at Chelsea Football Club have clearly been to Vicenzo Morabito's benefit and the whole situation begins to smell decidedly whiffy.

Admittedly, it would take a more detailed investigation of the paper trail to discover who Morabito does and does not represent. But if it is true that Hasselbaink, Bogarde and Ranieri share the same agent, it makes it hard to believe that the decision to dispose of Vialli was taken on September 12 2000. If on their travels any investigators also discovered that Morabito not only represents both the manager and players at Chelsea but also influential non-playing members of staff as well - the waters surrounding Luca's departure could get murkier still.

So who is the new manager of Chelsea? Claudio Ranieri was born in Rome in 1951 and his playing career took him from his home club Roma to Catanzaro and later Catania. After making his name as a coach at Cagliari, Ranieri moved to Napoli in

1991 where one of the players in his side was a young Gianfranco Zola. After coaching Napoli for two seasons he joined Fiorentina in 1993 and earned them promotion to Serie A in his first season. Soon after, Ranieri's won the Coppa Italia and followed that by winning the Italian Super Cup the same year.

He was headhunted by Spanish side Valencia in 1997 where he won the Coppa Del Rey (Spanish Cup) and gained qualification to the Champions League. It was the Ranieri constructed Valencia side that set the Champions League a light last season where they made the final only to lose to Real Madrid. By then, Ranieri had become coach of the other Madrid side Athletico. But in joining Athletico he found himself working for Jesus Gil, a chairman who makes Ken Bates look timid in comparison. Sadly his time at Madrid was not memorable. Madrid went into administration after Gil was sent to jail and Ranieri resigned as coach in March before his side were relegated at the end of the season.

So what will Ranieri bring to Chelsea? Despite not winning a title in all his years as coach, the Italian is clearly very experienced and has the distinct advantage of having worked previously with both Zola and Hasselbaink. His nickname in Italy was the 'Man of Steel' and he has a reputation as a strict disciplinarian. Clearly there are some players at Chelsea with rather large egos who need taking down a peg or two so he will have his work cut out but the early signs are promising.

Aside from the fiasco in Switzerland against St Gallen, Ranieri's early results have shown promise and despite the Blues poor start, most bookmakers are still only giving short odds on a Chelsea title win. The premature sacking of Vialli may still mean they have a transitional season. Let's hope our latest Italian manager receives longer shrift than the last one.

Chelsea Village - A Blue Tomorrow?

Back in the early 1970s Chelsea embarked on an ambitious ground development programme to build a soccer stadium second-to-none in Europe. The first stage involved the construction of the East Stand in 1974 which was proposed to be, in then chairman Brian Mears' words, 'the beginning of a new era in the history of Chelsea Football Club'. Instead Chelsea were relegated that season. Within two years, the club had accrued over £3 million worth of debts and Chelsea, in Mears' words, were 'in very serious trouble'.

The purchase of the freehold of Stamford Bridge from the J.T Mears Trustees had not been scheduled until May 1974. However, with Chelsea riding the crest of a wave both on and off the pitch, the board gave the go-ahead to purchase the freehold for £475,000 and began the redevelopment of Stamford Bridge.

The East Stand was the first stage of an ambitious project aimed at turning Stamford Bridge into an all-seater, 60,000 capacity stadium equipped with restaurants, executive boxes, and a direct pedestrian link from Fulham Broadway Station, an issue that has remained a bone of contention between the club and Hammersmith and Fulham Council ever since.

What Mears and his directors could not have foreseen was a deepening recession in the mid-seventies, the onset of the three-day week and soaring inflation that led to the stand being over budget and past its deadline. Unfortunately, the board of directors failed to insert any penalty clauses into the construction company's contract. As a result, when the recession kicked in, the board and the club had no comeback.

Although he would not thank me for saying it, the plans of Brian Mears and Ken Bates are very similar. In Mears' redeveloped stadium there were to be restaurants, a banqueting hall and 156 executive boxes. Like Bates, he recognised that football clubs were only making best use of their stadia on 25 to 30 days a year, during the rest of the year the stadium lay idle. The only difference and it is a major difference, is that Bates finished his ground redevelopment while Mears fell at the first hurdle.

As if to underline their similarity, read the following statement and see if you can work out which of the two made it. 'How we harness our earning power to maximum advantage is something to which we are giving the greatest thought at Chelsea. Most certainly ways and means of doing so need to be found. Naturally, we hope our all-seater arena will be considered for European finals and FA Cup semi-finals. I would like to think the new Stamford Bridge will have big earning potential in its off the field activities, with a restaurant open to the public for lunch and dinner every day of the week and a banqueting hall that should appeal to industry as a conference centre so near to London's West End.'

Close your eyes and you can imagine Ken Bates making that speech, bridling with ambition, at the centre of today's satellite powered football renaissance. Instead the words belong to his predecessor, Mr Mears, during the pre-recession early 70s. They clearly thought along similar lines, so Ken Bates' vision concerning Stamford Bridge as a commercial and leisure area and the creation of an income stream independent of supporters coming through the turnstiles, is not unique.

Bates' first ten years as chairman of Chelsea were spent battling the likes of Marler Estates and Cabra to keep football at Stamford Bridge. Since the Royal Bank of Scotland purchased the freehold of the ground in 1992 and effectively 'saved the Bridge' Bates has been able to concentrate on a more ambitious plan to turn Stamford Bridge into the leisure and entertainment complex outlined above.

The future Chelsea chairman was brought up in Hanwell, West London, the son of a London bus painter. He went to Ealing County Grammar School and played for Chase of Chertsey, a famous breeding ground for Arsenal. However a club foot and a motor cycle accident in 1952 saw him drift away from the game to devote his attention to running a quarry in Lancashire.

As a young man, he supported Queens Park Rangers, but living in the north he chanced upon Oldham Athletic and became the Football League's youngest-ever chairman when he took control of the club just before Christmas 1965. His fearsome reputation was swiftly built, as an Oldham director commented, 'Ken Bates believes in a committee of two, with one absent.' Bates' business commitments later took him away from Oldham and around the world. After living in Monte Carlo for a couple of years, he returned to England in 1981 and moved to Grange Farm, a 270-acre dairy farm in Beaconsfield, Buckinghamshire.

There his connection with Chelsea grew from an unlikely friendship between Bates' wife and the wife of the then chairman Brian Mears. A chance meeting became a friendship and Bates and his wife Pam were soon regular guests at Stamford Bridge. Almost inevitably Bates swiftly fell out with Mears but succeeded in making enough friends at the club to maintain contact with the club's financial controller Martin Spencer. Spencer kept Bates abreast of the looming financial crisis about to hit Chelsea and within a matter of months, Mears' chairmanship became untenable when he was unable to pay the players' wages. Things looked bleak at Stamford Bridge.

With the club facing extinction, Spencer set up a meeting

at Amhurst Brown's offices in Duke Street. Bates met the Chelsea board of David Mears, Viscount Chelsea and Spencer himself on Friday 1 April 1982 to determine the future of the club. By 8.45pm that evening Bates had bought Chelsea Football Club for £1 but inherited debts of more than £2 million. In the process he had taken on an enormous task. The club was losing £12,000 a week and had a group of players who had not been paid for several weeks.

As part of the purchase of the football club, however, Bates did not buy the ground from Stamford Bridge property company but opted instead to take it on a seven-year lease. Meanwhile, behind Bates' back, Mears sold the freehold of the ground to property developers Marler Estates. With the boom in the eighties property market, the value of Stamford Bridge rose. Marler Estates soon passed on their interest to another developer, Cabra, and they asked Chelsea for £40 million to buy the freehold. The only alternative to raising the asking price was for Chelsea to vacate the ground and find a new home. Clearly Chelsea were nowhere near raising the £40 million required.

In apparent desperation Bates appealed to the club's supporters to help raise the money for the freehold. The 'Save the Bridge' campaign was born and Colin Hutchinson was brought in as its chief. Bates had calculated that on the club's average gate of 17,000, sufficient money could be raised if every supporter made a donation to the campaign. In the programme for the home game against Southampton on 20 April 1987 he made this plea:

'The future of Chelsea Football Club is under threat, as you well know, from property speculators who intend to terminate football at Stamford Bridge in order to develop the site for commercial profit. It isn't an idle threat, one that will blow away on the winds of time; it is a serious declaration of intention to destroy our very heritage. I don't intend to let that happen but it's going to be one hell of a battle. In my five years at Stamford Bridge, within reason, I have always tried to follow through with what was wanted for the good of Chelsea Football Club but this one is too big for one man. I need your help. Never before have you been able to be such an important part of history because believe me; the future of Stamford Bridge lies in your hands.

'Our average gate this season is around 17,000. If you all gave £1000 then we will have more than achieved our target. Obviously I don't expect you all to cough up that sort of money for there are poor people, old people and children amongst you, but there are some who can afford more than that and their donations will help compensate for those who are not so well off.'

With Chelsea fans already paying the highest prices in the country, Bates' suggestions found little favour among supporters so he was soon looking to alternative methods to raise the money to keep Chelsea at the Bridge. Aided by the slump in the late eighties London property market, Bates survived until the early nineties when he set up Chelsea Village. From there his dream finally began to take shape.

Bates' vision, as has been mentioned, had always been to transform Stamford Bridge from somewhere where football was played 25 to 30 times a year, to an all-year round leisure and entertainment complex with such a variety of income streams that the club need not be dependent on fickle supporters and footballing fortune. Following the end of his battle with Cabra, when the Royal Bank of Scotland purchased the freehold in December 1992, the chairman's (and the club's) fortunes changed for the better. Bates took out a lease ensuring that Chelsea could purchase the site at any time before 2012 for £16.5 million. At last, the deal offered Chelsea the opportunity to catch up on their Premiership rivals and re-develop the ground into a 40,000 all-seater stadium.

Soon after, Bates put Chelsea Football and Athletic Club (the old company that owned the club) into liquidation and set up a new company, Chelsea Village. The Village aimed to provide a new complex at the home of Chelsea Football Club, which would include shops, offices, bars, restaurants, a hotel and a sports and leisure centre. Bates' ambition was for Chelsea Village to be, 'the Covent Garden of West London, the profits from which should enable Chelsea Football Club to implement a policy of continuous improvement of playing staff and facilities towards achieving our soccer ambitions.' Under Bates' plans, even if the team hit bad times once again and heaven forbid, were relegated, the club would retain a sound financial footing irrespective of attendance figures, buoyed by the revenue from their bars, restaurants, shops and hotels.

The new Stamford Bridge development began with the building of the North Stand in November 1994, financed primarily by the late Matthew Harding whose name the stand now bears. £2.06 million of the money came in the form of a grant from the Football Trust, while the remaining £5 million came from Harding in the form of convertible loan stock. In return, Harding was invited to join the Board of both Chelsea Village Limited and Chelsea Football Club as a non-executive director.

In the early days of their relationship things went well between Bates and Harding. By 1995, Bates had even confided in Harding that by 2002, having been in charge for twenty years, he planned to stand down as chairman. He advised the chairman-in-waiting that he would go on a three-month cruise, time enough for Harding to establish himself as chairman of the club. Soon however, Harding and Bates fell out over the direction Chelsea Village should take. Bates was keen to develop non-football related activities, while Harding felt the chairman should be developing the playing side, convinced that a successful team would bring in additional revenue.

Harding was also unhappy about who actually owned Chelsea Village and, despite many man-hours and thousands of pounds devoted to the trail, he never got a satisfactory answer.

Bates' answer, from that day to this, is that the people who own Chelsea Village are those who have been there since the start of his reign. In his programme notes for the Champions League game against Marseille last season he wrote: 'For the information of the great majority of Chelsea supporters, they are the same people who backed my appointment in 1982 when I completed the purchase of Chelsea Football Club and became

Chairman. If they are now sitting on a nice profit following their 18-year-old investment, good luck to them.'

The people involved include Stewart Thompson and Dr Ashraf Marwan. Bates describes Marwan as an Egyptian financier, whereas the News of the World claimed in November 1995 that Marwan was 'an international arms dealer who has been quizzed by Special Branch'. Irrespective of who Marwan is, he owns 1.4 million shares in Chelsea Village and he gave Bates £2 million to assist him in his battle with Harding. Meanwhile Thompson, who invested £500,000 in Chelsea Village in the early days, is another of Chelsea Village's owners. Both Marwan and Thompson helped Bates when he needed it most and he has never forgotten the vital assistance their finances have offered – without this help it is almost certain that Bates would not still be Chelsea chairman.

Following the deterioration of his relationship with Harding, Bates went looking elsewhere to raise the money for Chelsea Village. In 1996 he floated Chelsea Village on the Alternative Investment Market (AIM). At the launch, Chelsea Village announced that of the 102 million shares in existence, 9 million were to be made available at 55p each. Four years later the shares are worth between 60 and 70 pence (64p at the time of writing), although in January 2000 they fell back to their original 55p level

When Chelsea Village was floated on AIM in 1996 several thousand Chelsea fans bought shares, partly out of loyalty, partly because they thought they were doing their bit for the club. Clearly the majority of these fans did not purchase these shares with a view to making a quick profit (if you did, shame on you) so will not be too disturbed that the value of their shares remains the same as it was four years ago.

However, most of the Chelsea Village shares have been bought by City investors rather than supporters. They will be looking for profit and these investors have had nothing to show for their money to date. The share price has remained steady for most of the current year, which has done Bates no harm whatsoever. However the fact remains that the

City will expect dividends sooner rather than later.

To add to this uncertainty, there remains the question of the future of the Chelsea chairmanship. Inevitably, Bates will soon retire or pass on – even he cannot live forever, although I'm in no doubt that he will have a damn good try. As he has said in the past, 'I don't care what's written on my tomb. Not that I'm thinking of going. In fact, I'm still negotiating with the guy upstairs but we haven't agreed terms yet because Heaven may not be big enough for the both of us.' But when Bates has his judgement day what will happen then? Will the new chairmen put the interests of the shareholders of Chelsea Village before the interests of the fans? As an example of the frustrations facing investors let us analyse two people desperate for a dramatic rise in the price of Chelsea Village shares. They also happen to be employees of Chelsea Village.

In 2000, the new Chelsea Village chief executive Peter Bewsey and his financial secretary Michael Russell have both invested in the company they work for.

Between March and May, Bewsey invested £29,700 of his own money as the table below indicates:

Date	Shares Bought	Price	Total Cost
8/3/00	10,000	77p	£7,700
13/3/00	10,000	83p	£8,300
29/3/00	10,000	77p	£7,700
19/5/00	10,000	60p	£6,000
Total			**£29,700**

Michael Russell, Chelsea Village Financial Secretary, knows a thing or too about accounting and investment so he erred on the side of caution, buying one batch of shares in March which set him back the smaller sum of £2,850.

Perhaps this investment was all part of Ken Bates' employment criteria that employees must hold a minimum stake in Chelsea Village... Whatever the reason, both investors have seen the value of their shares plummet faster than Chris Sutton's transfer value. Clearly, like the supporters, they are not investing in Chelsea Village to make a fast profit. Indeed the only person who has made a clear profit from his shares is Ken Bates himself. On a personal note, I do not begrudge Bates the money; after all, he saved the club but not all supporters see things that way.

Fans who regularly surf the internet will have probably discovered the web site run by a group calling themselves the Chelsea Action Group. These individuals have, to date, remained anonymous but use nom-de-plumes of Chelsea players of yesteryear such as Alex Donald who played for Chelsea between 1930-1932, Joe Walton (1906-1911) and Charlie Cooke. This is what they had to say about Ken Bates and his shares in Chelsea Village:

'This week's Sunday Times UK rich list placed current Chelsea chairman Ken Bates 878th with a personal wealth of £34million. The question is, why does such a wealthy man never put any money back into the club from whence his wealth came? His current wealth is the result of gradually selling off his shares in the club, er... sorry, Chelsea Village, over the past three years making large personal profits which are now lost to the club. Between Bates and his 'Mystery Shareholders' they have reduced their shareholding from 100% to approximately 54%, mostly between 1996/97 when the share price was at its most buoyant. A conservative figure for these profits would be £70-£100 million pounds – all in their offshore pockets and never to return to the Bridge. In fact, this is a similar figure to the amount of debt that Bates has saddled Chelsea Village with due to the ludicrous high interest bonds taken out, which will have to be repaid long after Bates has retired to his offshore island.'

Ironically, the money Bates earned through a rise in Chelsea Village's share price can be traced to the fate of his old adversary Matthew Harding. Chelsea Village's shares had their highest rise in October 1996 when Harding, who had invested substantially in the club, was killed in a helicopter crash. By that time, Bates had severed his ties both personally and financially with the man he at one stage had groomed as his successor.

Following Harding's death there remained the small matter of funding the rest of the Chelsea Village development. To achieve this, Bates borrowed and borrowed big. He agreed a ten-year Euro bond deal with SBC Warburg Dillon Read that meant Chelsea could purchase the freehold of Stamford Bridge for £16.5 million and he borrowed £75 million in total to cover the costs of the Chelsea Village development.

The result is the current situation at Chelsea, where in order to pay for the development of hotels, apartments and restaurants, Chelsea Village must repay £6 million interest per year over ten years which means that Bates and his board will have paid back £135 million by 2007. Chelsea Village's daily interest payments come to £16,000 – a figure that dwarfs the wages of Desailly, Leboeuf, Hasselbaink and Zola. It remains a cause for concern that in this age of hyper-inflated players' wages, the biggest individual outgoing at the club remains the huge interest on this loan.

If, as a concerned supporter, you wish to test the popularity of Chelsea's latest investments and the reason we pay £112,000 a week in interest nip into Arkles, Fishnets or the Shed Bar on a non-match day and take a look at the shiny new face of Chelsea Village. You will swiftly establish that none of these establishments are bursting at the seams. Indeed in Arkles and Fishnets be prepared to be outnumbered by the staff. It is still only on a match day that these places fill to the brim and, although they are undoubtedly popular fans – form a lengthy and orderly queue to get into the Shed Bar and you are lucky if you can get a table at any of the club's restaurants – Bates' dream of expanding the number of days the ground turns a profit is still some way off.

Which brings us neatly around to the conundrum of what exactly Chelsea Village is and where the football club fits into the equation. At the last count there were 39 subsidiary companies of Chelsea Village, which included the following:

Chelsea Village Catering Ltd
Chelsea Village Merchandising Ltd
Chelsea Vintners Ltd
Chelsea Village Hotels Ltd
Chelsea Car Parks Ltd
Chelsea Worldwide Travel Ltd
Bulmer Travel Associates Ltd
Elizabeth Duff Travel Ltd
EDT European Travel Ltd
Chelsea Leisure Services Ltd
Chelsea Television Ltd
Chelsea Village Travel Ltd
Chelsea Pensioner Ltd
Fulham Securities Ltd
Stamford Bridge Properties Ltd
Stamford Bridge Securities Ltd
Chelsea Financial Consultants Ltd
Chelsea Pacific Ltd
London Voice Ltd
Chelsea Ltd
Chelsea Stadium Ltd

Chelsea Football Club is a subsidiary company under the Chelsea Village moniker and it has, in recent years, followed the trend towards 'expanding the brand', following the example of Manchester United. But Chelsea have gone much further than their Mancunian rivals – you can now book your holiday, insure your car, insure your house, use your Chelsea credit card, take out a loan or open a building society account under the umbrella of Chelsea Football Club.

As far as the football club itself is concerned, the future impact of pay-per-view and the money recently negotiated in the latest television deals means football is now talked about in terms of billions rather than millions. Chelsea's continued on-field success should mean that serious money should fall into the club's coffers over the next few years. There is also continued talk of a European Super League but if that fails to materialise, Chelsea's continued presence in the Champions League will become a necessity if the club are to survive.

All of which means that while qualification for the 2000/01 UEFA Cup was wonderful for supporters with bad memories of our struggles against relegation, it still left Chelsea short of the type of funds which would make Ken's accountants happy. Put simply, for Chelsea Village to thrive the club need to play in the Champions League every season, rather than once every forty-four years.

Some fans worry about the club's debt. In particular they are concerned that if the hotel and restaurants fail to produce and the non-football related income predicted in the original estimates fails to materialise, the club could find themselves in the same near-bankrupt position as they suffered throughout the mid-70s.

From his earliest days as chairman, Bates has always described Chelsea as being 'only fifteen minutes from Harrods', his vision that Chelsea should not just be a football club. He has more recently described Chelsea Village as the 'Covent Garden of West London' while his vision for the club was one where the subsidiary businesses of Chelsea Village would subsidise the football side of the business.

Therefore it was always intended that Chelsea Village with its hotels, restaurants and luxury apartments would be a thriving community to rival the West End on any Friday, Saturday or Sunday night.

So why isn't Chelsea Village making a fortune? After all, at no time in their history have Chelsea been as successful as they are now. Every game is a sell-out, there is regular revenue from playing in European, the apartments have all been sold, there are two hotels on site, two megastores (one at the ground and one in Guildford) there are restaurants, a nightclub, car parks, the Galleria, a radio station, the TV channel, the travel companies, banking and insurance, the credit card, the Gourmet Club, the

Racing Club and other 'high-class revenue streams' – they should all be pouring their profits into the Village. Oh, and the team's not bad either, pulling in 42,000 fans every week. Add to this the fact that despite only finishing fifth in the Premier League last season Chelsea are, after Manchester United, the second biggest club in the country and the gloom and despondency surrounding Chelsea Village plc enters the world of the unexplained.

Clearly the football side of the business is not the problem and despite Chelsea Football Club being a subsidiary of Chelsea Village, football remains the 'core business' of the company – if the team is successful then the company should profit accordingly. Conversely, if the football club fails, Chelsea Village fails - but the board's vision has always held that a successful football club was something that would be enhanced by the other companies. At the moment the football club is enhancing Chelsea Village and despite the success on the pitch the share price stubbornly refuses to rise or fall. Even the departure of Gianluca Vialli in September has had little impact.

In 1996/97 Chelsea's turnover was £23.7 million, which represented a 49% increase on the previous year. However the wage bill at the time saw to it that Chelsea recorded a loss of £376,000. By 1999, the club's turnover had risen to a staggering £88.3 million (although £30 million came as a result of the acquisition of EDT), the turnover on the football side was £37.1 million as the accounts below indicate.

Chelsea Village accounts	**1998**	**1999**
Turnover (£m)	**91.5**	**88.3**
Gross Profit	**20.7**	**20.4**
Operating Profit	**4.9**	**4.8**
(Loss)/Profit Before Taxation	**(0.5)**	**2.1**
Earnings per share	**(0.4p)**	**1.3p**
Adjusted earnings per share	**1.3p**	**3.3p**
Fixed assets	**140.3**	**121.9**
Shareholders' funds	**69.5**	**64.7**

This was the highest turnover of any of the Premiership plcs. It was higher than Manchester United's turnover of £87.8 million, more than rivals Tottenham and equal to Arsenal, despite the Gunners doing the domestic double the previous season. Alan Shaw, group secretary of Chelsea Village, said at the time, 'Ken Bates' vision was always to make us a Premier League Club, but one that didn't rely on gate receipts.' So has his vision approached reality?

At Chelsea Village's Annual General Meeting last October, the end of year accounts were presented with a loss of half a million pounds. Although the operating profit (£4.9m) was slightly higher than the previous financial year (£4.8m), the albatross round the club's neck in the shape of £7 million-worth of interest repayments saw the Village lose money.

In 1998/99 Chelsea Football Club was the most profitable part of Chelsea Village plc earning £44 million. However, although it was the most profitable part of the organisation it also incurred the most expenditure as, during the 1998/99 season players' wages increased by 18% from £22.5 million to £26.5 million. The wages of Desailly and co represent nearly 30% of Chelsea Village's current turnover or 60% of the Football Club's turnover.

Credit has to be given to the Chelsea board who, a few years ago, decided to speculate to accumulate and, while other Premier League chairmen such as Sir Alan Sugar pontificated about Carlos Kickaballs, Chelsea have reaped what they have sown. There is no doubt that the decision to purchase quality foreign internationals has put Chelsea into the big time. So while George Graham seems intent on turning Tottenham into Wimbledon Mark II, Chelsea continue to challenge for the unofficial title of top London club. The result can be seen at each sell-out home game. The club now has 19,000 season ticket holders, 40,000 club members and according to the Chelsea directors, a support base that has risen from 650,000 to 900,000 in the last three years. Chelsea also play in Europe every season so the players can test themselves against some of the best sides on the continent.

So why do some Chelsea fans remain pessimistic about Chelsea Village? After all with the signings of Jimmy Floyd Hasselbaink, Gudjohnsen, Panucci, and Stanic, Chelsea have spent £25 million on transfers during the summer, surely the financial side of the club has never looked better. Season ticket sales have brought in a staggering £16 million this season, an amount that clearly helped the recently-departed Gianluca Vialli's spending over the summer. The 2000/01 season is the first time in Chelsea's history that they have sold out of season tickets.

Part of the reason for disquiet among supporters is the loss of fellow fans who find themselves unable to afford to watch their beloved team these days. Although season ticket prices have remained steady in recent years, one of the costs of bringing big name players to Chelsea, building a new stadium and creating the financial viability to take Chelsea into the next century is that some less well-off Chelsea fans have found it impossible to afford to come to Chelsea as often as they would like, if at all.

These are the same fans that supported the club through thick and thin, spent their whole lives following the team all over the country and now find themselves frozen out by both ticket prices and availability. They have probably spent thousands of pounds on the club over the years but more and more of them find it difficult to keep going.

Bates has always defended the club's pricing policy robustly and when the prices of Chelsea's season tickets and the reintroduction of Category A and Category B games incurred fans' wrath before the start of the season, he was quick to respond:

'We are not the highest priced club for season tickets,' he said. 'We are behind Arsenal and we are behind Tottenham. As for fans that pay on the day, there has been an increase. We have reverted back to the category system for each of our home matches. There are six Category A games, Arsenal, Leeds, Tottenham, West Ham, Liverpool and Manchester United and for these matches, the prices have gone up £5. But for the B matches, they have gone up by a pound. I would not call those increases outrageous.'

In response, one anonymous Chelsea fan spoke for many when he pointed to the ever-increasing prices and Bates' obsession with Chelsea Village as an example of how supporters feel more alienated and less welcome at a club they love dearly.

'I have not renewed my season ticket because I felt that I should show some solidarity with my pals (who were unable to afford the continual increase), and to be honest after fifty years of going together I could not face going on my own. Last season, half the ground seemed to be full of tourists and first-timers. It goes without saying that a crowd of strangers is not going to create the same atmosphere as a crowd of friends. In the old days it was football, it was special. In the old days it was a Club, as a fan you felt you mattered. Today it is Chelsea Village, a leisure activity, and loyalty is measured by how much you can spend rather than how much you care. The life long emotional bond that forms between a football club and its supporters is now almost a weakness, there to be exploited by the money drunk millionaires that have taken over our sacred game. And we are Chelsea supporters, the most loyal and most committed of the lot! I must admit I caught myself a few times last season almost wondering where I was, it just felt so different to the Stamford Bridge that I had spent so much of my life in.'

Another issue that has cast a shadow over Bates' plans has been the long drawn-out planning enquiry regarding the upper tier of the West Stand. Plans were put in three seasons ago but the debate went on for two years. Although the building work is now going ahead at a rapid pace, Chelsea fans will not get to sit in the upper tiers of the West Stand until towards the end of the current season at the earliest.

The planning enquiry came about as a result of a dispute between Bates and his former allies at Hammersmith and Fulham Council regarding the extra commercial activity taking place at Chelsea Village.

The saga came to an end on 11 November 1999 when Chelsea finally received planning permission from Christopher Jarvis of the Independent Planning Inspectorate for the completion of the West Stand. Ken Bates immediately claimed victory,. 'It's been a long drawn out enquiry but we have got 85% to 90% of what we wanted. We now plan to start work in March and the West Stand should be finished by the end of next season. We got our sports and leisure centre,' he added, 'we got our museum, we got our hotels, we got our nightclubs, and we got the Galleria. You have to ask yourself what the fuss was about.'

However, if you logged onto Hammersmith and Fulham Council's web site the local council were also celebrating victory with some of the conditions the inspector had granted to limit the use of Chelsea Village on non-match days. 'We are very pleased with the outcome, the inspector has come up with some very sensible conclusions that will please both residents and the club,' said Cllr Michael Cartwright, who sat on the council's Environment Committee.

'Ken Bates called for the inquiry and if he had not been so stubborn throughout our protracted negotiations, the West Stand could have been sorted out two years ago. This council has always supported the football club and completion of the West Stand. However, Chelsea constantly delayed matters by not coming clean about the amount of commercial activity they envisaged taking place outside of normal match days. Residents expect disturbance and disruption in and around Stamford Bridge for home games. But it was unreasonable for Chelsea not to divulge the full extent of their plans for further development that may have included conferences, concerts, parties and other commercial activities to the council. The council has already successfully prosecuted the club over misuse of its facilities when a New Year's Eve party, due to finish at 1.00am, was still swinging at three in the morning. This sort of behaviour has caused local residents no end of grief and the council has a responsibility to protect the quality of their lives. If we had granted permission for the West Stand without proper conditions there would have been no way back.

'Chelsea now have a football ground with leisure activities attached. Our great fear was that they would have a massive leisure complex with a football ground attached. I am pleased with the inspector's findings and now hope we can enjoy good relations with the club once again.'

Hammersmith and Fulham Council had been negotiating with Bates and Chelsea Village and despite a good working relationship over the years, they had fallen out about the use of the function rooms at Chelsea Village. Before the results of the planning enquiry were known, Bates had his own views on the likely outcome.

'We have got six function rooms and an exhibition hall. We want to be able to use them away from match days. I also think we will get consent for that. The argument will be around the hours of use and again I think that's somewhat academic because 'unofficially' that has been agreed. So if the inspectorate puts the rubber stamp on it we can't be buggered about by any jobsworth at the Town Hall. We have had good relations with the Council for years and, rather like a marriage, it's going through a bad patch.'

In the end the Planning Inspectorate's main findings were:

- **PLANNING PERMISSION GRANTED FOR THE WHOLE WEST STAND DEVELOPMENT BUT WITH NOISE MITIGATION LEVELS EXTENDED BEFORE ITS USE**
- **PERMISSION GRANTED FOR THE COURT HOTEL AND THE USE OF THE RESTAURANT BETWEEN 6.00 AM AND 12 NOON, BUT SUBJECT TO REVIEW**
- **PERMISSION GRANTED FOR BLUEBELLS NIGHTCLUB TO STAY OPEN UNTIL 1.00AM MONDAY TO FRIDAY AND TO 2.00 AM SATURDAY TO SUNDAY.**
- **PERMISSION GRANTED FOR THE SPORTS AND LEISURE CLUB.**
- **PERMISSION GRANTED FOR THE GALLERIA TO BE USED FOR FUNCTIONS OTHER THAN ANCILLARY TO FOOTBALL.**

Although he had granted planning permission to most Chelsea Village demands, the Planning Inspector restricted late night activities within the Chelsea Village complex. In addition, he severely restricted the total number of people using Chelsea

Village, other than on match days, by a third of the number Ken Bates and Chelsea Village had asked for. This could have long term ramifications if the Village development really takes off as it will severely restrict the number of people able to use the its services and, in turn, it will restrict any fresh income stream Chelsea Village may have hoped for. Hammersmith and Fulham Council were happy about these restrictions, 'We are very satisfied with the result,' added Cllr Cartwright. 'We have won all the key arguments over sensible precautions to protect local residents and are pleased Chelsea will have a great stadium at last. We look forward to the team's continuing success on the pitch and peace of mind for local people who now know the stadium can only be used within reasonable limits.'

For the club, the two years spent arguing with the council have proved costly. Had the West Stand been completed two seasons ago with its additional executive boxes, the ground would have had a 42,000 capacity rather than its current 35,000 limit. It would also, according to Bates, have meant a reduction in the rise on ticket prices. On many occasions he has claimed that the reason for Chelsea's higher ticket price rises over the last couple of seasons stems from the loss of income on an additional 7,000 spectators during each home game for the last two years. Take last season, Chelsea played 31 games at Stamford Bridge in all competitions, so working on an average of £30 a ticket, taking into account those executives paying top dollar, Chelsea lost out on approximately £6.5 million last year. This is, conveniently, precisely the same amount as the annual interest on that £75 million loan. This significant amount would have put the club £6 million in the black - so if there is a thin line between love and hate, there seems to be an even thinner one between profit and loss.

Another area that has failed to keep Uncle Ken amused has been the dismal failure of the club's in house travel company which made a loss of £1 million in 1998/99. For a man not known to admit he is wrong, Ken Bates' comments in the Chelsea Village Annual report were refreshingly honest. 'Achievements elsewhere have been somewhat overshadowed by the problems that came to light at our travel agency EDT.' EDT remains a subsidiary of Chelsea Village, a subsidiary which continues to inspire more hatred than most among Chelsea fans.

Elizabeth Duff Travel (EDT) was an independent travel agency owned by Chelsea fan and executive Gary Pinchen, which the club bought in 1997. Pinchen remained after the take over but failed to endear himself to fans when EDT were handed responsibility for arranging travel for fans wishing to watch Chelsea in Europe. Aside from the expensive prices EDT charged, they have been found wanting on more than one occasion. For example, there was the fiasco of the mass invasion of Stockholm by Chelsea fans in 1998. Many fans had flights delayed both going out and coming home, which, although not specifically the travel company's fault, was not helped by EDT's lack of concern for their customers – their handling of the situation was a huge own goal.

The only success EDT seemed to have was convincing Chelsea fans that it was far easier, less stressful and far cheaper for them to travel independently. However, every time a Chelsea fan makes the sound economic decision to make his own arrangements this means less money in Chelsea's coffers. Also, if they were not impressed enough to travel with EDT when their team was playing in Europe, no Chelsea fan will be convinced to book his holiday through EDT out of loyalty as was perhaps first envisaged. One of the final nails in EDT's coffin, from the fans' point of view, came on one of the best European away trips of recent years when Chelsea beat Real Betis 2-1 in Seville. On a hot night in Southern Spain, with the Costa Del Sol just a few miles down the road, 4,000 Chelsea fans made the journey with many making a holiday of it by staying on in Torremolinos. Many independent travelling Chelsea fans stayed in the luxury five star hotel next to the ground, which they had managed to book themselves. From there they waited until a few minutes before kick off before strolling to seats bought from the Betis box office. With only about 500 Chelsea fans travelling with the club it seemed that the great majority of Chelsea fans had finally had enough and decided to ignore EDT and make their own arrangements to get to the match. On a rough calculation, if all those Chelsea fans had travelled with the club it would have meant at least another one million pounds into the club's coffers. If Ken Bates had a calculator handy in the directors box that night he would have been kicking himself to discover the loss of such a large amount of revenue to the club.

In contrast, the official club party were confined to a corner of the terraces and forced into the stadium a staggering three hours before kick-off. That night proved to many that they need not travel with the club to see Chelsea play in Europe and that it was probably much cheaper and much more fun travelling independently. As a final insult, as the night wore on, the San Miguel soaked Chelsea fans were heard to cry. 'you can stick Duff travel up your arse'. Soon after, Chelsea took the common sense approach that fans would no longer be forced to travel with EDT to see Chelsea in Europe provided they gave their travel details to the club when purchasing tickets. Clearly the club have seen the light on this issue and they now sell European match tickets without travel packages on most occasions. However, from a public relations point of view the damage has already been done and fans now only travel with the club out of necessity as they did for the Barcelona game when tickets were like gold dust.

As a possible suggestion for a way back for EDT and Chelsea Village, I would have to quote these words from a match programme between Chelsea and Queens Park Rangers on 10 April 1982, 'I would love to hear from you and how you think the club can be improved. No comments on the team please, that is the province of the Manager who must stand and fall on his own efforts without outside influence but any other topic i.e. accommodation, the social side, away travel, anything at all – I would be delighted to hear from you if you write to me care of the Club. Chelsea belongs to you, the fans – without you there would be no Chelsea and it's about time your opinions were considered when formulating future policy.'

The author of that excellent piece of customer awareness was one Ken Bates who had just bought the club for £1 and was writing his first-ever column in the match day programme. That Chelsea belongs to the fans and that their opinions should be considered when formulating policy are sentiments with which I whole-heartedly agree. In this consumer age, it still appears that the likes of EDT and Chelsea Village have little knowledge of their client group, their aspirations and desires. If they had, they would not be offering the type of 'cattle' packages as described at the Real Betis match. Forcing fans into a stadium three hours before the game and herding them onto planes straight afterwards is simply not good enough.

For a start, they could send out questionnaires to club members and season ticket holders who have travelled with the club inviting them to focus groups at the Bridge to get their views on what they would like to see from Chelsea when organising travel in Europe in future. As a personal suggestion, they could hold the focus groups in Drakes and as an incentive to attend, maybe a free pint could be thrown in. With Chelsea planning to be in Europe for many years to come, it's not too late for EDT and Chelsea Village to start thinking about it right now.

It was also refreshing to read Bates' final thoughts on EDT: 'We discovered that many of the controls that should have been in operation had either broken down or were not in place. As a result of this and other concerns we have taken a realistic view over financial provisions, resulting in a loss of £1 million before group charges. Subsequently, the managing director of EDT has left.'

If only the club and EDT had a bit more imagination about them and relaxed their rules, I imagine a lot more Chelsea fans would use them for European matches. There are many fans who have said that they would happily travel with the club but are put off for a variety of reasons.

Firstly, by shopping around they can do it much cheaper themselves. Secondly, they feel insulted by the club's insistence that fans meet three to four hours before kick-off, be herded in coaches to the ground and only then be issued with match tickets. And, although some of the EDT prices for last season's away trips to Italy and Spain game were much cheaper than they had been in the past, they failed to sell out all the club's packages, as people found they could still do it cheaper off their own back. Barcelona away was a sell out for EDT but only because so few tickets were available to Chelsea. The only way you could guarantee a ticket therefore was to reluctantly travel with the club – an offer 1500 lucky punters took up on this occasion. Contrast that with the Skonto Riga qualifier at the start of the season when EDT were forced to cancel one of their packages as so few people had booked with them. Yet out in Latvia, several hundred Chelsea fans made the long journey under their own steam.

The other major player in the Chelsea Village development is the Chelsea Village Hotel or Hotels, as there are now two on site bringing the total number of hotel rooms at the ground to 291. Occupancy rates at the first hotel were running at 70% last year which, despite the annual report's claim that the 'current year's performance is encouraging' must be an invalid figure as the second establishment will have eaten into this occupancy rate. The problem for Bates is that despite his repeated claim that 'we are only 15 minutes from Harrods', the majority of foreign tourists who come London want to stay in the centre of town, which for them means the West End, ruling out Stamford Bridge. The other major area of profit for the hotel industry is the corporate conference market and clearly this is a sector Chelsea Village have attempted to develop.

Despite complaints from many people who believe the rooms are too expensive, many people who work in the training/conference field feel that Chelsea Village's hotel room rates are competitive and no more expensive than other hotels in London. The one negative factor they talk about with regard to Chelsea Village's hotels is that the only people amongst their client group who would like the idea of staying at the Village are Chelsea fans. The majority of respondents typically lament the fact the hotel backs onto a football ground In addition, most people in the training/conference market like to unwind at the end of a hard day and although the facilities are clearly in place, people remain put off because there are so few other people.

A single guy I know, who is often on training courses and whose company has spurned Chelsea Village's marketing ploys, said this to me one night: 'Look, after we have finished our course or seminar we want to hit the town, drink a skinful and then pull a bird – now tell me: what chance have you got of getting a shag in Chelsea Village?' Now this might be a very narrow-minded view but Chelsea Village clearly have an image problem as far as the corporate conference market is concerned – the only people interested in staying there are Chelsea fans. I know, I can speak from experience as a relative of mine, who has a successful business booked all his staff into the Village Hotel after his company's Christmas party last year. His company is based near the West End but he chose Chelsea as, from a fan's point of view, he would rather Chelsea had his company's money than some other London hotel.

The marketing staff at Chelsea Village have tried, God bless them and I would love to know the take up on their Valentines' Weekend special at the hotel. For £400 per couple, you got to stay in the hotel, have breakfast, dinner and champagne and flowers in the room. The lucky couple would also get a couple of tickets for the Chelsea home game that weekend. The only down side was that Chelsea were due to play Wimbledon on the Saturday.

Earlier this year, *Business Age* magazine ran a feature on Chelsea Village with particular regard to the two hotels. According to *Business Age*, Chelsea Village 'hopes' to attract 200,000 non-football visitors a year to the site, which works out at some 4,000 a week and, discounting weekends, that would mean an average of 800 people a day. As a result they are banking on their 291 hotel rooms to attract visitors. Unfortunately, room rates are in the same bracket as the London Hilton which means they must produce similar standards of customer service.

As far as *Business Age* are concerned the hotels are just too expensive compared to others in their market place and not of sufficient quality to justify four-star prices. In terms of aesthetics, *Business Age* were less than impressed, describing the buildings as 'instantly forgettable, indistinguishable from the hundreds of others of their ilk in London.'

Financial secretary Michael Russell, speaking in *Business Age*, boasted that 'It would appear that the signs are healthy' and that the hotels are 'fully booked in August.' Now, August is a peak time in the tourist and hotel trade. Frankly, if the two hotels at Chelsea Village could not fill it then they should knock the thing down now and add another 10,000 seats to the Shed End. The real test will be in the winter months of the year from November to January. If the hotels are still doing good business then that will be the most positive news to date to emanate from the 'marble mausoleum', as hotel staff refer to it.

The only other strand of the hotel industry where bookings are in constantly high demand is in providing temporary accommodation to homeless families and more recently asylum seekers. With the recent influx of asylum seekers to London many are being temporarily housed in hotels all over the City and with the Government picking up the tab for accommodation, any hotelier would be guaranteed 100% occupancy at all times and all your bills paid for by Her Majesty's Government!

So will Chelsea Village thrive in the new millennium? Respected City analyst William Davies, leisure analyst with Capel Cure Sharp, seems to think so. He sides with Bates on the one area that may yet be Chelsea Village's salvation – their asset base. On current market values, Chelsea Village has a value of £140 million – which manages to exceed rivals Manchester United's Old Trafford site.

'There is always a problem with Chelsea because they are so cagey about their financial data,' says Davies, 'but in the long term my guess is that they will come through and do very well. They are broadening their revenue base, they've appointed a decent name at the top and they are getting the European trade – they know that you have got to be in the Champions League to be secure.'

One significant achievement, so far as Chelsea's financial base is concerned, came in the shape of a £50 million investment from BSkyB. Representatives from Sky had been present at Chelsea's 4-0 destruction of Sunderland on the opening day of last season. From that day rumours began to circulate that Rupert Murdoch wanted Chelsea to join his ever-growing portfolio of Premier League club shares. At the time, Chelsea Village financial director Michael Russell was quick to dispel rumours that the Australian was attempting to buy into Chelsea Village, 'If Sky came in and wanted to talk to us, and say offered £5 million, I am sure Ken would tell them where to go. But if they offered serious money, like all business concerns, we would be duty bound to sit down and talk about it.'

By Friday 3 March 2000, it looked as if Sky had offered some serious money as Chelsea announced that they had signed a £50 million deal with the company.

Ken Bates was a decidedly happy man as he announced the deal, 'I am delighted for both the supporters and shareholders. This strategic alliance represents another milestone along the road of Chelsea becoming an enduring force in European football and strengthens our move into new media.'

Sky were equally happy as managing director of Sky Sports Vic Wakeling said with equal gusto, 'Chelsea Village PLC and BSkyB will combine their strengths to benefit fans and shareholders. The club will be able to maximise their return from media rights, sponsorship and advertising deals and develop new media opportunities whilst remaining focused on the pitch. BSkyB is delighted to be associated with Chelsea, a club with a great history, excellent support, strong management and a magnificent stadium.'

However, The Chelsea Action Group remained suspicious and smelt a rat. Their web site ran the following article, 'At about 3pm Chelsea Village issued a press release announcing that BSkyB were taking a stake in the Village Group. There was no press conference, no razzmatazz, no bottles of Chairman's Choice bubbly, just a bare press release from Chelsea Village. One effect of this news was the *News of the World* immediately pulling a planned story, which related to a 'high profile' Premiership chairman under the headline 'Liar!' The story buzzed on the wires for three hours before Radio 5 Live picked it up. The whole thing was very low key, and almost slipped by unnoticed. The press release was taken down from the official Chelsea website after a few hours.

'Although both BSkyB and Bates appear delighted with the deal, what seems strange is that, at a time when Chelsea had secured a massive deal, why wasn't everyone shouting it from the rooftops? If you visited the Chelsea website and put BSkyB in the search engine, no references were found. The biggest deal in Chelsea's history and there was no mention of it anywhere! The previous day's news page completely ignored the 'BSkyB' deal. Then look at the press. When does *The Sun* ever miss an opportunity to plug Sky? Answer - never! Well you had to look long and hard to find any reference to the £40m deal, and it eventually turned up as the last sentence in a match preview! Blink and you would miss it! Murdoch's enemy *The Mirror*, on the other hand, splashed the story in two-inch capitals on its back page!

'So the actual chain of events appears to be like this: the deal is announced, the '*News of the World*' pull a story criticising Bates' business practices, and the Village half year losses of £4m are quietly announced and pass by almost unnoticed on the same day. The highly publicised 'purchase' of a ten-year debenture in the Millennium Suite was excellent publicity for Bates' ambitious scheme, and will no doubt be used extensively by the poor chap who has to try and get £10m off seventeen different people for a ten-year season ticket. A few weeks later, BSkyB win the TV bid, presumably with Bates' vote going in their favour.'

So with the money from BSkyB, will Chelsea Village finally have their Blue Tomorrow? Ken Bates seems to think so, 'We think that in the foreseeable future we will be the only club capable of taking on Manchester United in terms of capital and income growth. We are not a one-product company – and in the end that will make the difference.'

What will certainly make the difference for Chelsea Village is the completion of the remainder of the development. Next up, and a top priority for Ken, is the small matter of the completion of the West Stand and the successful outcome of his biggest gamble to date – the Millennium Suites. This stand contains seventeen of these executive suites. If you are thinking of purchasing one you will need to put down £10 million up front. If Chelsea have 25 home games in the 2001/02 season that works out a cost of £40,000 a suite or £1500 per person per game. Could it be that the real reason for Vialli's departure had less to do with his falling out with the players at the club and more to do with the need for Chelsea to be regularly challenging for the title and in the Champions League in order to put bums on these most expensive of seats?

Even by Chelsea's historically high prices, £10 million is a huge investment for any company. To invest that sort of money I imagine most companies would demand Chelsea success every season but as any long-standing Chelsea fan will tell you, it has not always been like it is today. Football goes round in cycles and Chelsea, having had so many lean and gloomy years, are enjoying their success now but it may not always be like that. A Chelsea side could be struggling mid-table in five years time or, God forbid, they could be in the Nationwide League again. If you doubt that, just look at the fortunes of Blackburn Rovers.

Who knows where any of us will be in ten years time? Living in another part of the country, another part of the world or dead and buried - a thriving company now could be bust in a few years, so who is prepared to splash out £10 million of their hard earned on a suite? Well, so far, there have been only two takers, BSkyB television and a 'mystery buyer'.

Let's examine what you get in return for your £10 million. You receive a ten-year lease on one of the suites for your personal use, your own personal seating area of 27 seats outside the suite so your guests will feel part of the 'atmosphere' and you get the opportunity 'to mingle with the Chelsea chairman's entourage as a VIP'. For £10 million up front I suspect you would not just want to mingle with the chairman's entourage but require the loan of Ken's Bentley whenever you wanted it, access to his yacht all-year round and be able to crash out at his penthouse any time you have too much drink in one of his club, bars or restaurants.

The bottom line, however, is that the future of Chelsea Village very much hinges on how well the seventeen Millennium Suites sell. The reality is that it is not a question of if they sell – they must sell. If Ken Bates succeeds in getting hold of that £170 million in the next twelve months it will probably give him more satisfaction than anything else he has achieved as Chairman. It is also probably the real reason behind the Vialli departure – the truth was Bates could no longer afford to wait for the Italian to turn Chelsea into Premier League champions. To ensure the continued success of Chelsea Village and the sale of the Millennium Suites this year, Chelsea must win the Premier League or at least guarantee Champions League qualification. His replacement, Claudio Ranieri, must win the Premier League title in what time remains of the Premier League season or get the Blues to a top three finish. That might prove a daunting task.

£170 million is not only the equivalent of two year's turnover at Chelsea Village, it would enable the club to pay off the £75 million they borrowed in 1997 to fund the whole development and more importantly, could save them paying a further £42 million in interest. Ranieri could no doubt use that £42 million to strengthen his side further. But with only two Millennium Suites sold to date (and one of them was part of the deal with Murdoch) Bates has his work cut out. If Bates manages to sell all seventeen it will surpass anything he has done in his time as Chairman of Chelsea Football Club or Chelsea Village. The £170 million earned would not only pay off the albatross of the Eurobond and its whopping great interest each year but it would also leave money in the bank.

I still owe Ken a drink from the time he bought a round in Verona when Chelsea played there in the Cup Winners' Cup in 1998; if those suites get sold I'll gladly buy him one back. Then we could all drink to a Blue Tomorrow.

Appendix - Vital Statistics

League Positions 1906-2000

Year	Div.	Pos	P	W	D	L	GF	GA	Pts
1906	2	3rd	38	22	9	7	90	37	53
1907	2	2nd	38	26	5	7	80	34	57
1908	1	13th	38	14	8	16	53	62	36
1909	1	11th	38	14	9	15	56	61	37
1910	1	19th	38	11	7	20	47	70	29
1911	2	3rd	38	20	9	9	71	35	49
1912	2	2nd	38	24	6	8	74	34	54
1913	1	18th	38	11	6	21	51	73	28
1914	1	8th	38	16	7	15	46	55	39
1915	1	19th	38	8	13	17	51	65	29
		(World War I)							
1920	1	3rd	42	22	5	15	56	51	49
1921	1	18th	42	13	13	16	48	58	39
1922	1	9th	42	17	12	13	40	43	46
1923	1	19th	42	9	18	15	45	53	36
1924	1	21st	42	9	14	19	31	53	32
1925	2	5th	42	16	15	11	51	37	47
1926	2	3rd	42	19	14	9	76	49	52
1927	2	4th	42	20	12	10	62	52	52
1928	2	3rd	42	23	8	11	75	45	54
1929	2	9th	42	17	10	15	64	65	44
1930	2	2nd	42	22	11	9	74	46	55

1931	1	12th	42	15	10	17	64	67	40
1932	1	12th	42	16	8	18	69	73	40
1933	1	12th	42	14	7	21	63	73	35
1934	1	19th	42	14	8	20	67	69	36
1935	1	12th	42	16	9	17	73	82	41
1936	1	8th	42	15	13	14	65	72	43
1937	1	13th	42	14	13	15	52	55	41
1938	1	10th	42	14	13	15	65	65	41
1939	1	20th	42	12	9	21	64	80	33
1940	1	12th	3	1	1	1	4	4	3
(Season abandoned due to World War II)									
1947	1	15th	42	16	7	19	69	84	39
1948	1	18th	42	14	9	19	53	71	37
1949	1	13th	42	12	14	16	69	68	38
1950	1	13th	42	12	16	14	58	65	40
1951	1	20th	42	12	8	22	53	65	32
1952	1	19th	42	14	8	20	52	72	36
1953	1	19th	42	12	11	19	56	66	35
1954	1	8th	42	16	12	14	74	68	44
1955	1	1st	42	20	12	10	81	57	52
1956	1	16th	42	14	11	17	64	77	39
1957	1	13th	42	13	13	16	73	73	39
1958	1	11th	42	15	12	15	83	79	42
1959	1	14th	42	18	4	20	77	98	40
1960	1	18th	42	14	9	19	76	91	37
1961	1	12th	42	15	7	20	98	100	37
1962	1	22nd	42	9	10	23	63	94	28
1963	2	2nd	42	24	4	14	81	42	52
1964	1	5th	42	20	10	12	72	56	50
1965	1	3rd	42	24	8	10	89	72	56
1966	1	5th	42	22	7	13	65	53	51
1967	1	9th	42	15	14	13	67	62	44
1968	1	6th	42	18	12	12	62	68	48

1969	1	5th	42	20	10	12	73	53	50
1970	1	3rd	42	21	13	8	70	50	55
1971	1	6th	42	18	15	9	52	42	51
1972	1	7th	42	18	12	12	58	49	48
1973	1	12th	42	13	14	15	49	51	40
1974	1	17th	42	12	13	17	56	60	37
1975	1	21st	42	9	15	18	42	72	33
1976	2	11th	42	12	16	14	53	54	40
1977	2	2nd	42	21	13	8	73	53	55
1978	1	16th	42	11	14	17	46	69	36
1979	1	22nd	42	5	10	27	44	92	20
1980	2	4th	42	23	7	12	66	52	53
1981	2	12th	42	14	12	16	46	41	40
1982	2	12th	42	15	12	15	60	60	57
		(3 points for a win)							
1983	2	18th	42	11	14	17	51	61	47
1984	2	1st	42	25	13	4	80	40	88
1985	1	6th	42	18	12	12	63	48	66
1986	1	6th	42	20	11	11	57	56	71
1987	1	14th	42	13	13	16	53	64	52
1988	1	18th	40	9	15	16	50	68	42
1989	2	1st	46	29	12	5	96	50	99
1990	1	5th	38	16	12	10	58	50	60
1991	1	11th	38	13	10	15	58	69	49
1992	1	14th	42	13	14	15	50	60	53
		(Premier League Formed)							
1993	P	11th	42	14	14	14	51	54	56
1994	P	14th	42	3	12	17	49	53	51
1995	P	11th	42	13	15	14	50	55	54
1996	P	11th	38	12	14	12	46	44	50
1997	P	6th	38	16	11	11	58	55	59
1998	P	4th	38	20	3	15	71	43	63
1999	P	3rd	38	20	15	3	57	30	75

A SEASON TO REMEMBER
1999-2000

Date	Opponent	Score	Attendance	Scorers
07/08/99	Sunderland (H)	4 - 0	34,831	Poyet(2), Zola, Flo
14/08/99	Leicester City (A)	2 - 2	21,068	Wise, Own Goal
21/08/99	Aston Villa (H)	1 - 0	35,071	Own Goal
28/08/99	Wimbledon (A)	1 - 0	22,167	Petrescu
11/09/99	Newcastle U (H)	1 - 0	35,092	Leboeuf (pen)
18/09/99	Watford (A)	0 - 1	21,244	
25/09/99	Middlesbro (A)	1 - 0	34,183	Lambourde
03/10/99	Man Utd (H)	5 - 0	34,909	Poyet (2), Sutton, Own Goal, Morris
16/10/99	Liverpool (A)	0 - 1	44,826	
23/10/99	Arsenal (H)	2 - 3	34,958	Petrescu, Flo
30/10/99	Derby County (A)	1 - 3	28,614	Lebouef
07/11/99	West Ham (H)	0 - 0	34,935	
20/11/99	Everton (A)	1 - 1	38,225	Flo
28/11/99	Bradford City(H)	1 - 0	31,951	Flo
04/12/99	Sunderland (A)	1 - 4	41,377	Poyet
19/12/99	Leeds Utd (H)	0 - 2	35,106	
26/12/99	Southampton (A)	2 - 1	15,232	Flo (2)
29/12/99	Sheffield Wed (H)	3 - 0	32,938	Wise, Flo, Morris
04/12/99	Coventry City (A)	2 - 2	20,164	Flo (2)
08/01/00	Bradford City (A)	1 - 1	18,276	Petrescu
12/01/00	Tottenham H (H)	1 - 0	34,969	Weah
15/01/00	Leicester City (H)	1 - 1	35,063	Wise
22/01/00	Aston Villa (A)	0 - 0	33,704	
05/02/00	Tottenham H (A)	1 - 0	36,041	Lambourde
12/02/00	Wimbledon (H)	3 - 1	34,826	Poyet, Weah, Morris

26/02/00	Watford (H)	2 - 1	34,928	Desailly, Harley
04/03/00	Newcastle U (A)	1 - 0	36,448	Poyet
11/03/00	Everton (H)	1 - 1	35,113	Wise
18/03/00	West Ham (A)	0 - 0	26,041	
25/03/00	Southampton (H)	1 - 1	34,956	Own goal
01/04/00	Leeds Utd (A)	1 - 0	40,162	Harley
12/04/00	Coventry City (H)	2 - 1	32,316	Zola, Own goal
15/04/00	Sheffield Wed (A)	0 - 1	21,743	
22/04/00	Middlesbro' (H)	1 - 1	33,467	Poyet
24/04/00	Man Utd (A)	2 - 3	61,593	Petrescu, Zola
29/04/00	Liverpool (H)	2 - 0	34,957	Weah, Di Matteo
06/05/00	Arsenal (A)	1 - 2	38,119	Poyet
14/05/00	Derby County (H)	4 - 0	35,084	Zola, Poyet, Di Matteo, Flo

Worthington Cup

13/10/00	Huddersfield (H)	0 - 1	21,008	

FA Cup

Round 3				
11/12/99	Hull City (A)	6 - 1	0,279	Poyet(3), Sutton, Wise, Di Matteo
Round 4				
19/01/00	Nott'm Forest (H)	2 - 1	30,125	Lebouef, Wise
Round 5				
30/01/00	Leicester City (H)	2 - 1	30,141	Poyet, Weah
Round 6				
19/02/00	Gillingham (H)	5 - 0	34,205	Flo, Terry, Weah, Morris, Zola (pen)
Semi-final				
09/04/00	Newcastle Utd	2 - 1	73,876	Poyet(2)
Final				
20/05/00	Aston Villa	1 - 0	78,217	Di Matteo

Chelsea in Europe

1958/59 Inter Cities Fairs Cup

1st Round		Bk Frem (Denmark)		
1st leg	(A)	W	3-1	Harrison Greaves Nicholas
2nd leg	(H)	W	4-1	Greaves (2) Sillet Own Goal
2nd Round			Ville de Belgrade (Yugoslavia)	
1st leg	(H)	W	1-0	Brabrook
2nd leg	(A)	L	1-4	Brabrook

1965/66 Inter Cities Fairs Cup

1st Round		AS Roma (Italy)		
1st leg	(H)	W	4-1	Venables (3) Graham
2nd leg	(A)	D	0-0	
2nd Round			Wiener Sport Club (Austria)	
1st leg	(A)	L	0-1	
2nd leg	(H)	W	2-0	Murray Osgood
3rd Round		AC Milan (Italy)		
1st leg	(A)	L	1-2	Graham
2nd leg	(H)	W	2-1	Graham Osgood
Play Off	(A)	D	1-1	Bridges
		Chelsea won on toss of a coin		
4th Round		TSV Munchen 1860 (West Germany)		
1st leg	(A)	D	2-2	Tambling
2nd leg	(H)	W	1-0	Osgood
Semi Final		Barcelona (Spain)		
1st leg	(A)	L	0-2	
2nd leg	(H)	W	2-0	Own goal (2)
Play off	(A)	L	0-5	

1968/69 Inter Cities Fairs Cup

1st Round		Greenock Morton (Scotland)		
1st leg	(H)	W	5-0	Osgood Birchenall Cooke Boyle Hollins
2nd leg	(A)	W	4-3	Baldwin Birchenall Houseman Tambling
2nd Round			DWS Amsterdam (Holland)	
1st leg	(H)	D	0-0	
2nd leg	(A)	D	0-0	

Chelsea lost tie on toss of a coin

1970/71 European Cup Winners' Cup

1st Round		Aris Salonika (Greece)		
1st leg	(A)	D	1-1	Hutchinson
2nd	(H)	W	5-1	Hollins (2) Hutchinson (2) Hinton
2nd Round			CSKA Sofia (Bulgaria)	
1st leg	(A)	W	1-0	Baldwin
2nd leg	(H)	W	1-0	Webb
3rd Round		FC Bruges (Belgium)		
1st leg	(A)	L	0-2	
2nd leg	(H)	W	4-2	Houseman, Osgood (2,) Baldwin
Semi-final		Manchester City (England)		
1st leg	(H)	W	1-0	Smethurst
2nd leg	(A)	W	1-0	Own goal
Final		Real Madrid (Spain)		
In Athens		D	1-1	Osgood
Replay		W	2-1	Dempsey, Osgood

1971/72 European Cup Winners' Cup

1st Round		Jeunesse Hautcharage (Luxembourg)		
1st leg	(A)	W	8-0	Osgood (3) Houseman (2) Hollins Webb Baldwin

2nd leg	(H)	W	13-0	Osgood (5,) Baldwin (3) Hudson, Hollins (pen) Webb Harris Houseman
2nd Round			Atvidaberg (Sweden)	
1st leg	(A)	D	0-0	
2nd leg	(H)	D	1-1	Hudson

Atvidaberg won on away goals

1994/95 European Cup Winners' Cup

1st Round		Viktoria Zizkov (Czechoslovakia)		
1st leg	(H)	W	4-2	Furlong, Sinclair, Rocastle, Wise.
2nd leg (A)D 0-0				
2nd Round			Austria Memphis (Austria)	
1st leg	(H)	D	0-0	
2nd leg	(A)	D	1-1	Spencer

Chelsea won on away goals rule

3rd Round		FC Bruges (Belgium)		
1st leg	(A)	L	0-1	
2nd leg	(H)	W	2-0	Stein Furlong
Semi-final		Real Zaragoza (Spain)		
1st leg	(A)	L	0-3	
2nd leg	(H)	W	3-1	Furlong, Sinclair, Stein

1997/98 European Cup Winners' Cup

1st Round		Slovan Bratislava (Slovakia)		
1st leg	(H)	W	2-0	Di Matteo, Granville
2nd leg	(A)	W	2-0	Vialli, Granville
2nd Round			Tromso (Norway)	
1st leg	(A)	L	2-3	Vialli (2)
2nd leg	(H)	W	7-1	Vialli (3,) Petrescu (2), Zola, Lebouef

3rd Round		Real Betis (Spain)		
1st leg	(A)	W	2-1	Flo (2)
2nd leg	(H)	W	3-1	Sinclair Di Matteo Zola
Semi final		Vicenza (Italy)		
1st leg	(A)	L	0-1	
2nd leg	(H)	W	3-1	Poyet, Zola, Hughes
Final		Stuttgart (Germany)		
Stockholm		W	1-0	Zola

1998/89 European Cup Winners' Cup

1st Round		Helsingborg (Sweden)		
1st leg	(H)	W	1-0	Leboeuf
2nd leg	(A)	D	0-0	
2nd Round			FC Copenhagen (Denmark)	
1st leg	(H)	D	1-1	Desailly
2nd leg	(A)	W	1-0	Laudrup
3rd Round		Valerenga (Norway)		
1st leg	(H)	W	3-0	Babayaro, Zola, Wise
2nd leg	(A)	W	3-2	Vialli, Lambourde, Flo
Semi-final		Real Mallorca (Spain)		
1st leg	(H)	D	1-1	Flo
2nd leg	(A)	L	0-1	

1999/2000 UEFA Champions League

3rd Qualifying Round			Skonta Riga (Latvia)	
1st leg	(H)	W	3-0	Babayaro Poyet Sutton
2nd leg	(A)	D	0-0	

Group H First Phase

AC Milan	(H)	D	0-0	
Hertha Berlin	(A)	L	1-2	Lebouef
Galatasary	(H)	W	1-0	Petrescu
Galatasary	(A)	W	5-0	Flo (2,) Zola, Wise, Ambrosetti

AC Milan	(A)	D	1-1	Wise
Hertha Berlin	(H)	W	2-0	Deschamps Ferrer
	Group D Second Phase			
Feyenoord	(H)	W	3-0	Babayaro Flo (2)
Lazio (Italy)	(A)	D	0-0	
O. Marseille	(A)	L	0-1	
O. Marseille	(H)	W	1-0	Wise
Feyenoord	(A)	W	3-1	Zola Wise Flo
Lazio	(H)	L	1-2	Poyet
Quarter-final	Barcelona			
1st leg	(H)	W	3-1	Zola, Flo (2)
2nd leg	(A)	L	1-5	Flo